SMITH,
MARX, & AFTER

SMITH, MARX, & AFTER

Ten Essays in the Development of Economic Thought

Ronald L. Meek

Tyler Professor of Economics at the
University of Leicester

London
CHAPMAN & HALL

A Halsted Press Book
John Wiley & Sons, New York

First published 1977
by Chapman and Hall Ltd
11 New Fetter Lane, London EC4P 4EE

© 1977 Ronald L. Meek

Printed by William Clowes & Sons, Limited
London, Beccles and Colchester

ISBN 0 412 14360 7

Distributed in the USA by Halsted Press,
a division of John Wiley & Sons, Inc., New York

Library of Congress Cataloging in Publication Data
Meek, Ronald L
   Smith, Marx, and after.

   "A Halstead Press book."
   Includes index.
   1. Economics—History—Addresses, essays, lectures.
   2. Smith, Adam, 1723–90—Addresses, essays, lectures.
   3. Marxian economics—Addresses, essays, lectures.
   I. Title.
HB75.M42 1977   330'.09   77–5345'·
ISBN 0–470–99161–5

To the Memory of
Maurice Dobb

CONTENTS

PREFACE

With one exception, all the essays in this collection have been written during the last seven or eight years. Two of them (*Smith and Marx* and *A Plain Person's Guide to the Transformation Problem*) are essentially new; the others have already been published in one form or another, in most instances in academic journals. In the case of the majority of the items which have already been published I have made various amendments, partly in order to minimize the amount of repetition, and partly in order to bring the views expressed into conformity with those which I now hold.

The exception is the final essay, which consists of the inaugural lecture I gave at Leicester University in 1964. Inaugural lectures, generally speaking, should be heard and not seen; but I felt on re-reading it that it might serve quite usefully as the final item in this collection. I have omitted two or three passages of largely local interest, but otherwise have left the text unaltered: if one foists a thirteen-year-old inaugural lecture on one's readers, I do not think one should cheat by excising any defects which time may since have revealed. If it is found to be good for nothing else, it can be studied as a typical example of the *genre* – erudite literary references, self-deprecatory comments, comical jests for the groundlings, and all.

The book as a whole is, I hope, a little larger than the sum of its parts, in the sense that the essays, although written at different times and for different purposes, have been put together in a way which is designed to emphasize the relationship between their themes. In Part One, I am concerned in particular with the work of Adam Smith, with which in a very real sense both Marxian and modern economics began. In Part Two, the main theme is Marx's theory of value and distribution, with particular reference to the so-called 'transformation problem' around which so many of the modern debates are centred. In Part Three, I turn to modern economics, discussing some of its links with the past and prospects for the future.

I am greatly obliged to the editors of the *Economic Journal* and *History of Political Economy*, to Cambridge University Press, and to Leicester University Press, for allowing me to reproduce material published by them. I am also greatly obliged to Andrew Skinner for giving me permission to reprint, in a volume published under my name alone, an article (*The Development of Adam Smith's Ideas on the Division of Labour*) which was in fact written jointly by the two of us.

R.L.M.

PART ONE

SMITH

I

Smith and Marx

I

'I bring you greetings from Adam Smith, who is alive and well and living in Chicago.' It was in this engaging way that Professor George Stigler opened his speech at a banquet at Glasgow University during the *Wealth of Nations* bicentennial celebrations held there in 1976.

The picture which this genial proprietary claim was meant to conjure up, of course, was of the Adam Smith who stood out as the great pioneering advocate of competitive capitalism, free trade, and the price mechanism, and whose *Wealth of Nations* was destined to become the Bible of the liberal bourgeoisie. And – let us face it – the picture drawn by Professor Stigler is not *too* misleading. The tremendous Smithian sentences ring down the centuries still:

All systems either of preference or of restraint, therefore, being thus completely taken away, the obvious and simple system of natural liberty establishes itself of its own accord. Every man, as long as he does not violate the laws of justice, is left perfectly free to pursue his own interest his own way, and to bring both his industry and capital into competition with those of any other man, or order of men.[1]

The uniform, constant, and uninterrupted effort of every man to better his condition, the principle from which publick and national, as well as private opulence is originally derived, is frequently powerful enough to maintain the natural progress of things toward improvement, in spite both of the extravagance of government, and of the greatest errors of administration.[2]

Every individual is continually exerting himself to find out the most advantageous employment for whatever capital he can command. It is his own advantage, indeed, and not that of the society, which he has in

[1] Adam Smith, *Wealth of Nations* (edited by R. H. Campbell and A. S. Skinner, Oxford University Press, 1976), Vol. II, p. 687.
[2] *Ibid.*, Vol. I, p. 343.

view. But the study of his own advantage naturally, or rather necessarily leads him to prefer that employment which is most advantageous to the society . . . I have never known much good done by those who affected to trade for the publick good.[3]

Monopoly, besides, is a great enemy to good management, which can never be universally established but in consequence of that free and universal competition which forces every body to have recourse to it for the sake of self-defence.[4]

And these are not exceptional statements torn from their contexts: Smith's great message of good cheer – that competitive capitalism is, if not the best of all economic systems, at any rate the best of all *possible* systems – is echoed, with a greater or lesser degree of academic qualification, in almost every chapter of the *Wealth of Nations*. Do away with most, if not all, monopolies and restrictions on internal and external trade; allow each man to do as he wants to with his own (and in particular with his own capital); give 'the obvious and simple system of natural liberty' its head, and the famous invisible hand will automatically maximize the rate of growth of the national product and promote the diffusion of the increasing opulence among the populace. No fears here, apparently, that free competition might sooner or later breed a new type of monopoly; not *much* fear that the process of development might eventually come to an end; no worries that a more or less unfettered capitalism might generate chronic unemployment, or severe inflation, or gross disparities in income, or war; and no hint at all, of course, that capitalism might at some time or other be replaced by a different type of economic system.

When we move from the fundamentally approving and optimistic view of capitalism in Smith's *Wealth of Nations* to the highly disapproving and pessimistic view of it in Marx's *Capital,* we seem at first sight to be in a completely different world. The capitalism described by Marx is monopolistic rather than competitive; 'machinery and modern industry' have replaced the division of labour as the main means of increasing productivity; and the system as a whole is racked with internal contradictions which are manifesting themselves in the form of a whole number of unpleasant tendencies – notably a falling rate of profit, a worsening of the lot of the working class, and an intensification of the trade cycle. Fortunately, however, relief is at hand in the shape of the impending proletarian revolution: the capitalist system has almost had its day, and socialism is not very far around the corner.

Two very different worlds, it would seem, and two very different men. Yet to Marx himself the matter never seemed anything like as simple as this. To Marx, although Smith was certainly a strong advocate of capitalism, he was

---

[3] *Ibid.*, Vol. I, pp. 454 and 456.
[4] *Ibid.*, Vol. I, pp. 163–4.

also at the same time one of the 'best representatives' of 'classical' political economy – 'that economy', as Marx put it, 'which, since the time of W. Petty, has investigated the real relations of production in bourgeois society'.[5] The great merit of classical political economy, in Marx's view, was that it dissolved the world of illusion implicit in what he called the 'trinity formula' – i.e., the apologetic notion that capital produced its own profit, land its own rent, and labour its own wages. Classical political economy 'destroyed this false appearance', Marx argued,

> by reducing interest to a portion of profit, and rent to the surplus above average profit, so that both of them converge in surplus-value; and by representing the process of circulation as a mere metamorphosis of forms, and finally reducing value and surplus-value of commodities to labour in the direct production process.[6]

To the extent that Smith's analysis was characterized by elements which led in this direction – i.e., in the direction of Marx's own theory of value and surplus value – the two men clearly inhabited the same intellectual world.

But even the 'best representatives' of classical political economy, Marx believed, remained 'more or less in the grip of the world of illusion which their criticism had dissolved, as can not be otherwise from a bourgeois standpoint'. The result was that they all fell more or less into 'inconsistencies, half-truths and unsolved contradictions'.[7] In Smith's case these manifested themselves in the fact that the elements of his analysis which led in the direction of Marx's own theory – the 'esoteric' (i.e. profound) elements, as Marx christened them – were developed only sporadically, running side by side, in a kind of 'perpetual contradiction', with a number of 'exoteric' (i.e. superficial) elements. On the one hand, Marx wrote, Smith

> traces the intrinsic connection existing between economic categories or the obscure structure of the bourgeois economic system. On the other, he simultaneously sets forth the connection as it appears in the phenomena of competition and thus as it presents itself to the unscientific observer who is actually involved and interested in the process of bourgeois production. One of these conceptions fathoms the inner connection, the physiology, so to speak, of the bourgeois system, whereas the other takes the external phenomena of life, as they seem and

---

[5] Karl Marx, *Capital*, Vol. I (Foreign Languages Publishing House, Moscow, 1954), p. 81 n. Marx goes on to contrast classical political economy with 'vulgar economy', which 'deals with appearances only, ruminates without ceasing on the materials long since provided by scientific economy, and there seeks plausible explanations of the most obtrusive phenomena, for bourgeois daily use. . .'

[6] *Ibid.*, Vol. III (Foreign Languages Publishing House, Moscow, 1959), p. 809. Cf. Marx, *Theories of Surplus Value*, Part III (Lawrence and Wishart, London, 1972), pp. 500–1.

[7] *Capital*, Vol. III, p. 809.

appear and merely describes, catalogues, recounts and arranges them under formal definitions.[8]

The presence of these 'exoteric' elements in Smith's thought, in Marx's view, was historically speaking of great significance – not only because Smith's defence of capitalism was up to a point based upon them, but also, and more importantly, because in Marx's own time the 'vulgar' opponents of Ricardo were largely taking their stand upon them and attacking Ricardo (and therefore, by implication, Marx himself) in the name of Smith. To Marx, therefore, it seemed very necessary to emphasize something that seemed to be in danger of being forgotten – namely, that there was another side of Smith's thought, a side in which the origins of the Ricardian (and Marxian) approaches to value and distribution theory were fairly clearly to be found.

II

The 'esoteric' side of Smith's thought was rooted in his simple but epoch-making delineation of the tripartite structure of classes and class incomes in capitalist society, which was made (for the first time) in a passage near the end of Book I of the *Wealth of Nations*:

> The whole annual produce of the land and labour of every country, or what comes to the same thing, the whole price of that annual produce, naturally divides itself . . . into three parts; the rent of land, the wages of labour, and the profits of stock; and constitutes a revenue to three different orders of people; to those who live by rent, to those who live by wages, and to those who live by profit. These are the three great, original and constituent orders of every civilized society, from whose revenue that of every other order is ultimately derived.[9]

Before the *Wealth of Nations*, the socio-economic structure had almost always been defined in terms of a pattern which either virtually ignored the existence of the third of these 'orders', or implicitly denied its 'great, original and constituent' character by including it in some other 'order'. Smith's unambiguous assertion of the 'original' (i.e. independent) status of the capitalist class and the profit-income by which it lived, coupled with his insistence on the crucial social importance of the activities of this class, meant that a number of traditional economic concepts had to be amended or discarded.

In particular, the social surplus or 'net revenue' of society, out of which

---

[8] *Theories of Surplus Value*, Part II (Lawrence and Wishart, London, 1969), p. 165. Marx goes on to say that with Smith this dualism was justifiable, 'since his task was indeed a twofold one. On the one hand he attempted to penetrate the inner physiology of bourgeois society but on the other, he partly tried to describe its externally apparent forms of life for the first time, to show its relations as they appear outwardly and partly he had even to find a nomenclature and corresponding mental concepts for these phenomena. . .'

[9] *Wealth of Nations*, Vol. I, p. 265.

alone new capital could be accumulated, could no longer be conceived (as it had been by the French Physiocrats) as consisting exclusively of land rent, with profit being considered – when it was considered at all – as a secondary and derivative income which in some sense or other was 'paid out of' rent. Clearly, the social surplus had now to be conceived as consisting of two equally 'independent' forms of income – rent and profit. And since profit was now manifestly yielded in manufacture as well as in agriculture, it followed that the *origin* of profit could no longer plausibly be explained in terms of the 'productivity' (i.e. surplus-producing capacity) of land, or of nature, or of the Author of nature. It could in fact only be explained, or so Smith (and Ricardo) came to believe, in terms of the productivity of *labour* – not, be it noted, this or that specific kind of labour, but what Marx was later to call 'general social labour'.[10] Profit was, in fact, generated by the capital-labour relation, and was earnable (at an average rate) in whatever occupation this relation happened to exist. Profit arose, in other words, whenever the labourer – i.e. the *wage*-labourer – was obliged to share what Smith called 'the produce of his labour' with the capitalist who employed him. Profit was actually a 'deduction' from the produce of labour. In manufacture it was the first and only such deduction; in agriculture it was the second – the other of course being rent. And in all occupations profit itself might be subject to a deduction, in the shape of the interest paid on borrowed capital.[11]

Looking at the passages in the *Wealth of Nations* in which these ideas are elaborated, one sees that Smith did indeed go quite a long way towards what Marx called 'reducing interest to a portion of profit, and rent to the surplus above average profit, so that both of them converge in surplus-value'.[12] When it came to 'reducing value and surplus-value . . . to labour in the direct production process',[13] however, Smith's analysis was much less 'Marxian' – if only because he specifically rejected the embodied-labour theory of value as an explanation of the determination of prices in a capitalist (as distinct from a pre-capitalist) society,[14] and replaced it in effect with a kind of cost-of-production theory.

It would be wrong, however, in an essay on the relation between Smith and Marx, to leave this statement about Smith's rejection of the embodied-labour theory of value unqualified. For one thing, Smith not infrequently forgot that he had rejected it – as, for example, when he stated quite unequivocally that

the proportion between the value of gold and silver and that of goods of any other kind . . . depends upon the proportion between the quantity

[10] *Theories of Surplus Value*, Part I (Foreign Languages Publishing House, Moscow, n.d.), p. 83.
[11] See, e.g., *Wealth of Nations*, Vol. I, pp. 65–7, 82–3, 105–6, 160, and 331.
[12] Above, p. 5.
[13] *Ibid.*
[14] *Wealth of Nations*, Vol. I, p. 67.

of labour which is necessary in order to bring a certain quantity of gold and silver to market, and that which is necessary to bring thither a certain quantity of any other sort of goods.[15]

Then again, Smith did in certain contexts come quite close to 'reducing surplus-value to labour', or at any rate to the difference between two quantities of labour – the quantity required to bring the annual produce to market, and that greater quantity which the annual produce will normally 'purchase or command'.[16] This is not the same as Marx's concept of surplus value by any means, but it is nevertheless surely recognizable as a species belonging to the same genus. And finally – and most important of all – Smith *posed the problem* of exchange value in a way which set the pattern for all subsequent labour theorists. Given that the embodied-labour theory worked straightforwardly in a pre-capitalist commodity-producing society, Smith asked in effect, did it still work when capitalism arrived on the historical scene? Smith answered this question in the negative, whereas Ricardo and Marx were later to answer it (with modifications) in the affirmative. The important point, however, is that by and large it was one and the same question which all three economists were trying to answer, and that Smith was the first to ask it.[17]

III

The links between Smith and Marx, it is sometimes argued, extend appreciably beyond the rather inchoate anticipations of the Marxian theories of value and surplus value which are to be found in the *Wealth of Nations*. Smith, it is said, in fact made a large number of individual statements about the motives and behaviour of the capitalists and landlords, about the exploitative origin of their incomes, and about the long-run effects of capital accumulation on wages, profits, and the lot of the working class, which were distinctly radical and 'Marxian' in character. Some commentators have even gone so far as to claim that when one adds up all these statements they amount to a serious indictment of capitalism rather than a defence of it, and to a profoundly pessimistic view of its prospects rather than an optimistic one.

Marx himself was not above making capital (in more senses than one!) out of these statements of Smith's. I am accustomed to tell my students, when I feel that a little provocation may be called for, that Marx was in fact converted to communism in the 1840s by none other than that great apostle of private enterprise, Adam Smith. As evidence of this I refer them to Marx's *Economic and Philosophic Manuscripts of 1844*, a major part of which consists of direct and indirect quotations from Smith's *Wealth of Nations* – quotations which prove conclusively (or so it would appear) that

[15] *Ibid.*, Vol. I, pp. 328–9.
[16] See, e.g., *ibid.*, Vol. I, p. 71.
[17] Cf. below, p. 129.

the capitalist system is based on the exploitation of the workers by scheming capitalists and idle landlords; that even at the best it is liable to impoverish and degrade the masses of the people; and that it is doomed in the end to decline to a stationary state marked by zero net investment, extremely low wages and profits, and the 'mental mutilation' of the workers.

Marx's quotations from Smith in the 1844 *Manuscripts* were designedly very selective, and they are not always readily distinguishable from the numerous glosses added by Marx himself. But most of the individual statements which Marx attributed to Smith in the *Manuscripts* were in fact made by him somewhere or other in the *Wealth of Nations*; and many of these statements do indeed have certain *relatively* critical and pessimistic implications which at first glance may seem inconsistent with Smith's powerful advocacy of a system of 'perfect liberty'. Before we decide to label these statements as 'Marxian', however, we should look at them carefully in the context of Smith's thought as a whole, and, even more importantly, in the context of the historical period in which Smith made them.

Let us consider, for a start, some of the better-known of Smith's uncomplimentary characterizations of the capitalists and landlords:

> Masters are always and every where in a sort of tacit, but constant and uniform combination, not to raise the wages of labour above their actual rate.[18]

> The interest of the dealers, however, in any particular branch of trade or manufactures, is always in some respects different from, and even opposite to, that of the publick . . . [This order of men] have generally an interest to deceive and even to oppress the publick, and [they] accordingly have, upon many occasions, both deceived and oppressed it.[19]

> Those who live by rent . . . are the only one of the three orders whose revenue costs them neither labour nor care, but comes to them, as it were, of its own accord, and independent of any plan or project of their own. That indolence, which is the natural effect of the ease and security of their situation, renders them too often, not only ignorant, but incapable of that application of mind which is necessary in order to foresee and understand the consequences of any publick regulation.[20]

> The rent of land, therefore, considered as the price paid for the use of the land, is naturally a monopoly price. It is not at all proportioned to what the landlord may have laid out upon the improvement of the land, or to what he can afford to take; but to what the farmer can afford to give.[21]

These statements are unequivocal enough, and there is no doubt that in

---

[18] *Wealth of Nations*, Vol. I, p. 84. See also p. 145.
[19] *Ibid.*, Vol. I, p. 267. See also p. 115.
[20] *Ibid.*, Vol. I, p. 265.
[21] *Ibid.*, Vol. I, p. 161.

making them Smith meant exactly what he said. But at any rate so far as the capitalists are concerned, the characterizations just quoted are to some extent offset by others in which the virtues of this class, rather than their vices, are stressed.[22] It is also important to note that Smith's harshest condemnations of the 'merchants and manufacturers' were reserved for their 'monopolizing spirit' and the 'interested sophistry' with which they persuaded governments to introduce or maintain restrictions on trade. Simply by removing these restrictions, Smith argued – i.e., by fostering *competitive* capitalism –

> the mean rapacity, the monopolizing spirit of merchants and manu-facturers . . . though it cannot perhaps be corrected, may very easily be prevented from disturbing the tranquillity of any body but themselves.[23]

And so far as the indolent landlords are concerned, it should be remembered that according to Smith their interest, in contrast to that of the 'merchants and manufacturers', was 'strictly and inseparably connected with the general interest of the society'.[24]

Also relevant here, perhaps, is the fact that in Smith's view the economic machine would operate to produce good results not simply *in spite of* the vices and follies of the economic agents but also in part *through* them. The ancient Stoics, said Smith in the *Theory of Moral Sentiments*,

> were of opinion, that as the world was governed by the all-ruling provi-dence of a wise, powerful, and good God, every single event ought to be regarded, as making a necessary part of the plan of the universe, and as tending to promote the general order and happiness of the whole: that the vices and follies of mankind, therefore, made as necessary a part of this plan as their wisdom or their virtue; and by that eternal art which educes good from ill, were made to tend equally to the prosperity and perfection of the great system of nature.[25]

In Smith's own eighteenth-century version of this notion, the private vices of the capitalists and landlords – and, for that matter, those of the wage-labourers as well – could readily be transmuted into public benefits through the operation of the economic machine, if only men would learn to leave it alone.

But how far could the operation of the machine be said to be based on exploitation? The passages (referred to above)[26] about the labourers having to share the produce of their labour with the capitalists and land-

[22] See David A. Reisman, *Adam Smith's Sociological Economics* (Croom Helm, London, 1976), pp. 93–5.
[23] *Wealth of Nations*, Vol. I, pp. 493–4.
[24] *Ibid.*, Vol. I, p. 265.
[25] Adam Smith, *The Theory of Moral Sentiments* (edited by D. D. Raphael and A. L. Macfie, Oxford University Press, 1976), p. 36.
[26] P. 7.

lords, and about profit and rent representing deductions from the labourers' 'natural recompence',[27] certainly seem at first sight to suggest this. Forms of words of this kind were used by Smith so regularly, and in such a variety of different contexts, that one can hardly regard them as unintended; and Marx was undoubtedly correct in adducing them as evidence that Smith was at least looking in the direction of a general theory of surplus value. Relevant in this connection too is the fact (also frequently referred to by Marx) that Smith went out of his way to emphasize that the profits of stock were *not* simply 'a different name for the wages of a particular sort of labour, the labour of inspection and direction'. At any rate in large enterprises, said Smith, the owner of capital, even though he is 'discharged of almost all labour', still expects that 'his profits should bear a regular proportion to his capital'.[28]

Nor can it be said that Smith was particularly happy about this state of affairs, 'The labour and time of the poor', Smith told his students at Glasgow, 'is in civilized countries sacrificed to the maintaining the rich in ease and luxury'[29] – words which could hardly have been used by one whose sympathies did not lie with the labouring classes. But however unfortunate this necessity might be, it *was* in Smith's view a necessity. Without the deduction of profit from 'the value which the workmen add to the materials', he said, the capitalist 'could have no interest to employ them'.[30] Nor, at any rate in normal circumstances, was the deduction either undeserved or unreasonably large: net profit, said Smith, 'is the compensation, and in most cases it is no more than a very moderate compensation, for the risk and trouble of employing the stock'.[31] The moral Smith drew from the frank discussion in his Glasgow lectures of the great inequality in the distribution of wealth and effort in 'civilized countries' was *not* that this inequality should be done away with, or even reduced: rather, the moral was that *in spite of* the prevalence of this 'oppression and tyranny' even the most disadvantaged members of society enjoyed a far greater 'plenty and opulence' that that which they could have expected in 'a savage state'.[32] And this fortunate circumstance was the result of the extension of the division of labour in modern society, which was dependent upon the accumulation of capital – which was in its turn dependent upon the size of the deductions the capitalists were able to make from the produce of labour. It is surely clear that in the context of this kind of argument, put forward as it was at a time when capitalism had not yet come under serious

[27] 'The produce of labour constitutes the natural recompence or wages of labour' (*Wealth of Nations*, Vol. I, p. 82).
[28] *Wealth of Nations*, Vol. I, pp. 66–7.
[29] The quotation is from p. 26 of Vol. VI of the recently-discovered set of student's notes of Smith's Glasgow lectures on Jurisprudence, which is shortly to be published by Oxford University Press in the Glasgow edition of Smith's works and correspondence.
[30] *Wealth of Nations*, Vol. I, p. 66.
[31] *Ibid.*, Vol. II, p. 847.
[32] See pp. 24–5 of Vol. VI of the set of notes referred to in [29].

attack, a 'deduction' theory of profit could not have had the same derogatory connotations as those which it was to acquire in Marx's time, in the context of a very different kind of argument and a very different period of history. The deduction of *rent*, of course, was – or could have been – a rather different matter; but Smith confused this particular issue by claiming (at least in some places) that rent was in fact 'the produce of those powers of nature, the use of which the landlord lends to the farmer'.[33] The landlord, therefore, although he might possibly be accused of appropriating the gifts of nature without making any corresponding return, could not quite so easily be accused of the more heinous crime of exploiting the labourers employed on the land.

Let us now turn to Smith's views about the effects of capital accumulation on the level of wages. Smith, as is well known, argued that there was 'a certain rate below which it seems impossible to reduce, for any considerable time, the ordinary wages even of the lowest species of labour'. A workman's wages 'must at least be sufficient to maintain him', and in most cases must in fact be higher than this, since otherwise 'it would be impossible for him to bring up a family, and the race of such workmen could not last beyond the first generation'.[34] In addition, as is equally well known, Smith argued that since population will increase when the demand for labour and therefore the wage-rate increase, 'the demand for men . . . necessarily regulates the production of men', and the operation of this demand-and-supply mechanism will ensure that the wage-rate is constantly adjusted to 'that proper rate which the circumstances of the society require'.[35] If one puts these two arguments side by side, as Marx did for his own purposes in the 1844 *Manuscripts*,[36] it is tempting to read the elements of an 'iron law' or 'subsistence theory' of wages into Smith's analysis.

Before we succumb to this temptation, however, we should recall that the context in which these two arguments are set is a lengthy discussion of the way in which wages are affected by 'the advancing, stationary, or declining state of the society'.[37] The crucial point is that according to Smith the *level* of 'that proper rate which the circumstances of the society require' – i.e., the rate which equilibrates demand and supply in the labour market – will vary according to which of these three states the society happens to find itself in. In a stationary state (i.e., a state in which the country has acquired its 'full complement of riches'), it is true, the labourer's wages will soon be reduced to a level which is 'barely enough to enable him to bring up a family, or to continue the race of labourers'; and in a declining state they

[33] *Wealth of Nations*, Vol. I, p. 364. Cf. p. 363: 'In agriculture too nature labours along with man; and though her labour costs no expence, its produce has its value, as well as that of the most expensive workmen.'
[34] *Ibid.*, Vol. I, p. 85.
[35] *Ibid.*, Vol. I, p. 98.
[36] *Economic and Philosophic Manuscripts of 1844* (Foreign Languages Publishing House, Moscow, n.d.), p. 22.
[37] *Wealth of Nations*, Vol. I, p. 80.

will fall even below this.[38] In an advancing state, however, the condition of the labouring poor will be 'the happiest and the most comfortable',[39] since the rate of wages which equilibrates demand and supply in the labour market will be appreciably above the subsistence level. And this, Smith argues, is in fact the actual situation in Britain. Over the present century, he says, the 'real recompence' of labour has been rising (due largely, of course, to the steady accumulation of capital), and it is now appreciably above the subsistence level.[40] This is definitely advantageous to society, on grounds not only of equity[41] but also of efficiency;[42] and the process can readily be continued by adopting the appropriate measures required to encourage the further accumulation of capital. Provided such measures are in fact adopted, Smith apparently believed, one need not worry too much about the prospect of reaching a stationary state: after all, 'perhaps no country has ever yet arrived at this degree of opulence'; and even a country like China, which at first sight appears to have done so, might be able to increase its wealth further by means of an appropriate alteration in its 'laws and institutions'.[43] Nor, a fortiori, need one worry about the prospect of a declining state. The only example of the latter which Smith gives is 'the present state of Bengal, and of some other of the English settlements in the East Indies' – and this he blames specifically on the policies adopted by 'the mercantile company which oppresses and domineers in the East Indies'.[44] Nor, finally, need one worry unduly about the fact that 'the increase of stock, which raises wages, tends to lower profit'.[45] One can certainly find in the *Wealth of Nations* the germs of the influential notion that the long-run tendency of the rate of profit is to fall;[46] but there appears to be no hint anywhere that this will ever be sufficiently serious to threaten the future prospects of capitalism.[47]

To conclude this section, something should be said about the celebrated passages in the *Wealth of Nations*, to be found in a section entitled 'Of the Expence of the Institutions for the Education of Youth',[48] in which Smith talks about the way in which the extension of the division of labour in the manufactory exposes those whose whole life is spent in performing a few simple operations to a process of 'mental mutilation',[49] which may result in their becoming 'as stupid and ignorant as it is possible for a human

---

[38] *Ibid.*, Vol. I, pp. 111 and 266; and cf. also pp. 91 and 99.
[39] *Ibid.*, Vol. I, p. 99.
[40] *Ibid.*, Vol. I, pp. 91–3, 95–6, and 106.
[41] *Ibid.*, Vol. I, p. 96.
[42] *Ibid.*, Vol. I, p. 99.
[43] *Ibid.*, Vol. I, pp. 111–12.
[44] *Ibid.*, Vol. I, p. 91.
[45] *Ibid.*, Vol. I, p. 105.
[46] The most relevant passages will be found in Vol. I, pp. 144–5 and 352–3.
[47] Cf. David A. Reisman, *op. cit.*, pp. 173–4.
[48] Vol. II, pp. 758 ff.
[49] *Wealth of Nations*, Vol. II, p. 787.

creature to become'.[50] Marx was fond of quoting from these passages,[51] and some echoes of them are probably to be found in his descriptions of the effects of 'the general law of capitalist accumulation' (e.g., when he speaks of the way in which under capitalism all methods for the development of production 'mutilate the labourer into a fragment of a man').[52] It is not unduly misleading, therefore, to suggest that this Smithian idea may well have been the source of *one* of the ingredients of Marx's concept of 'alienation'.

What *is* misleading, however, is to suggest that Smith himself visualized this 'mental mutilation' as a fatal flaw in the capitalist system itself – a flaw which predestined it to some kind of all-embracing moral decay at the end of its developmental journey. The idea that the division of labour may have bad effects as well as good ones first appears in Smith's work, not in the *Wealth of Nations*, but in his Glasgow lectures on Jurisprudence. It makes its appearance there in a lecture dealing with 'the influence of commerce on the manners of a people', in which Smith begins by describing the 'principal virtues' of a commercial nation. He then goes on to remark that 'there are some inconveniences, however, arising from a commercial spirit', the first of these 'inconveniences' being that the division of labour 'confines the views of men'.[53] And when the idea reappears in a developed form in the *Wealth of Nations*, this bad effect of the division of labour is still considered as no more than an inconvenience; a cost of growth, certainly, but not really a very heavy one. The essential virtues of the 'commercial spirit' and the division of labour are still extolled; the advancing state (in which the division of labour is of course being further extended) is described as one in which the condition of the labouring poor is 'cheerful' and 'hearty';[54] and Smith suggests that the effects of 'mental mutilation' can be mitigated – and for 'a very small expence', too – by means of a measure of state aid to education.[55] It should also perhaps be added that in advocating this policy of state aid to education Smith seems to have been concerned not only with the happiness of the labourers, but also, to at least as great an extent, with the maintenance of the country's defence capacity and the prevention of 'faction and sedition'.[56]

IV

Another link between Smith and Marx, which has been less commented upon than those considered above, arises from the fact that both men can

[50] *Ibid.*, Vol. II, p. 782.
[51] See, e.g., *Capital*, Vol. I, p. 362.
[52] *Capital*, Vol. I, p. 645.
[53] *Lectures on Justice, Police, Revenue and Arms* (edited by E. Cannan, Oxford University Press, 1896), pp. 253–5.
[54] *Wealth of Nations*, Vol. I, p. 99.
[55] *Ibid.*, Vol. II, pp. 785–6.
[56] *Ibid.*, Vol. II, pp. 782 and 786–8.

be said (with appropriate qualifications in each case) to have been 'economic determinists'.[57] In Smith's case this 'economic determinism' reflected itself first and foremost in his view of the development of society, although its influence can also be detected in a number of other parts of his analysis.

Smith's view of the development of society, which was embodied mainly in his version of the four stages theory, is dealt with in some detail in the next essay in this volume,[58] and there is therefore no need for me to say very much about it at this juncture. Let us note only that Smith was probably the first thinker to put forward in a coherent form the immensely influential notion that societies normally tended to progress over time through four more or less consecutive and distinct socio-economic stages, each based on a different mode of subsistence, namely, hunting, pasturage, agriculture, and commerce. To each of these economic bases, in Smith's account, it was assumed that there corresponded a different superstructure of political, moral, and legal ideas and institutions. Movement from one of the stages to the next, although the result of human action and in an important sense law-governed, was not consciously directed or designed: rather, in Smith's view, it was a kind of unintended by-product of the conflict of individual wills and actions, which were often directed towards quite different (usually self-regarding) ends. As Adam Ferguson was later to put it, 'nations stumble upon establishments, which are indeed the result of human action, but not the execution of any human design'.[59] The mechanism involved in this process was similar in its character to that which Smith envisaged as operating in the more narrowly 'economic' sphere, where the net effect of the self-regarding activities of the economic agents was the maximization of the national product at any given moment of time, the maximization of its rate of growth over a period of time, and a reasonably adequate and efficient distribution of income among the different social classes.

This set of ideas, around which a great deal of Smith's thinking was oriented, was not of course identical with Marx's materialist conception of history. Marx's 'mode of production' was by no means the same as Smith's 'mode of subsistence'; his sociology was completely emancipated from theology whereas Smith's was not; and his 'laws of motion of capitalism' acted maleficently whereas Smith's by and large acted beneficently. But Smith's general attitude towards the problem of the determination of the structure and development of society is surely recognizable as a logical ancestor of Marx's; and I have always found it surprising that Marx himself should have said so little about this aspect of Smith's thought. It is true, of course, that Marx did not have access to Smith's lectures on Jurisprudence, in which the four stages theory appeared much more prominently than it was later to do in the *Wealth of Nations*. But it is still

[57] Cf. Reisman, *op. cit.*, p. 10 and *passim*.
[58] Below, pp. 18 ff.
[59] Adam Ferguson, *An Essay on the History of Civil Society* (6th edn., London, 1793), p. 205.

fairly clearly visible in the latter book; and Smith's published work as a whole is chock-full of 'materialist' statements of which one might have expected Marx to take rather more notice than he in fact did. It could very plausibly be argued, indeed, that it is in Smith's numerous remarks about the influence exerted upon the character of individuals, social classes and nations by the manner in which the people concerned get their living, about the relativity of manners and morals to time and place, and about the socio-economic determinants of political attitudes, literary styles, consumption patterns, etc.,[60] that the main similarities between his approach and Marx's are to be found.

V

How then can we sum up this question of the relation between Smith and Marx? It will be clear from what I have said in Section III of this article that I do not think Smith can properly be regarded as a kind of premature eighteenth-century Marxian socialist. Most of the Smithian propositions that are usually relied upon in order to support such a view take on a much less radical hue when they are seen in the perspective of Smith's argument as a whole. Also, of course, it must be remembered that many of Smith's critical statements about capitalism and the capitalists, although they might well have seemed inflammatory or even revolutionary if they had been made in Marx's time, must have seemed merely honest and realistic in Smith's time, when capitalism had not yet come under serious attack. Nevertheless, as we have seen, there are certain respects in which there is no doubt at all that Smith must be regarded as a precursor of the intellectual tradition within which Marx worked. Smith provided Marx (and of course Ricardo) with a model of the new tripartite framework of class relationships characteristic of capitalist society; he formulated a new concept of surplus in which profit was emancipated from its former dependence upon rent and ascribed to the productivity of labour in general; and he outlined a new theory of the development of society and the nature of socio-historical processes in general which, whether Marx himself was aware of it or not, set the stage for the eventual emergence of the materialist conception of history.

These ideas of Smith's were embodied in the general *economic methodology* which he employed, at any rate for part of the time, in his analysis of the determination of class incomes and the prices of finished commodities. The distinguishing feature of this methodology was that it stressed the determining role of the *techniques and relationships of production* – in much the same kind of way as the more developed methodologies of Ricardo and Marx were later to do. Up to a point, therefore, Smith can be regarded as the founder of what has today come to be known as the Ricardo–Marx tradition in value and distribution theory. But as we have already seen

[60] Cf. Reisman, *op. cit.*, pp. 88–101 and *passim*.

there was an 'exoteric' as well as an 'esoteric' side to Smith's thought, which economists like Malthus were soon to seize upon and develop. Thus Smith can also, perhaps, be regarded as the founder of the other main tradition in value and distribution theory – the tradition which takes as its starting-point the *conditions of exchange* rather than the conditions of production. This curious ambiguity in Smith's position in the history of economic analysis is discussed more fully in a later essay in the present volume.[61]

Finally, it should be emphasized once again that when we turn our attention from the economic methodology employed by Smith to his moral and political attitude towards the capitalist system, there is not really any ambiguity at all about his position. Although he did not neglect to consider a number of the social costs of the system, about which (to the extent that he recognized them as such) he was always honest and forthright, there is no doubt that he envisaged the benefits of the system as very greatly exceeding these costs. From the Marxian point of view, I suppose that this attitude of Smith's towards capitalism was in a sense historically justifiable – not simply because capitalism was a necessary stage on the road to socialism, but also because in Smith's time, when capitalism was still up to a point in its 'manufacturing' stage and could still be conceived as basically competitive, it was in fact quite plausible to regard the benefits of the system as exceeding the costs. A century later, however, when the age of 'manufacture' had given way to the infinitely more dynamic and disturbing age of 'machinery and modern industry', and competition was beginning to be replaced by monopoly, everything (at any rate as Marx saw it) was turned upside down. The innate contradictions of the capitalist system, which Smith's bourgeois limitations had prevented him from apprehending, had begun to manifest themselves on the surface of economic reality in various extremely unpleasant ways.[62] Thus the very features of capitalism which had appeared to Smith as the main sources of its strength and stability – atomism in production, the private accumulation of capital, the inequality of wealth and income, and so on – appeared to Marx as the main sources of its weakness and instability. Also, of course, whereas Smith, writing in the 1770s, was unable to conceive of the working class ever being capable of playing an active role in politics, or of anything like an 'Oceana or Utopia' ever being established in Britain,[63] Marx, writing a century later, was for obvious reasons able to take a radically different view. But he himself would probably have been the first to acknowledge that it might have been much more difficult for him to arrive at this view if he had not had the shoulders of Adam Smith to stand on.

[61] Below, pp. 156–8.
[62] Cf. p. 4 above.
[63] *Wealth of Nations*, Vol. I, p. 471: 'To expect, indeed, that the freedom of trade should ever be entirely restored in Great Britain, is as absurd as to expect that an Oceana or Utopia should ever be established in it.'

II

Smith, Turgot, and the 'Four Stages' Theory[1]

I

In the early years after the war, when I was a lecturer in the Department of Political Economy at Glasgow University, I became very interested in the work of the members of the so-called Scottish Historical School, which Roy Pascal had rescued from oblivion in his remarkable article of 1938.[2] I was impressed in particular by John Millar, whose work was pervaded by a theory of history and society which seemed to me to be a kind of preview of the materialist conception of history upon which I had been brought up in my revolutionary youth. I was interested also, of course, in the work of the other members of the School – notably that of Adam Ferguson, William Robertson, and Adam Smith; but these three seemed to be rather shadowy, peripheral figures in the face of the gigantic presence of the great John Millar.

The basic ideas which I detected, or believed I detected, in the work of Millar and his associates, taken as a whole, were roughly as follows, to proceed from the more to the less general:

1. Everything in society and its history was bound together by a succession of causes and effects. Thus the task of the historian was to seek for reasons

[1] This essay owes its origin to a lecture given under the same title at a History of Economic Thought Conference at Sheffield University on 3 January 1970. In its first published version (*History of Political Economy*, 3, 1971) some of the arguments of the lecture were extended and a number of references were added, but I made no real attempt to transform what was originally an informal talk into a formal paper. The same goes for the present version, in which I have allowed most of the colloquialisms and bits of autobiography to remain. I have, however, ventured to add a few footnote references to some more recent work of my own in this field. In addition, I have taken this opportunity to make two or three additional entries in the 'calendar' described in Section II; to remove a paragraph in which I had wrongly adduced two fragments of Smith's on the division of labour as evidence for the back-dating of the four stages theory to the Edinburgh period; and, most important of all, to rewrite a number of passages in which I had seriously underestimated the part played by Montesquieu in the development of the four stages theory. It was Andrew Skinner who finally convinced me that I was wrong about the dating of the fragments; and it was a former student of mine, David Allen, who drew my attention to the importance of Book XVIII of the *Spirit of Laws*.

[2] Roy Pascal, 'Property and Society: The Scottish Historical School of the Eighteenth Century', *Modern Quarterly*, 1, 1938.

and causes, with the aid of the new scientific methodology which had already proved so fruitful in other spheres of enquiry.

2. Society developed blindly, but not arbitrarily. As Ferguson put it: 'Every step and every movement of the multitude, even in what are termed enlightened ages, are made with equal blindness to the future; and nations stumble upon establishments, which are indeed the result of human action, but not the execution of any human design.'[3] But social changes did occur, and in the process of change certain uniformities and regularities were observable. The great task was to explain these, in terms of the *laws* which lay behind social development.

3. In the process of development the key factor was the 'mode of sub-sistence'. As Robertson said: 'In every inquiry concerning the operations of men when united together in society, the first object of attention should be their mode of subsistence. Accordingly as that varies, their laws and policy must be different.'[4]

4. In tracing out the process of development, particular emphasis should be placed on the reciprocal interconnection between property and govern-ment. Smith put the point magistrally: 'Property and civil government very much depend on one another. The preservation of property and the inequality of possession first formed it, and the state of property must always vary with the form of government.'[5]

5. Emphasis should also be placed on the emergence and growth of a social surplus, upon which depended the rise of towns, the arts, manu-factures, new social classes, etc.

6. Development should be regarded as proceeding through four nor-mally consecutive socio-economic stages, each based on a particular 'mode of subsistence', namely, hunting, pasturage, agriculture, and commerce. To each stage there corresponded different ideas and institutions relating to both property and government, and in relation to each, general state-ments could be made about the state of manners and morals, the social surplus, the legal system, the division of labour, and so on.

All these ideas were tied up together with a sensationalist psychology or theory of knowledge derived in one way or another from Locke; and even making allowances for my youthful ardour I do not think I was all that wrong in describing this theoretical system as *a*, if not *the*, materialist conception of history.

At this period of my life I misguidedly regarded myself as a kind of naturalized Scot, and it was thus with a glow of patriotic pride that I proclaimed the emergence of this theoretical system as an exclusively Scottish phenomenon, explaining its origin in terms of the rather special

[3] Adam Ferguson, *An Essay on the History of Civil Society* (6th edn., London, 1793), p. 205.
[4] William Robertson, *Works* (Thomas Nelson, Edinburgh, 1890), Vol. II, p. 104.
[5] *Lectures on Justice, Police, Revenue and Arms* (edited by E. Cannan, Oxford University Press, 1896), p. 8.

social and economic situation of Scotland at the time.[6] A little later, however, when I started working on the French Physiocrats, I came to realize that this was too parochial a view. For Quesnay and Mirabeau, as well, had put forward *a* materialist conception of history. When you knew what you were looking for, it was there as clear as crystal, not only in Quesnay's marginal notes on Mirabeau's early economic manuscripts but also in cold print, particularly in Chapter 8 of *Rural Philosophy* (1763) and in *Natural Right* (1765).[7] And when Andrew Skinner revealed the existence of a rather similar set of ideas in the work of Sir James Steuart – who had had, so to speak, a foot on either side of the English Channel – this seemed finally to confirm that the phenomenon in question was in fact a joint Scottish and French one. The Auld Alliance, it appeared, was riding again.

But that was not to be the end of the story. Shortly after this I embarked upon two editorial jobs, which were to occupy me for some years. The first of these related to the new set of student's notes of Adam Smith's Glasgow lectures on Jurisprudence which was discovered some years ago in Aberdeen.[8] The second related to certain early sociological works written by the young Turgot during his period at the Sorbonne.[9] Carrying out these two editorial jobs more or less simultaneously, I naturally looked at the Scottish and French material concerned to see if there were any traces in it of the particular view of history and society in which I was interested. It was not necessary, I soon found, to look very far. Almost immediately it became evident that two further reorientations of my notions were going to be required.

First, it was clear from the new set of notes of Smith's lectures on Jurisprudence that those of us who had put Smith down as a more or less peripheral member of the Scottish Historical School were simply wrong. In the new notes the set of basic ideas outlined above appears more clearly, extensively, and sharply than it does in the Cannan notes. In particular, the 'four stages' theory is given considerable prominence; and it is perhaps

---

[6] See Ronald L. Meek, *Economics and Ideology and other Essays* (Chapman and Hall, London, 1967), pp. 47–8.

[7] See R. L. Meek, *Economics of Physiocracy* (Allen and Unwin, London, 1962), pp. 43–71.

[8] I am editing these notes jointly with Professor D. D. Raphael and Professor P. G. Stein for the Glasgow bicentennial edition of the works and correspondence of Adam Smith. The views expressed in the present essay, however, are mine alone, and neither of my two collaborators should be held responsible for them.

[9] See R. L. Meek, *Turgot on Progress, Sociology and Economics* (Cambridge University Press, 1973). I should perhaps make it clear at this point that the present essay is not meant as a contribution to the so-called Turgot–Smith controversy. It is true that I shall be impliedly claiming that the Turgot–Smith controversialists have tended to overlook one of the most important of the new ideas developed and held in common by Turgot and Smith. But the idea in question was more 'sociological' than 'economic' in character, and in any event the two men almost certainly developed it quite independently of one another – two facts which take what I have to say right outside the orbit of the traditional controversy. (I reserve the right, however, to prove incontrovertibly in a subsequent essay that Smith was the author of the famous translation of Turgot's Six Edicts into Sanskrit.)

not too much to say that it is revealed as the basic conceptual framework within which the major part of Smith's argument in the lectures is set.[10]

It was with new eyes, therefore, that I went back to Dugald Stewart's biographical memoir of Smith to re-read the contemporary descriptions of his Glasgow lectures which it contains. In the account of the lectures which John Millar supplied to Stewart, the following passage relating to the section on Justice occurs:

> Upon this subject he followed the plan that seems to be suggested by Montesquieu; endeavouring to trace the gradual progress of jurisprudence, both public and private, from the rudest to the most refined ages, and to point out the effects of those arts which contribute to subsistence, and to the accumulation of property, in producing correspondent improvements or alterations in law and government.[11]

I must confess that I had always felt that in this passage Millar was exaggerating a little, perhaps describing more what he would have liked to see in Smith's lectures than what was actually there. With the new notes in front of one, however, the accuracy of Millar's description is rather spectacularly confirmed. And one can also better appreciate the significance of that remarkable section of Stewart's memoir[12] in which he talks for several pages about Smith's great interest in 'Theoretical or Conjectural History', which is claimed to have pervaded most of his writings, his conversation, and in particular his lectures on Jurisprudence.

This line of inquiry, says Stewart, began with Montesquieu, who 'attempted to account, from the changes in the condition of mankind, which take place in the different stages of their progress, for the corresponding alterations which their institutions undergo'.[13] As a description of Montesquieu's approach this is a little inept: few clear traces of a stadial view of this type can in fact be found in the *Spirit of Laws*. As a description of Smith's approach, however, it is very accurate indeed;[14] and the passage as a whole enables us to understand better Millar's well-known statement that if Montesquieu was the Bacon in this field of inquiry, Adam Smith was the Newton.[15] The moral of all this, surely, is that it

---

[10] Some of the key passages are reproduced in R. L. Meek, *Social Science and the Ignoble Savage* (Cambridge University Press, 1976), pp. 116–26.
[11] Dugald Stewart, *Biographical Memoir of Adam Smith* (Kelley reprint, New York, 1966), p. 12.
[12] *Ibid.*, pp. 32–7.
[13] *Ibid.*, p. 35.
[14] See Duncan Forbes, "'Scientific' Whiggism: Adam Smith and John Millar" (*Cambridge Journal*, 7, 1954), p. 646.
[15] John Millar, *An Historical View of the English Government* (London, 1787), p. 528. The full quotation, which appears in a footnote, reads as follows: 'I am happy to acknowledge the obligations I feel myself under to this illustrious philosopher [Adam Smith], by having, at an early period of life, had the benefit of hearing his lectures on the History of Civil Society, and of enjoying his unreserved conversation on the same subject.– The great Montesquieu pointed out the road. He was the Lord Bacon in this branch of philosophy. Dr. Smith is the Newton.'

would be unwise to underestimate the seminal character of Smith's own contribution in this field, and the extent to which he influenced other members of the School, including Millar himself.

The second reorientation of my notions which was required became clear when I passed from a reading of these new lecture notes to a reading of those early writings of Turgot which I had undertaken to edit. What suddenly became obvious to me was the crucial role which the 'four stages' theory must have played in the emergence of the new Franco–Scottish view of socio-historical development.

My starting-point here was the two lectures which the young Turgot gave at the Sorbonne in 1750, the second of which is quite well-known because of the doctrine of perfectibility which is clearly stated in it. Much more important, however, is another document, dating apparently from the same period, entitled *Plan of Two Discourses on Universal History*.[16] Here we find many of the ingredients of the new view, including most notably a quite advanced statement of the four stages theory – or at any rate of a three stages theory, with a distinct hint of the fourth stage. Hunting, pasturage, and agriculture are very clearly defined and distinguished, and Turgot describes the way in which population, property, slavery, the social surplus, the system of government, etc., change as mankind proceeds from one stage to the next. The development of this idea in Turgot's mind during the two or three years immediately prior to its relatively mature expression in this document can up to a point be traced, but this is not the place for such an exercise.[17] Suffice it to say that in the *Plan* (and in one or two other documents composed by Turgot at this time), the stadial view of social development is beginning to become a kind of general conceptual framework, in much the same way as it did in Smith's lectures on Jurisprudence.

This rather startling fact led me to realize that I had hitherto tended to underestimate the role of the four stages idea in the emergence of the eighteenth-century version of the materialist conception of history. This idea was not, it now appeared, a kind of end-product, a particular proposition which emerged only after a more general proposition had been developed and applied: rather, it was the idea whose emergence *made possible* many of the remarkable developments in the science of society which took place during the last half-century of the Enlightenment.[18]

II

On the assumption, then, that the four stages theory was in fact much more important than has generally been appreciated, let us try to construct a kind of calendar of the first decade of its development. The great problem

[16] See *Turgot on Progress, Sociology and Economics*, pp. 61–118.
[17] See *ibid.*, pp. 4–10.
[18] I would have got on to this a great deal earlier if I had treated with the respect they deserved a number of inspired hints in the early pages of the article by Duncan Forbes which is referred to in [14].

here is where we should put Smith. Let us therefore proceed for the moment as if Smith had not existed, leaving until later the question of where he should actually be fitted in.

The first date on our calendar is 1750–1, when Turgot's contributions appear to have been written. I have tried to find earlier expressions of the four stages theory, or of ideas closely akin to it,[19] but apart from the case of Montesquieu (who receives separate treatment below)[20] I have had hardly any success. I can find remarkably little, for example, in the Greeks, Cantillon, Mandeville, Bolingbroke, Hume, Hutcheson, Voltaire, or Priestley which could really be said to rank as a definite anticipation. All I have been able to discover are certain fairly general streams or traditions of thought which could conceivably have led, either directly or indirectly, to the emergence of the four stages theory round about 1750. (These lines of thought are discussed at the end of the present essay.) But the theory as such would seem to have had few, if any, real ancestors.

If we are prepared to skip over Rousseau's *Discourse on the Origin of Inequality*, which I think we are justified in doing,[21] the second date on our calendar must surely be 1757. This was the year of the appearance of what would seem to be the first *published* version of the four stages theory, in Sir John Dalrymple's *Essay Towards a General History of Feudal Property in Great Britain*.[22] It was also the year of the celebrated interview between Quesnay and Mirabeau at Versailles, at which – if we can believe Mirabeau's rather suspect account[23] – Quesnay put forward the notion of a more or less orderly progression through the hunting, pasturage, and agricultural stages.[24]

The third date on our calendar is 1758, the year in which Lord Kames's *Historical Law-Tracts* was published.[25] The four stages theory appears suddenly in the form of a lengthy footnote in the first essay in the book, that on the history of the criminal law.[26] It comes in again at the beginning of the second essay, on the history of promises and covenants;[27] and in

[19] The results of a later and more sustained effort to discover the antecedents of the theory are recorded in Chapter 1 of *Social Science and the Ignoble Savage*.

[20] P. 29.

[21] The reasons for my view on this point are spelt out in detail in *Social Science and the Ignoble Savage*, pp. 76–91.

[22] See *ibid.*, pp. 99–102.

[23] In a letter to Rousseau written about ten years afterwards. See *Economics of Physiocracy*, pp. 16–18.

[24] 1757 was also the year in which the Italian economist Antonio Genovesi put forward, in an essay entitled *Digressioni Economiche*, a theory of stadial development containing several of the elements of the four stages theory. I owe this reference to Dr Enzo Pesciarelli, the author of an article (which it is hoped will shortly be published) on the Italian contribution to the four stages theory.

[25] Although not published until 1758, it seems probable that Kames's book was started, and parts of it finished, several years earlier. Cf. A. F. Tytler, *Memoirs of Kames* (2nd edn., Edinburgh, 1814), Vol. I, p. 299.

[26] Kames, *Historical Law-Tracts* (Edinburgh, 1758), Vol. I, pp. 77–80.

[27] *Ibid.*, Vol. I, pp. 92–3.

the third essay, on the history of property, it becomes all-pervasive. In the earlier works of Kames, so far as I can see, there were no more than the vaguest hints of the idea, even in contexts where one would most have expected to find it (e.g., in discussions of property).[28] In 1758, too, Helvétius made use of a version of the theory in a passage in his *De l'Esprit*, and Goguet made much more extensive use of it in his *De l'Origine des Loix, des Arts, et des Sciences.*[29]

If we were to extend our calendar beyond the late 1750s it would soon become very crowded indeed. In the 1760s and early 1770s the mature works of the Scottish Historical School began to appear – Ferguson's *Essay on the History of Civil Society*, for example, in 1767; Robertson's *History of the Reign of the Emperor Charles V* in 1769;[30] and Millar's *Observations Concerning the Distinction of Ranks in Society* in 1771. Other important works by authors associated with the School soon followed – notably, in 1774, Kames's *Sketches of the History of Man.* In most of these works – and in a large number of others by authors unconnected with the School – the four stages theory was used as an important frame of reference, and was linked up with some or all of the other ideas listed in the first part of this essay to form one or another variant of the 'materialist conception of history' of the eighteenth century.

III

The missing piece in this jigsaw puzzle is obviously Smith. Whereabouts in the calendar ought his contribution to be fitted? All that we really know for certain is that in the lectures on Jurisprudence which he gave at Glasgow University *in 1762–3* (the academic session to which the recently-found set of student's lecture notes specifically refers) he made extensive use of the four stages theory. But he had begun lecturing to the Moral Philosophy class at Glasgow as early as October 1751, and for three years before that he had given his famous public lectures in Edinburgh. From what period, then, does Smith's use of the four stages theory in fact date? It is unlikely that we shall ever find an absolutely certain answer to this question, but I think it is possible to move some distance towards one by the use of a little 'theoretical or conjectural history' of our own. What I hope to suggest, with its aid, is that Smith's use of the four stages theory *probably* dates from the latter part of his Edinburgh period.

Our starting-point here is Millar's description of the Justice section of Smith's Moral Philosophy lectures, which I have already quoted above.[31] From the context, and from certain other considerations, it seems very probable that Millar's description related to the lectures as Smith delivered them during his earliest years as a professor at Glasgow, which was when

[28] See *Social Science and the Ignoble Savage*, p. 106.

[29] *Ibid.*, pp. 92–7.

[30] Robertson's *History of Scotland* had already appeared in 1759.

[31] P. 21.

Millar himself attended them;[32] and, all things considered, it seems likely that the form and content of this particular part of the course were not essentially different in those early years from what they were in 1762–3. It seems very probable, then, that Smith was putting forward the four stages theory in his Moral Philosophy lectures at Glasgow at any rate by the mid 1750s.[33] This is of some importance, because as we shall see immediately the year 1755 is quite crucial in the story.

In 1755, Stewart tells us, Smith drew up and 'presented . . . to a society of which he was then a member' a 'short manuscript' giving 'a pretty long enumeration . . . of certain leading principles, both political and literary, to which he was anxious to establish his exclusive right'. The context in which Stewart's account of this manuscript appears is a discussion of the originality or otherwise of the doctrines of the *Wealth of Nations*, with particular reference to the question of whether the Physiocrats anticipated Smith's views on the freedom of trade and industry. Stewart reminds his listeners that 'Mr. Smith's Political Lectures, comprehending the fundamental principles of his *Inquiry*, were delivered at Glasgow as early as the year 1752 or 1753; at a period, surely, when there existed no French performance on the subject, that could be of much use to him in guiding his researches'.[34] Shortly afterwards there follows the account of the 'short manuscript', which account is so important that it must be reproduced in full:

I am aware that the evidence I have hitherto produced of Mr. Smith's originality may be objected to as not perfectly decisive, as it rests entirely on the recollection of those students who attended his first courses of Moral Philosophy at Glasgow; a recollection which, at the distance of forty years, cannot be supposed to be very accurate. There exists, however, fortunately, a short manuscript drawn up by Mr. Smith in the year 1755, and presented by him to a society of which he was then a member; in which paper, a pretty long enumeration is given of certain leading principles, both political and literary, to which he was anxious to establish his exclusive right, in order to prevent the possibility of

---

[32] The most important piece of evidence on these points is John Craig's account of Millar's early contacts with Smith at Glasgow. See the *Account of the Life and Writings of John Millar, Esq.* prefixed to the 4th edn. of Millar's book, *The Origin of the Distinction of Ranks* (Edinburgh, 1806), pp. iv–v. If one reads this in conjunction with the description of Smith's lectures given by Millar to Stewart, and with the acknowledgement of his obligation to Smith made by Millar in his *Historical View of the English Government* (see [15]), it is difficult not to reach the conclusion stated in the text.

[33] Some additional evidence to this effect, which has only very recently come to light, is surveyed in the fourth essay in this volume. See in particular pp. 80–1 below.

[34] Stewart, *Biographical Memoir of Adam Smith*, p. 66. In a long note to this section written in 1810 (pp. 88–95) Stewart states that when his memoir was first written he 'was not fully aware to what an extent the French Economists had been anticipated in some of their most important conclusions by writers (chiefly British) of a much earlier date'. He still defends Smith's originality, however; and it is perhaps significant that at the very end of the note the following sentence appears: 'Mr. Smith's Lectures, it must be remembered (to the fame of which he owed his appointment at Glasgow), were read at Edinburgh as early as 1748.'

some rival claims which he thought he had reason to apprehend, and to which his situation as a Professor, added to his unreserved communications in private companies, rendered him peculiarly liable. This paper is at present in my possession. It is expressed with a good deal of that honest and indignant warmth, which is perhaps unavoidable by a man who is conscious of the purity of his own intentions, when he suspects that advantages have been taken of the frankness of his temper. On such occasions, due allowances are not always made for those plagiarisms, which, however cruel in their effects, do not necessarily imply bad faith in those who are guilty of them; for the bulk of mankind, incapable themselves of original thought, are perfectly unable to form a conception of the nature of the injury done to a man of inventive genius, by encroaching on a favourite speculation. For reasons known to some members of this Society, it would be improper by the publication of this manuscript, to revive the memory of private differences; and I should not have even alluded to it, if I did not think it a valuable document of the progress of Mr. Smith's political ideas at a very early period. Many of the most important opinions in *The Wealth of Nations* are there detailed; but I shall quote only the following sentences: – 'Man is generally considered by statesmen and projectors as the materials of a sort of political mechanics. Projectors disturb nature in the course of her operations in human affairs; and it requires no more than to let her alone, and give her fair play in the pursuit of her ends, that she may establish her own designs.' – And in another passage: – 'Little else is requisite to carry a State to the highest degree of opulence from the lowest barbarism, but peace, easy taxes, and a tolerable administration of justice; all the rest being brought about by the natural course of things. All governments which thwart this natural course, which force things into another channel, or which endeavour to arrest the progress of society at a particular point, are unnatural, and to support themselves are obliged to be oppressive and tyrannical ... A great part of the opinions', he observes, 'enumerated in this paper, is treated of at length in some lectures which I have still by me, and which were written in the hand of a clerk who left my service six years ago. They have all of them been the constant subjects of my lectures since I first taught Mr. Craigie's class, the first winter I spent in Glasgow, down to this day, without any considerable variation. They had all of them been the subjects of lectures which I read at Edinburgh the winter before I left it, and I can adduce innumerable witnesses, both from that place and from this, who will ascertain them sufficiently to be mine'.[35]

The last three sentences of this account, purporting to be a direct quotation from Smith's own words in the paper, are of primary importance in the present connection. One notes, first, the careful reference to 'Mr.

[35] *Biographical Memoir of Adam Smith*, pp. 67–8.

Craigie's class', which Smith would not have singled out in this way if it had been his 'literary' rather than his 'political' principles to which he wished to draw particular attention. One notes, second, Smith's insistence on the fact that *all* the opinions enumerated in the paper had not only been the 'constant subjects' of his lectures at Glasgow but had also been the subjects of lectures given at Edinburgh the winter before he left it (1750–1). And one notes, third, that 'a great part' (not 'all') of these opinions had been treated of at length in some lectures 'written in the hand of a clerk who left my service six years ago' – i.e., presumably, in 1749. The implication of the latter statement is perhaps ambiguous: in the context, it could be taken to imply either that Smith gave lectures on 'political' subjects at Edinburgh before the winter of 1750–1 in which a great part, but not all, of the opinions concerned were put forward, or simply that the documentary evidence he was able to produce in 1755 concerning what he said in the winter of 1750–1 was incomplete. But the central point is not ambiguous: all the 'political' opinions enumerated in the paper, Smith is claiming, date from the Edinburgh period.

The only real question at issue, therefore, is whether this list of opinions included the four stages theory. I would myself think it most unlikely that it did not do so. It is true that Stewart's account concentrates attention on 'economic' rather than 'sociological' principles. It must be remembered, however, that Stewart was mainly concerned at this point in his memoir of Smith with the question of the originality of the doctrines of the *Wealth of Nations*; and it is noteworthy that even in the presence of this constraint the second of the two actual opinions of Smith's which Stewart quotes should perhaps be construed as being basically sociological rather than economic.[36] The point is, surely, that in 1755 the *Wealth of Nations* was still almost a quarter of a century away, and the danger of plagiarization of such economic ideas as Smith might have arrived at by 1755 could hardly have been very serious. But if Smith had by 1755 arrived at the main sociological ideas which we know for certain he was putting forward in his lectures only seven years later, then he might very reasonably have feared the plagiarization of these. Studies in the general field of the 'history of civil society' were being given a considerable impetus in France at this time by the work of Rousseau, as Smith himself pointed out in the *Edinburgh Review* in that same crucial year 1755; and nearer home, men like Robertson and Kames were also showing signs of a developing interest in 'the first beginnings and gradual progress of society'. Even to one without Smith's rather suspicious and volatile temperament, it might have seemed advisable at this time to stake a claim to originality in respect of sociological ideas as novel and important as the four stages theory.

There is another reason, of a more intriguing if at the same time more

---

[36] There is an interesting – and perhaps deliberate – link between this 'opinion' and the one ascribed to Smith earlier in Stewart's narrative (p. 36) in the course of his discussion of Smith's excursions into the field of 'Theoretical or Conjectural History'.

conjectural kind, why Stewart may have felt it advisable to disguise or soft-pedal the predominantly sociological character of the leading principles in respect of which Smith had apprehended 'rival claims' in 1755. It may well be that the mysterious 'private differences', the memory of which Stewart was so anxious not to revive, had in fact been with Robertson – who was in the final stages of his last illness at the very time when Stewart delivered his memoir of Smith to the Select Society,[37] and who was of course the Principal of Stewart's own university. We know that Smith accused Robertson of borrowing the 'first vol.' of his *History of the Reign of the Emperor Charles V* from his lectures;[38] and although this particular book of Robertson's did not appear until 1769 there are a number of reasons why Smith, even as early as 1755, might have feared that Robertson was about to make some 'rival claims'. Robertson had quite probably attended the lectures which Smith gave at Edinburgh;[39] in January 1755 he preached his famous sermon, *The Situation of the World at the Time of Christ's Appearance*, with its strong socio-historical overtones; in 1755 he published a review of a book about America which showed him already making sociological generalizations about early society on the basis of an account of the Indian nations;[40] and in 1754–5, too, he was playing a prominent part, along with Smith, in the activities of the Select Society, which was then debating such questions as 'Whether the difference of national characters be chiefly owing to the nature of different climates, or to moral and political causes?'[41]

[37] See Stewart's 'Memoir of Robertson', reprinted in the Kelley edition of *Biographical Memoir of Adam Smith*, pp. 198–9.

[38] The reference here is to the account given (at second hand) by John Callander of Craigforth (Edinburgh University MSS., La. II, 451(2)). The 'first vol.' referred to is clearly the long introductory section entitled *A View of the Progress of Society in Europe, from the Subversion of the Roman Empire, to the Beginning of the Sixteenth Century*, together with the even longer set of notes appended to it under the title *Proofs and Illustrations*. The sixth note is of particular importance, and will be referred to again below (see [44]).

[39] It seems probable on a number of grounds that Robertson attended, but I know of no definite evidence to this effect. Scott, it is true, in his *Adam Smith as Student and Professor* (Jackson, Son and Co., Glasgow, 1937) includes him in the list of definite attenders (p. 63). But this seems to be based on a gross misquotation from the Callander document (*ibid.*, pp. 54–5), in which it is made to appear that the word 'here' in the phrase 'which he here gave' must necessarily refer to Edinburgh. When read in the full context it seems much more likely to refer to Glasgow. The Callander document cannot in fact be used as evidence either for or against Robertson's attendance at the Edinburgh lectures.

[40] *The Edinburgh Review for the Year 1755* (2nd edn., 1818), pp. 103–5.

[41] See the first note to Stewart's *Memoir of Robertson*, pp. 203–5. Another possibility, of an equally conjectural kind, is that one of the people from whom Smith in 1755 apprehended 'rival claims' was none other than Lord Kames – who, as we have already seen, was to produce the four stages theory out of the blue in his *Historical Law-Tracts* in 1758. It is true that Smith later referred to Kames (in a letter to him) as 'so old and so good a friend'; and it is *possibly* true that Smith on another occasion said that 'we must every one of us acknowledge Kames for our master' (Tytler, *Memoirs of Kames*, Vol. I, pp. 271 and 218). It is also true, however – at any rate if we are to believe Boswell – that Smith on yet another occasion wholeheartedly endorsed Hume's description of Kames as 'the most arrogant Man in the world'. See *The Private Papers of James Boswell* (edited by Scott and Pottle), Vol. 15 (1934), p. 12.

IV

If Smith's version of the four stages theory can in fact be dated back to the winter of 1750–1, we are clearly in the presence of one of the most remarkable coincidences in the whole history of social and economic thought, since it was precisely at this time that the young Turgot was writing down his own version of the same theory. There was no possibility at this point of either of the two men being able to influence the other, and there was no common literary source – or at any rate none that I have been able to find – upon which they might have drawn, at least for *direct* inspiration. We would seem to be face to face with the genuinely original and independent discovery by two young men in their twenties, in two different countries but at exactly the same time, of an extremely important conceptual principle.

Part of the reason for the temporal coincidence, in all probability, is that both men were strongly influenced by Montesquieu's *Spirit of Laws*, which had appeared in 1748. They both certainly saw the *Spirit of Laws* as providing a kind of green light, an authoritative 'go ahead', for the new social science which was forming in their minds. And their attention was no doubt caught by the remarkable passages in Book XVIII where Montesquieu makes sustained use of the notion that differences in manners and social institutions are related to differences in the mode of subsistence. Montesquieu certainly distinguished more precisely than any of his predecessors between societies based on hunting, pasturage, agriculture, and commerce. But there is no clear indication in the *Spirit of Laws* that he visualized these different modes of subsistence as marking *successive stages of development* through which societies normally progressed over time. Nor, of course, is there any indication that he regarded the mode of subsistence as being in any sense the *key* factor in the total situation: it was only one of a large number of factors to which the laws should properly be related. Why, then, was it that Smith and Turgot reacted so positively to the isolated passages in Book XVIII where Montesquieu dealt with the mode of subsistence, and so negatively to the much larger number of passages in the remainder of the work where he dealt (for example) with government and climate? Why, having seized upon the more or less static analysis in Book XVIII, did they proceed to dynamize it (as it were) and transform it into a new theory of socio-economic development?

When a new conception of this kind arises in the mind of a thinker, there are usually two types of influence which operate – first, the great global or environmental causes which in some way encourage or engender the general attitudes lying behind the new idea; and second, the literary traditions or streams of thought from which the actual building-blocks are derived. So far as the first of these sets of causes is concerned, I do not feel that I have much to add or take away from what I have already written in various places on this question, although I would now wish to place

more emphasis on the important connection between the four stages theory
and the concepts of progress and of the perfectibility of mankind – a
connection which was of course particularly evident in the work of Turgot.[42]
But on the second set of causes there are a few brief remarks which I think
I can usefully make in conclusion. As I now see it, there are three streams of
thought in particular which may well have had an important influence.

The first stream of thought was provided by a long line of lawyers
writing on the historical origin of property in what may be called the
Pufendorf–Locke tradition. The seminal idea here was Pufendorf's notion
that 'not all things passed into proprietorship at one time, but successively',[43]
and his hints that the successive stages were related to different modes of
subsistence. This idea was filled out a little by Locke in his famous chapter
on property in the second *Treatise*, with some interesting biblical illustrations which were later to become widely used, and also some illustrations
from America which were destined to become of even greater importance.
The tradition was carried on in the eighteenth century by writers like Hume,
Hutcheson, and Kames when they were dealing with the origin of property,
and it may well be that the young Smith was influenced by it. Certainly,
at any rate, it was in connection with the problem of the origin and development of property that the four stages theory was most extensively illustrated
and applied by Smith in his Glasgow lectures.

The second stream of thought was provided by a succession of studies of
the Indian tribes of America, in particular the well-known books by
Charlevoix and Lafitau, which were very frequently quoted by almost all
the historians of civil society in the latter half of the eighteenth century.
The works concerned comprised a heterogeneous mixture of travellers'
tales, genuine anthropological research, and argument and speculation
about the genetic origins of the Indians. They were important for three
reasons:

1. The contrast between the primitive, static state of the Indian tribes
and the advanced, relatively dynamic societies of western Europe which
they revealed was so striking that it stimulated an interest in the causes of
these differences, and through this a more general interest in the causes of
development as such.

2. A number of the works concerned made it clear that there were strong
resemblances between the Indians and certain ancient peoples – for example
the early Greeks. Thus the view arose that in America one could see,
re-created as in a laboratory and laid out conveniently for study, the true
infancy of the world.

3. The early controversies about the origin of the Indians were almost

---

[42] Sidney Pollard has emphasized this in a very interesting way in his book *The Idea of Progress*
(Watts, London, 1968).
[43] Samuel Pufendorf, *De jure naturae et gentium libri octo* (translated by C. H. and W. A.
Oldfather, Oxford University Press, 1934), p. 551. The whole of Chapter 4, 'Of the Origin of
Dominion', is interesting in this connection. See in particular pp. 539–40, 550–1, and 554.

all based on the assumption that if it could be proved that the Indians had the same basic habits and characteristics as, say, the early Greeks, then it followed that they must in fact have descended from the early Greeks. This must surely have provoked, by way of reaction, the idea that any such similarities were in fact due to similarities of situation – that, as Robertson put it, 'the character and occupations of the hunter in America must be little different from those, say, of an Asiatic, who depends for subsistence on the chase'.[44] It seems very likely that Smith and Turgot – and also, perhaps, Quesnay – reacted in much the same way, although at an earlier date than Robertson.[45]

The third stream of thought was provided by those writing in the tradition of the so-called providential view of history, which up to the middle of the eighteenth century was more or less orthodox in France and of which the best-known example was Bossuet's *Histoire Universelle*. The influence of this tradition may have been particularly important in the case of Turgot, not because he accepted it but precisely because he tried to substitute something else for it, and, like most people in such a situation, was more influenced than he knew by the doctrine he was rejecting. Bossuet had claimed that although God makes history, he very seldom does this by intervening directly: he works through 'chains of particular causes' and, as Bossuet put it, 'prepares the effects in the most distant causes'. Now the 'chains of particular causes' which Bossuet and other writers in the same tradition postulated were up to a point materialist in character, which meant that a historian like Turgot could push God out of the picture as a historical agent, concentrate on the analysis of the 'chains of particular causes', and still have something interesting and important to say. Bossuet had talked in terms of a succession of religious epochs; Turgot could talk in terms of a succession of socio-economic stages.

[44] The quotation is from a passage near the beginning of Book 4 of Robertson's *History of America*, in which the view concerned is spelt out very explicitly. Cf. also the sixth note in the *Proofs and Illustrations* appended to his *History of the Reign of the Emperor Charles V*.
[45] So far as Smith is concerned, we know at any rate that he approved of a work in which this reaction was strongly expressed. I refer to John Logan's *Elements of the Philosophy of History* (Edinburgh, 1781), which is a kind of short sketch or analysis of a course of lectures given by Logan in Edinburgh in 1779–81 under the patronage of Robertson, Blair, and others. 'Similar situations produce similar appearances', wrote Logan, 'and, where the state of society is the same, nations will resemble one another. The want of attention to this hath filled the world with infinite volumes. The most remote resemblances in language, customs, or manners, has suggested the idea of deriving one nation from another' (pp. 16–17). Smith's favourable opinion of Logan's historical work is contained in a letter dated 29 September 1783, which John Rae published on pp. 396–7 of his *Life of Adam Smith* (Macmillan, London, 1895). Logan's *Elements* contains quite a number of other interesting 'materialist' statements – as also does his later book *A View of Antient History*, Vol. I (London, 1788) and Vol. II (London, 1791), which he published under the curious pseudonym of William Rutherford, D. D., and for which he solicited Smith's contribution (see *Adam Smith as Student and Professor*, p. 304). The question of Logan's connection with Smith – and with the Scottish Enlightenment in general – has not yet been sufficiently explored. It is a subject which would make a good Ph.D. thesis, and possibly something rather more.

Bossuet had emphasized the way in which law-givers and conquerors were subject to a major force outside themselves: they made history, but since God worked *through* them they did not make it as they wished. Turgot, similarly, could emphasize the way in which certain immanent historical laws and necessities worked *through* individuals to produce a regular, law-governed, developmental process.

All in all, then, I think that these three streams of thought[46] may have been of particular importance in forming in the minds of Smith and Turgot a *predisposition* to be struck by the ideas put forward by Montesquieu in Book XVIII of the *Spirit of Laws*. To paraphrase Millar, Montesquieu may in a general sense have pointed out the road, but it was Smith and Turgot, building their new theory out of these earlier materials – and out of their own genius – who were the real Newtons.

[46] Dr Pesciarelli, in the article referred to in [24], has shown that the versions of the four stages theory put forward by Genovesi were influenced also by another stream of thought – that associated with what Dr Pesciarelli calls 'the Bruno–Vico tradition'.

III

The Development of Adam Smith's Ideas on the Division of Labour[1]

Most of the accounts hitherto given of the development of Adam Smith's ideas on the division of labour prior to the appearance of the *Wealth of Nations* have been based on a number of crucial assumptions made by early Smith-scholars concerning the dating of the relevant documents – notably the so-called *Early Draft of the 'Wealth of Nations'* and the two fragments on the division of labour discovered by Scott. The recent discovery of a new set of student's notes of Smith's Glasgow lectures on Jurisprudence, relating to the 1762–3 academic session, has made it possible to reconsider these assumptions. It will be our contention in the present essay that in the light of the new evidence the documents should probably be placed in a date order very different from that which has up to now been accepted, and that if this is done the traditional picture of the way in which Smith's ideas on the division of labour developed is radically altered. In the appendices to the essay we present some of the more important of the materials upon which the argument rests, including an extract from the new lecture notes and what we believe to be the first printed text of the two fragments.

I

Let us begin with a brief review of the main documents which Scott had before him when he wrote his *Adam Smith as Student and Professor*,[2] and the main assumptions which he made concerning their dates.

First, there were 'four documents, amounting to fifteen folio pages' which Scott discovered 'amongst letters kept by Adam Smith'.[3] One of these documents, as Scott himself indicated, is very probably not by Smith, but

---

[1] This essay was written jointly by Andrew Skinner and myself, and originally appeared in the *Economic Journal*, **83**, 1973. In the present version very few amendments of substance have been made.
[2] W. R. Scott, *Adam Smith as Student and Professor* (Jackson, Son and Co., Glasgow, 1937).
[3] *Ibid.*, p. 58.

a copy of a paper on prices which he had received from Lord Hailes.[4] A second, on moral philosophy, has recently been edited by Professor Raphael, who has quite properly questioned Scott's judgement as to the date of its composition, while indicating that it was probably written before the first edition of the *Theory of Moral Sentiments* in 1759.[5] The two remaining documents – the really relevant ones so far as the present essay is concerned – deal more or less exclusively with the division of labour, and were thought by Scott to be of such interest as to deserve reproduction in facsimile.[6] The longer of these two pieces, which begins with a discussion of the interdependence of the philosopher and the porter as representatives of distinct trades, will henceforth be cited as Fragment A (FA). The second of the pieces (FB) is somewhat shorter, and opens with a discussion of the relative merits of land and water carriage. Upon examination, Scott concluded that these two fragments were 'specimens of Adam Smith's earliest economic work',[7] and the captions to the facsimiles describe them specifically as coming from 'one of the Edinburgh lectures'. This judgement of Scott's was based in part upon his interpretation of their content, but also, apparently, on the very curious ground that 'the many avocations of Adam Smith during the first eight years he was at Glasgow make it highly improbable, if not impossible, that they [the four documents] could have been written then, and thus they may be assigned to the Edinburgh period'.[8]

Second, there was the well-known set of student's notes of Smith's Glasgow lectures on Jurisprudence which Cannan discovered and published in 1896.[9] On the basis of internal evidence, Cannan had opined that it was probable that 'the actual lectures from which the notes were taken were delivered either in the portion of the academical session of 1763–4 which preceded Adam Smith's departure [from Glasgow], or in the session of 1762–3, almost certain that they were not delivered before 1761–2, and absolutely certain that they were not delivered before 1760–1'.[10] On his title-page, however, Cannan had ventured to describe the lectures as having been 'reported by a student in 1763'. Scott concluded that the lecture course concerned 'must have been given in the session 1762–3', apparently basing this judgement on 'an experiment made by an expert

[4] In a letter to Hailes dated 5 March 1769 Smith asked him for 'the papers you mentioned upon the price of provisions in former times' (John Rae, *Life of Adam Smith* (Macmillan, London, 1895), p. 247). Smith returned the original manuscript to Hailes, after having 'taken a copy' of it, on 23 May 1769 (Scott, *op. cit.*, p. 265).

[5] D. D. Raphael, "Adam Smith and 'the infection of David Hume's society'", *Journal of the History of Ideas*, **30**, 1969.

[6] Scott, *op. cit.*, pp. 379–85. The manuscripts themselves are located in the Bannerman Papers, Glasgow University Library.

[7] *Ibid.*, p. 59.

[8] *Ibid.*, pp. 57–8.

[9] *Lectures on Justice, Police, Revenue and Arms*, (edited by E. Cannan, Oxford University Press, 1896).

[10] *Ibid.*, p. xx.

note-taker' which allegedly proved that it was 'not possible that the notes could have been taken in the part of the next session during which Adam Smith was at Glasgow'.[11]

Third, there was the so-called *Early Draft of the 'Wealth of Nations'* which Scott discovered among Charles Townshend's papers at Dalkeith House and the text of which he published in an appendix to *Adam Smith as Student and Professor*.[12] This document begins with an extended and fully written-out section on the division of labour (under the heading 'Chap. 2. Of the nature and Causes of public opulence') which occupies just over thirty pages of the manuscript; and the remaining eighteen pages are taken up with what appears to be a summary (under the heading 'Contents of the following Chapters') of the major part of the remaining 'economic' materials in Smith's lecture course. Scott, asking himself the question 'Is this manuscript that of the *Glasgow Lectures* or an early revision of these?', answered that 'many reasons point to the latter' – among these reasons being, apparently, 'the very much greater prominence which is given to questions of Distribution here as compared with the report of the Glasgow Lectures'. Since in Scott's opinion, as we have just seen, the latter report related to lectures given in 1762–3, he concluded that 'the probable date of the revision, represented by this manuscript, would be 1763, probably the summer or later'.[13]

Summing up, the view put forward by Scott, which has been accepted by the great majority of later Smith-scholars, was that FA and FB dated from the very early Edinburgh period; that the Cannan notes related to lectures delivered in the 1762–3 session; and that the *Early Draft* was probably written in 1763, fairly soon after these lectures had been delivered.

Our review of these assumptions in the remaining part of the present essay is organized as follows. In Section II, we begin by provisionally ascribing the Cannan notes to the 1763–4 session. We then summarize the treatment of the division of labour in the newly discovered 1762–3 notes, and compare it with the treatment of this subject in the Cannan notes. Finally, we put the two sets of notes side by side and compare them with the *Early Draft*, arriving at the tentative conclusion that the latter was probably written before April 1763. In Section III, we turn to the two fragments. We first describe their form and content in more detail, and then compare them with the *Early Draft* on the one hand and Chapter III of Book I of the *Wealth of Nations* on the other, arriving at the conclusion that the fragments probably date from the 1760s rather than from the Edinburgh period. Finally, in Section IV, we survey some of the important *differences* between the fragments and the *Wealth of Nations*, drawing from this comparison certain conclusions regarding the nature and development of Smith's ideas on the division of labour.

---

[11] Scott, *op. cit.*, p. 319.
[12] *Ibid.*, pp. 322–56.
[13] *Ibid.*, p. 319.

II

The first thing which emerges as a result of the discovery of the new set of notes mentioned above is that the lectures to which the Cannan notes related (assuming that they were all of a piece) could not possibly have been given in the 1762–3 session. This is a point which will be documented more fully when the new notes are published:[14] here we need only say that so far as they go[15] they are very much fuller than the Cannan notes; that most of the lectures are separately reported *and dated*; that all the dates relate to the 1762–3 session; and that the whole order of treatment of the main subjects is radically different from that in the Cannan notes. The only question now really at issue, therefore, is whether the Cannan notes relate to 1761–2 or to 1763–4. And on this point, fortunately, the reference to Florida on p. 70 of the published edition of the Cannan notes would seem to be fairly decisive. A comparison of the passage in which this reference occurs with the corresponding passage in the 1762–3 notes shows that it must relate to the cession of Florida at the end of the Seven Years War, which could obviously not have been referred to in the 1761–2 session. It seems very likely indeed, therefore, *pace* Scott, that the lectures to which the Cannan notes refer were in fact delivered in 1763–4 – the session during which Smith left Glasgow, his course being continued and completed by Thomas Young.[16] If this is so, the intriguing question arises as to the extent, if any, to which Young's views as well as Smith's may be reported in the Cannan notes; but this is not a question which need concern us in the present essay.

Let us turn, then, to the treatment of the division of labour in the new 1762–3 lecture notes, numbering the successive points made so as to facilitate later comparison with the other documents concerned.[17] After a discussion of the secular growth of wants, and a very interesting development of the idea that 'all the arts, the sciences, law and government, wisdom and even virtue itself, tend all to . . . the providing meat, drink, raiment, and lodging for men', Smith comes directly to the division of labour, dealing with it as follows:

1. The fact that the 'ordinary day-labourer' in Britain has a higher standard of living than 'an Indian prince at the head of 1000 naked savages' is due to the 'joint assistance' of hundreds of different people who have in

[14] The notes are being edited by Professor D. D. Raphael, Professor P. G. Stein, and myself for the Glasgow bicentennial edition of the works and correspondence of Adam Smith.

[15] The notes stop short a little over half-way through the 'economic' section of Smith's lectures. More specifically, the material in them corresponds roughly to that in the Cannan notes up to but not beyond p. 208 of the published edition of the latter.

[16] If Young was in fact furnished by Smith with the latter's lecture notes, as A. F. Tytler asserts (*Memoirs of Kames* (2nd edition, Edinburgh, 1814), Vol. I, p. 272), and as would indeed seem very probable, it follows that the experiment by Scott's 'expert note-taker' (above, pp. 34–5) proves nothing at all.

[17] In the quotations from the 1762–3 notes which follow in the present essay, and in Appendix A, some of the imperfections of grammar, punctuation, spelling, etc. in the student's report have been cleaned up in the interests of readability.

effect co-operated to produce his 'blue woollen coat', his tools, his furniture, etc.

2. It may not seem surprising that 'the moneyed man and man of rank' should be so much better provided for than the most wealthy savage, since 'the labour and time of the poor is in civilised countries sacrificed to the maintaining the rich in ease and luxury'. Among the savages, however, there are 'no landlords, no usurers, no tax gatherers', and we should therefore expect that 'the savage should be much better provided than the dependent poor man who labours both for himself and for others'. But the case is in fact 'far otherwise'.

3. The difficulty in accounting for this is increased by the fact that labour is not 'equally proportioned to each', so that 'of 10 000 families which are supported by each other, 100 perhaps labour not at all'. The 'rich and opulent merchant' lives better than his clerks who 'do all the business'; the latter better than the artisans; and the latter in turn better than the 'poor labourer' who 'supports the whole frame of society'. How then can we account for 'the great share he and the lowest of the people have of the conveniences of life'?

4. The division of labour among different hands can alone account for this. Let us consider the effects the division of labour can have on 'one particular branch of business' – pin-making – with a view to judging from this the effect it will have on the whole. If one man had to do all the work of making a pin from beginning to end, it would take him at least a whole year to make a pin, so that its price would be £6, the value of a man's labour for a year. Even if he were given the wire ready made, he would not be able to make more than twenty pins a day, and the pins would sell at not less than one penny each. As things actually stand, however, the labour is normally divided among eighteen persons; 36 000 pins can be made in a day; and the pin-maker can as a result afford both to increase the workman's wages and to sell his pins more cheaply.

5. Agriculture 'does not admit of this separation of employment in the same degree as the manufactures of wool or lint or iron work'. Though an opulent state will no doubt far exceed a poorer one both in agriculture and in manufacture, 'yet this will not be so remarkable in the produce of the soil as the handicraft trades'.

6. When these improvements have been made, 'each branch of trade will afford enough both to support the opulence and give considerable profit of the great men, and sufficiently reward the industry of the labourer'. If, for example, the pin-maker can contrive that each man produces 2000 pins per day, and if he sells these at one penny per hundred, he can pay the artisan fifteen pence and still have '5 for his share'.[18]

---

[18] This is in fact the second of two numerical examples which are given in this section. In the first, it is assumed that each man produces 1000 (instead of 2000) pins per day, and that these are sold at the rate of three-halfpence per 100. In this case 'the whole thousand will then be worth 15d., of which the artisan can afford 3 to his master and have 12 as the price of his labour'.

7. Thus 'the price of labour comes to be dear while at the same time work is cheap' – two things which 'in the eyes of the vulgar appear altogether incompatible'; and 'that state is opulent where the necessaries and conveniences of life are easily come at'.

8. The extension of the division of labour cheapens commodities. Thus we see that the price of almost all commodities has fallen since the Revolution, 'notwithstanding the supposed abundance of money'. 'We are not to judge whether labour be cheap or dear by the moneyed price of it, but by the quantity of the necessaries of life which may be got by the fruits of it.' Gold and silver, however, 'can not be so easily multiplied as other commodities'.

9. The increase in 'the stock of commodities' arising from the division of labour has three causes: '1st, the dexterity which it occasions in the workmen; 2dly, the saving of time lost in passing from one piece of work to another; and 3dly, the invention of machines which it occasions'.[19]

10. In relation to the invention of machines, those 'general observers whom we call philosophers' play an important role, as for example in the case of the fire engine and wind and water-mills. And in time 'philosophy itself becomes a separate trade . . . like all others subdivided into various provinces'.

11. The division of labour is not 'the effect of any human policy', but is rather 'the necessary consequence of a natural disposition altogether peculiar to men, viz., the disposition to truck, barter, and exchange'. This disposition is never found in animals: the hounds which help each other when chasing a hare do not do so as the result of any contract between them. It is only men who enter into bargains, and who, when they want beer or beef, address themselves not to the humanity of the brewer or the butcher but to his self-love.

12. This 'bartering and trucking spirit' is the cause of the separation of trades and the improvements in arts. A savage, for example, who finds that he can make arrows 'better than ordinary', may become a full-time arrow-maker.

13. It is not the difference of 'natural parts and genius' that occasions the separation of trades, but the separation of trades that occasions the diversity of genius, as is shown by the example of the philosopher and the porter.

The argument which we have just summarized takes us up to the end of the lecture which Smith gave on Tuesday, 29 March 1763. As we shall see directly, the argument was subsequently continued and developed – although in a very peculiar and significant manner – in the two following lectures on Wednesday, 30 March and Tuesday, 5 April. Let us pause here, however, to draw a mental line under the thirteenth point, for, as will be emphasized later, the section of the *Early Draft* dealing with the division of labour more or less exactly mirrors the argument of the 1762–3 lectures *up to but not*

---

[19] This point and its illustration occupy five pages of the manuscript.

beyond this point, whereas the Cannan notes in effect incorporate the subsequent material.

Under the date for the notes of the lecture given on Wednesday, 30 March the student has – quite unusually – written a note which reads 'continues to illustrate former, etc.' The notes of the lecture proper begin with Smith's customary summary of some of the main points in his previous lecture, which is fairly straightforward until he starts recapitulating point 11 above. Here he introduces some new material, of which there is no trace at all in the student's notes of the previous lecture, concerning a law made by Sesostris to the effect that 'everyone should for ever adhere to his father's profession'. The student's report of this new material takes up 172 words. Smith then goes straight on to summarize point 12; and from there directly proceeds to make another new point, also not made in the previous lecture, to the effect that the 'disposition of trucking' is founded on 'the natural inclination everyone has to persuade'. Men, the argument runs, 'always endeavour to persuade others to be of their opinion', and thus acquire 'a certain dexterity and address . . . in managing of men'. The activity of bartering, in which they 'address themselves to the self-interest of the person', is the result of their endeavours to do this 'managing of men' in the simplest and most effective manner.

Smith now leaves the subject of the division of labour, and announces the five main topics with which he is going to concern himself in the remaining parts of the 'economic' section of the course. The first of these is 'the rule of exchange, or what it is which regulates the price of commodities'; and he embarks immediately upon his discussion of this topic, continuing with it until the end of the lecture.

At the beginning of the *next* lecture, however, on Tuesday, 5 April, one is surprised to find Smith returning yet again, this time quite out of context, to the question of the division of labour, and developing for the first time (at any rate in the 1762–3 lectures) the crucial principle that the division of labour is limited by the extent of the market. This passage, which takes up nearly four pages of the student's manuscript, is clearly important, and is therefore reproduced in full in Appendix A at the end of the present essay. After it is finished, Smith proceeds calmly on his way, picking up the threads of his previous discussion of 'the rule of exchange' and carrying on with his exposition of it.

Let us now make a comparison between the treatment of the division of labour in the 1762–3 notes, as outlined above, and the treatment of it in the Cannan notes (which, as we have seen, very probably relate to the lectures delivered in 1763–4), the purpose of this comparison being to detect the differences, if any, between what was actually said about the division of labour in the lectures in 1762–3 and what was said about it in 1763–4.

One important point which must be stressed here is the big difference in the standard of note-taking between the two sets of notes. The 1762–3 notes as a whole are very full, and so far as one can judge extremely accurate: in all probability they were a student's transcription of *shorthand* notes taken down by him in class, and the student evidently took great pains to make this transcription as correct as possible a rendering of the words actually used by Smith. The Cannan notes, by way of contrast, are in many places very sketchy, and in some places – as it now turns out – rather unreliable: they bear all the marks of being a copyist's later transcription of a set of rather abbreviated notes originally taken down by a student in *longhand*. Thus one frequently finds that a point which occupies a whole page of the 1762–3 notes is represented in the Cannan notes by no more than a single sentence – and sometimes a rather incomprehensible one at that. Thus whereas the absence of a particular point from the 1762–3 notes can normally be assumed to indicate that this point was not in fact dealt with in that session's lectures, the same assumption can *not* safely be made in relation to the Cannan notes.

Bearing this in mind, and putting the two sets of notes side by side,[20] there is no evidence to suggest that what was actually said about the division of labour in the 1763–4 lectures was *substantially* different from what had been said in 1762–3, *at any rate up to (and including) point 10 above*. Some of the points concerned are very baldly summarized in the Cannan notes, but most of them (with the possible exception of point 6)[21] do in fact appear to be there, and they are presented in what seems to be the same order. The first difference which may be of importance occurs when we come to the counterpart in the Cannan notes of point 11.[22] Here the exposition begins with a discussion of that 'law made by Sesostris' of which we have already heard (above, p. 39), and only *after* this discussion does it proceed to the illustration of the hounds chasing a hare. In the 1762–3 lectures, by way of contrast, Smith when dealing with point 11 went straight to the hounds illustration, and as we have seen made no mention of the 'law made by Sesostris' until the recapitulation of the argument at the beginning of his next lecture on Wednesday, 30 March.

[20] The relevant passages in the Cannan notes will be found on pp. 161–72 of the published version.

[21] The only counterpart of point 6 in the Cannan notes would seem to be a single sentence on p. 164 reading 'When labour is thus divided, and so much done by one man in proportion, the surplus above their maintenance is considerable, which each man can exchange for a fourth of what he could have done if he had finished it alone.' There is no trace of the two numerical illustrations from pin-making which Smith used in 1762–3 to illustrate the point. There are a number of possible explanations of this omission, but they need not concern us here. What is more interesting is the fact that these illustrations clearly display the division of the product between wages and profits, and that they were carried over (in amended form – see [23]) into the *Early Draft*. If Scott had been able to compare the *Early Draft* with the 1762–3 notes as well as the Cannan notes, he would have found it much less easy, we think, to argue that the *Early Draft* 'contains much more on Distribution' than the lectures. Cf. Scott, *op. cit.*, pp. 319–20.

[22] See the published edition of the Cannan notes, pp. 168–9.

In the Cannan notes, the summary of point 11, expanded in this way, is followed immediately by a summary of points 12 and 13, and the notes then proceed directly to a discussion of the notion that the real foundation of the disposition to truck or barter is the 'principle to persuade'. This point was also made in the 1762–3 lectures, but only, as we have already seen, at the end of the recapitulation of the argument near the beginning of the lecture on Wednesday, 30 March. Immediately after this discussion, the Cannan notes proceed with a consideration of the crucial point that 'the division of labour must always be proportioned to the extent of commerce'. This point too, it will be remembered, was also made by Smith in the 1762–3 lectures, *but not at this place*: it was squeezed in, in a way which makes it look very like an afterthought, half-way through his exposition of the theory of price, at the beginning of his lecture on Tuesday, 5 April.

To sum up, then, the three additional points made by Smith in 1762–3 in his lectures on Wednesday, 30 March and Tuesday, 5 April – the 'law made by Sesostris' point, the 'principle to persuade' point, and, most important of all, the point that the division of labour depends on the extent of the market – were all incorporated *in their proper places* in the 1763–4 lectures.

How can we account for this difference? It *could* be argued, of course, that in his lecture on Tuesday, 29 March 1763, Smith did not have time, or perhaps forgot, to deal with the three points concerned; that he remembered to deal with the first two at the beginning of his next lecture; but that he forgot about the third until the beginning of the next lecture after that. This would have been uncharacteristic, but it is at least possible. More likely, however, we believe, is the suggestion that at any rate the third of the three points concerned – the idea that the division of labour depends on the extent of the market – really was a genuine afterthought, appearing for the first time in the 1762–3 course and assuming its proper place in the narrative only in 1763–4.

This suggestion is supported by a comparison between the two sets of lecture notes and the *Early Draft*. The latter document evidently represents a preliminary and rather tentative attempt by Smith to translate the 'economic' material in his Jurisprudence lectures into book form. It is very much the sort of document which any of us today might produce for a publisher whom we were wanting to interest in a projected book and who had asked us to submit a sample first chapter plus a summary of the remaining chapters. And there is of course no doubt that the document is directly based on the material in *some* set of Smith's lectures: the only question really at issue is *which* set. The main point here is that the chapter on the division of labour, which is fully written out and with which the *Early Draft* begins, corresponds very closely indeed – argument by argument, and often sentence by sentence and even word by word – with the treatment in the 1762–3 lecture notes, *up to but not beyond the end of the lecture on Tuesday, 29 March.*[23] In other words, there is no mention whatever in it of the 'law by Sesostris' point, the 'principle to persuade' point, or, more importantly, the point that the division of labour depends on the extent of the market. So far as the summary of the remaining chapters is concerned, it seems to us that this might equally well have been based on the lectures as reported in 1762–3 or in 1763–4. But the absence from the first part of the *Early Draft* of any mention of the point about the extent of the market (to say nothing of the two other points concerned) surely suggests that it could not have been based on the 1763–4 lectures – and, indeed, that it could not have been based on the 1762–3 lectures either, *unless it was written prior to April 1763.* It does not seem at all plausible that the *Early Draft* should have omitted all mention of the idea that the division of labour depends on the extent of the market if Smith had in fact arrived at this idea, and appreciated its full economic significance, at the time when the document was drawn up. What does seem plausible is that the *Early Draft* was a revised version of the 'economic' part of Smith's lecture notes as they stood at some date shortly before April 1763; that while thinking about the division of labour and the way in which he would treat it in his projected book Smith arrived at certain new ideas, including that concerning the dependence of the division of labour on the extent of the market; and that he explained the latter idea to his students for the first time in his lecture on 5 April 1763.

III

The reader who has already had a look at Appendix A, in which the 1762–3 report of Smith's apparent afterthought on the dependence of the division of labour on the extent of the market is reproduced, will have noticed that it can be divided roughly into two halves. In the first half Smith introduces and illustrates the general point that the division of labour is 'greater or less according to the market'; in the second half he goes on to talk about the relative effects of sea and land carriage upon 'the greatness of the market'. The curious thing is that these are precisely the two subjects

[23] The main *differences* between the relevant sections of the *Early Draft* and the 1762–3 notes are as follows:

(a) *Point 6.* In the 1762–3 notes the two numerical illustrations are based respectively on the assumptions that 1000 pins and 2000 pins are produced per day. In the *Early Draft* the corresponding assumptions are that 2000 and 4000 pins are produced per day.

(b) *Point 8.* In the *Early Draft* the substance of point 8 seems to have been transferred from the division of labour section to the summary of 'Chap. 4th. Of money, its nature, origin and history' (cf. Scott, *op. cit.*, p. 347).

(c) At the end of the division of labour section of the *Early Draft*, after point 13, a new passage (not to be found, we believe, anywhere else in Smith's writings) is added. In this rather curious passage Smith discusses certain implications of the fact that almost everything we know is acquired second-hand from books.

It would take us too far out of our way to analyse these differences here: suffice it to say that in our opinion they are perfectly consistent with the view about the probable dating of the *Early Draft* given in the text.

dealt with respectively in the two fragments (FA and FB) mentioned on p. 34 above. The fact that the only two unpublished economic documents of Smith's (apart from the *Early Draft*) which have survived should deal with the same two subjects as the uncharacteristic 'afterthought' which we have just been considering can hardly be due to a mere coincidence, and cries out for some kind of explanation.

The text of FA and FB is reproduced in Appendices B and C below. In physical appearance, FA consists of a single folio sheet of four pages with the text extending almost, but not quite, to the bottom of the last page. FB consists of a single folio sheet with the text covering rather more than two and one-half pages. Both fragments begin in the middle of a sentence. Each page has a broad margin at the left-hand side, and in FA there is in one case a lengthy insertion written in this margin and preceded by a signal which also appears in the text. Similar insertions appear on the first and third pages of FB. In both cases there are a number of words struck out in the text with new ones substituted – occasionally, it would seem (as in the case of the *Early Draft*), by Smith himself. The bulk of the insertions, however, are in the hand of the amanuensis, and generally occur above the line. In addition, there are a number of cancelled words (and parts of words) without corresponding insertions, indicating in all probability that Smith often changed his choice of expression during dictation. It is evident, therefore, that the two fragments, unlike the *Early Draft*, are not in a finished form.

The two folios have the same watermark and were written in the same hand. The watermarks are quite clear, and would appear to be the same as those found in the *Early Draft*. On one sheet there is a circular emblem containing the motto *Pro Patria Eiusque Libertate*, surmounted by a crown, the whole containing a lion 'rampant and regardant'. The lion seems to be grasping a weapon in one hand, and a sheaf of corn or arrows in the other. The animal stands on a pedestal whose base appears to bear the letters VRYHYT. On the facing page, the countermark consists of a single circle, enclosing the letters GR, which are flanked by laurel leaves and again surmounted by a crown.[24]

In other words, the paper on which the two fragments were written would appear to be the same as that used for the *Early Draft*, although the hand does differ.

Turning now from the physical appearance of the fragments to their actual content, we find that FA is mainly concerned with the relationship between the division of labour and the extent of the market. Smith here illustrates the point by reference to small communities such as those found in the 'mountainous and desart' Highlands of Scotland, where individuals are forced to exercise a number of different trades. His basic argument

---

[24] Scott's description of the *Early Draft* watermarks (which is rather inaccurate) will be found in *Adam Smith as Student and Professor*, p. 322.

is that the extent of the market must be affected by the size of the community, and he goes on to provide further illustrations drawn from the experience of North American Indians, Tartars, Arabs, and Hottentots. In FB the same theme is considered from a rather different point of view: here the extent of the market is analysed in relation to the ease of communication, especially by sea. Smith indicates that economic development was historically dependent on foreign or inland navigation, citing the experience of Greece and ancient Egypt as instances. Economic development round the coasts of the colonies in America is also mentioned in support of the general thesis; the colonies being likened (in the manner of King James's description of the county of Fife) to 'a coarse woollen coat edged with gold lace'.

Are these fragments the work of the Edinburgh period, as Scott believed? Three main considerations seem to us to tell against the ascription of them to such an early date.

The first consideration is suggested by a comparison of the opening paragraphs of FA with the concluding part of the section of the *Early Draft* dealing with the division of labour, which consists of a long analysis of the interdependence of, and mutual advantage to be derived from, the separate trades of the philosopher and the porter. The final portion of this concluding part is reproduced in Appendix D; and a comparison with the opening paragraph of FA in Appendix B will show that the latter is virtually identical with a passage in the former. Starting with the words 'who, for an equal quantity of work' in the first line of FA and in the third sentence of the extract from the *Early Draft*, the two texts continue in more or less exact parallel down to the sentence ending (in the *Early Draft*) 'usefull knowledge to diminish', so that there are about 25 lines of the *Early Draft* which reappear at the beginning of FA with only four very minor substantive changes and one handwritten alteration. At this point, however, the two texts part company: FA continues directly with a discussion of the dependence of the division of labour on the extent of the market, whereas the division of labour section of the *Early Draft* carries on with the general theme of the philosopher and the porter for a further 35 lines and then finishes. The final 35 lines constitutes that curious passage, mentioned above,[23] in which Smith discusses certain implications of the fact that almost everything we know is acquired second-hand from books. What may have happened is that Smith decided to rewrite the final part of the division of labour section of the *Early Draft*, and in the process of revision judged it proper to omit the passage just mentioned. In other words, it seems at least possible that the fragments represent an alternative conclusion to the division of labour section of the *Early Draft*.[25]

[25] The very fact that the fragments have survived, and that they were apparently found among letters kept by Smith, lends *some* support (although probably not very much) to the suggestion that they were linked in some way with the *Early Draft*. We are not prepared, however, to hazard any guess as to the exact reasons for their survival.

The second consideration relates more directly to the question of the content of the fragments. It will be remembered that in the *Early Draft* Smith did not formally consider the relationship between market size and the division of labour at all. The subject *was* considered in the 1762–3 lectures, but only, apparently, as an afterthought, and not at any great length.[26] In the 1763–4 lectures it was also considered, this time in its proper place, but there is no evidence to suggest that it was then considered either more extensively than in 1762–3 or in any substantially different way. Certainly there is nothing in either set of lecture notes suggesting a treatment of the subject which remotely approaches, either in length or in sophistication, the treatment found in the fragments, extending as the latter do to over six and one-half closely written folio pages. If, therefore, we adopt the plausible hypothesis that work which is analytically more developed is likely to come later in time, the possibility begins to emerge that the fragments were in fact written *after* that version of the lecture notes which contains the most elaborate account of the subject, i.e., the version of 1762–3.

The third consideration is suggested by a comparison of FA and FB with Chapter III of Book I of the *Wealth of Nations*, which brings to light a close parallel as regards the order and content of the argument. In both cases, for example, we find the point about the extent of the market illustrated in terms of community size before Smith goes on to examine the issue of transportation and its contribution to the development of commerce. Moreover, the form of words employed in certain passages is very similar – so similar, indeed, as to suggest that the fragments may have served at least as a preliminary basis for the chapter. In the *Wealth of Nations*, for example, paragraphs 1 and 2 of Chapter III appear to follow FA from the sentence in the latter beginning 'As it is the power of exchanging' (with which the second paragraph commences) to the end of the second page of the manuscript; and paragraphs 3–7 show the same close connection with the whole of FB.

Although the apparent link between the fragments and the *Early Draft*

---

[26] In his lecture on 24 February 1763, however, Smith did discuss the importance of the 'opportunity of commerce' in the developmental process, relating the comparative lack of advance in 'Tartary and Araby' to (*inter alia*) the fact that 'they are deprived in most places of the benefit of water carriage, more than any other nation in the world; and in some places where they would have an opportunity of it, the land carriage which would be necessary before it, debars them no less than the other'. And Smith went on from there to compare the situation of these countries with that of ancient Greece, which did not suffer from the same disadvantage. (Cf. the published edition of the Cannan notes, p. 22.) In an earlier lecture, too, in the context of a discussion of the original utility and necessity of the exclusive privileges of corporations, Smith drew attention to the fact that 'society must be pretty far advanced before the different trades can all find subsistence'. To this day, he said, 'in the remote and deserted parts of the country', a weaver or a smith, besides exercising his trade, may cultivate a small farm as well. The historical function of the exclusive privileges of corporations was 'to bring about . . . the separation of trades sooner than the progress of society would naturally effect'. (See pp. 39–41 of Vol. II of the MS.)

tends to suggest that Smith, at the time he wrote these documents, had not yet decided to accord the point about the dependence of the division of labour on the extent of the market a separate chapter in his proposed book, the close parallel between the *Wealth of Nations* and the fragments may perhaps suggest that the latter represent not just an *alternative* conclusion to the division of labour section of the *Early Draft*, but rather a *substitute* for it. There is also of course the possibility – which we would however regard as much less likely – that the fragments could be discarded pages from the manuscript of the *Wealth of Nations* itself. But however this may be, it seems fair to conclude from all the evidence that the balance of probability lies in favour of a date in the 1760s for the fragments and rather against the Edinburgh period of 1748–51. In placing FA 'almost midway between Hutcheson and the *Glasgow Lectures*', Scott relied in part on the point that while this fragment considers 'the nature' of the division of labour, 'there has yet to be worked out "its causes"'.[27] He does not seem to have examined the documents in relation to Smith's other work, or to have considered the possibility that 'its causes' had been worked out already and elsewhere.

IV

Apart from the parallels which exist between the fragments and the *Wealth of Nations*, there are also some interesting differences: materials, for example, which are present in one version of the argument but not in the other.

1. The opening passage of FA, illustrating the advantages of the division of labour in terms of the philosopher/porter example, was omitted from the analysis in the *Wealth of Nations* – most probably on the ground that it was redundant, i.e., concerned with a point which was already adequately established. At the same time, Smith must have decided to expand the new material included in the fragments and to give it the dignity of a separate chapter, beginning with the second paragraph of FA, as noted above.

2. As stated above, paragraphs 1 and 2 of Chapter III of the *Wealth of Nations* appear to follow FA from the sentence in the latter beginning 'As it is the power of exchanging' to the end of the second page of the manuscript, which takes us to about the middle of paragraph 2 of Chapter III. There is no counterpart in Chapter III of the material in pp. 3–4 of FA;[28] and the counterpart in it of FB begins at the eleventh word of the third sentence of paragraph 3. There is therefore a long passage in Chapter III, beginning 'Country workmen are almost everywhere' and ending 'a ship navigated by six', of which there is no counterpart in the fragments. This passage begins by elaborating on the theme of paragraph 1 in providing further illustrations of the point that rural communities are often too

---

[27] Scott, *op. cit.*, p. 59.
[28] We deal with the omission of this material under the last heading in this section.

small to permit a complete division of employments, and links the discussion of the relation between community size and the division of labour (the subject of FA, pp. 1–2) with that of the relative merits of land and sea carriage (the subject of FB). The passage amounts to approximately 300 words, which would make about one folio page in the hand of the amanuensis used. It is thus quite possible that Smith, having decided to omit the material in the two final pages of FA, later inserted a single page of material (now lost) linking the two fragments together.

3. Another addition in the *Wealth of Nations* is represented by the last paragraph of Chapter III, which continues a theme introduced in the previous part of the chapter. In FB the discussion of the importance of water carriage had reached a natural period in citing the examples of China and Egypt, but in the *Wealth of Nations* additional examples are provided – Africa, Austria, Bavaria, etc. From the standpoint of the discussion of the division of labour the new material is of limited significance, in that the point at issue had already been adequately established. But from other points of view the same material is important, and this for two reasons. First, it is interesting to note the weight of emphasis which Smith gave to ease of navigation as contributing to economic development and even as a precondition of it. It was in this place that Smith commented:

> All the inland parts of Africa, and all that part of Asia which lies any considerable way north of the Euxine and Caspian seas, the antient Scythia, the modern Tartary and Siberia, seem in all ages of the world to have been in the same barbarous and uncivilized state in which we find them at present.

Second, the point is also significant in relation to Smith's general theory of historical change, which features the use of four socio-economic stages through which communities are 'naturally' expected to pass in sequence over time. The emphasis on a *sequence* of stages tends to distract attention from the necessary preconditions of development (ease of defence, fertility, navigation) which Smith himself isolated, and thus from the point that socio-economic development may be *arrested* at a certain point – such as that reached by the Tartars.

4. Interestingly enough, the last point we wish to make is also connected with Smith's use of economic stages. We have already noted that the two final pages of FA were omitted from the *Wealth of Nations*, and that in this passage Smith had provided a number of historical illustrations of the point that community size must affect the scope for the extension of the division of labour. Smith probably had two reasons for making this omission: first, he had already illustrated the point at issue in terms of a modern example, so that additional material could be regarded as redundant; and second, the examples drawn from the experience of North American Indians, Tartars, Arabs, and Hottentots, while important in themselves, were all to receive attention elsewhere in the *Wealth of Nations*,

most notably in Book V.[29] Yet this particular decision is less obviously
an improvement, for a number of reasons. First, in the passage omitted
Smith *explicitly* established a connection between mode of subsistence,
size of community, and division of labour, illustrating the point in terms
of three distinct economic types (hunting, pasturage, and agriculture).
Second, Smith there provided hard evidence that the division of labour
was practised in primitive communities such as the Hottentots, pointing
out in the latter case that

> even in each village of Hottentots . . . there are such trades as those of
> a smith, a taylor & even a phisician, & the persons who exercise them,
> tho' they are not entirely, are principally supported by those respective
> employments . . .

Third, Smith's discussion, when taken in conjunction with the previous
chapters in the *Wealth of Nations*, helps to clarify just what he meant by
the term 'division of labour'. The point made in the omitted passage of
FA is really that even backward or barbarous communities will feature a
division of labour but not necessarily specialization in employments. The
Hottentots, for example, are 'principally', not 'entirely', supported by
their respective employments. But the division of labour properly so-called
only exists where there is *specialization* both in terms of area of employment

---

[29] There may have been another more general reason for this omission, related to what Scott
called Smith's 'epoch-making decision' to separate his economic material from 'the treatment
of Jurisprudence in which it had been previously embedded' (Scott, *op. cit.*, p. 319). After
making this decision, and as his economic work proceeded, it would have been natural for
Smith to purge the more 'analytical' parts of his material of some of the 'sociological' illustrations with which they had hitherto been associated.

There may be an interesting parallel here with Smith's decision to omit paragraphs 2 and 3 of
the *Early Draft* (the counterpart of points 2 and 3 in the 1762–3 notes) from the *Wealth of
Nations*. In the first paragraph of the *Early Draft* he had already noted that in a modern
society the unassisted labour of the individual could not supply him with his simple needs, and
that the poor man was in fact able to command enjoyments which placed him nearer to the
modern *rich* than 'the chief of a savage nation in North America' (Scott, *op. cit.*, p. 325). In the
Early Draft this is presented as part of a problem to be explained, while in the *Wealth of Nations*
the material is used to conclude the discussion of Chapter I. In the *Early Draft*, however, the
second and third paragraphs continue with the theme that while it is an easy matter to explain
why the rich of a modern state should be well provided as compared to the savage, it is not so
easily understood why this should also apply to the modern poor. By way of illustration Smith
proceeded to show that the peasants and labourers of the modern state were relatively badly
off due to inequality in the distribution of wealth (and effort). Smith really warmed to his task
in these two paragraphs: here we meet the 'slothful Landlord', the 'indolent and frivolous re-
tainers' of the court, and the monied man indulging himself in 'every sort of ignoble and sordid
sensuality' – and we are told that 'those who labour most get least', and of the 'oppressive
inequality' of the modern state. From the standpoint of the analytical discussion of the division
of labour the two paragraphs are probably redundant, thus explaining their omission; an
omission which probably does improve the flow of the argument and which lends to it a modern
air of technicality and detachment. Yet one wonders if the reaction of contemporary (and
modern) readers might have differed, had they been introduced to an inquiry into the nature
and causes of the wealth of nations by way of a by no means trivial polemic on the subject of
inequality.

and process of manufacture. For Smith, such *specialization* was the characteristic of the fourth socio-economic stage *alone*: a point which he makes plain in remarking that while the first three stages gave increasing scope to the division of labour, yet 'the compleat division of labour . . . is posteriour to the invention even of agriculture'. In the *Wealth of Nations* Smith was of course concerned with a form of economy characterized not merely by the division of labour, but by the 'compleat' form of that institution.

APPENDIX A

Extract from the 1762–3 lecture notes
Tuesday, 5 April, 1763

Having given an account of the nature of opulence and the things in which the riches of a state might consist, I proceeded to show that this was greatly promoted by the division of labour, which took its rise from the disposition to truck, etc., as well as the means by which it produced that effect. – We may observe on this head that as the division of labour is occasioned immediately by the market one has for his commodities, by which he is enabled to exchange one thing for every thing, so is this division greater or less according to the market. If there was no market every one would be obliged to exercise every trade in the proportion in which he stood in need of it. If the market be small he can't produce much of any commodity. If there are but ten persons who will purchase it he must not produce as much as will supply 100, otherwise he would reap no benefit by it; far less will he be induced to bring about the great increase which follows on the farther improvement of this division. The being of a market first occasioned the division of labour, and the greatness of it is what puts it in one's power to divide it much. A wright in the country is a cart-wright, a house-carpenter, a square-wright or cabinet-maker, and a carver in wood, each of which in a town makes a separate business. A merchant in Glasgow or Aberdeen who deals in linen will have in his warehouse Irish, Scots, and Hamburgh linens, but at London there are separate dealers in each of these. The greatness of the market enables one to lay out his whole stock not only on one commodity but on one species of a commodity and one assortment of it. This also lessens his correspondence and gives him less trouble; besides that as he deals in a large quantity he will get them cheaper and consequently can get the higher profit. Hence as commerce becomes more and more extensive the division of labour becomes more and more perfect. From this also we may see the necessity of a safe and easy conveyance betwixt the different places from whence the commodities are carried. If there is no conveyance of this sort the labour of the person will not be extended beyond the parish in which he lives. If the roads are infested by robbers the commodities will bear a higher price on account of the risk. If the roads are bad in winter the commerce is then greatly retarded, if not altogether stopped. A horse in a bad road in winter will take four times the time he took before to carry his loading of equal quantity, that is, will carry one-quarter of the goods he formerly did, whereas when they are good winter and summer makes no odds. And hence we see that the turnpikes of England have within these thirty or forty years increased the opulence of the inland parts. This may show us also the vast benefit of water carriage through the country. Four or five men will navigate a vessel betwixt Scotland and England, Norway, etc. which may contain perhaps 200 tons. The whole expense of the carriage is the tear and wear of the ship and the wages of these men backwards and forwards, that is, if we suppose she returns empty; but if she returns loaded this will be born in half by the second cargo. If we should suppose that this should be carried by land the expense is far greater. If a wagon carries five tons, it will be requisite to have forty wagons for 200 tons. Each of these have six or eight horses with two men. The expense here will be much greater. The tear and wear is much the same, but the wages is much higher, besides that the ship does it in a much shorter time. Land carriage therefore obstructs the supply of goods and the greatness of the market. Hence also we may see the great benefit of commerce, not as it brings in money into the country, which is but a fanciful advantage, but as it promotes industry, manufactures, and opulence and plenty made by it at home.

I had begun also to treat of the prices of commodities. There are in every species of goods two separate prices to be considered, the natural and the market price . . .

APPENDIX B

Fragment 'A'

who, for an equal quantity of work, would have taken more time and consequently[a] have required more wages, which must have been charged upon the goods. The philosopher, on the other hand, is of use to the porter; not only by being sometimes an occasional customer, like any other man who is not a porter, but in many other respects. If the speculations of the philosopher have been turned towards the improvement of the mechanic arts, the benefit of them may evidently descend to the meanest of the people. Whoever burns coals has them at a better bargain by means of the inventer of the fire-engine. Whoever eats bread receives a much greater advantage of the same kind from the inventers and improvers of wind and water mills. Even the speculations of those who neither invent nor improve any thing are not altogether useless. They serve, at least, to keep alive and deliver down to posterity the inventions and improvements which have been made before them. They explain the grounds and reasons upon which those discoveries were founded and do not suffer the quantity of useful science to diminish.

As it is the power of[b] exchanging[c] which[d] gives occasion to the division of labour, so the extent of this division will always be in proportion to the extent of that power.[e] Every species of industry will be carried on in a more or less perfect manner, that is, will be more or less accurately sub-divided into[f] the different branches according to[g] which it is capable of being split, in proportion[h] to the extent of the market, which is evidently the same thing with the power of exchanging. When the market is very small it is altogether impossible that there can be that separation of one employment from another which naturally takes place when it is more extensive. In a country village, for example, it is altogether impossible that there should be such a trade as that of a porter. All the burdens which, in such a situation, there can be any occasion to carry from one house to another would not give full employment to a man for a week in the year. Such a[i] business can scarce be[j] perfectly separated from all others in a pretty large market town. For the same reason, in all the small villages which are at a great distance from any market town, each family must bake their own bread and brew their own beer, to their own great expence and inconveniency,[k] by the interruption which is thereby given to their respective employments, and by being obliged, on this account, to main-tain[l] a greater number of servants than would otherwise be necessary. In mountainous and desart countries,[m] such as the greater part of the High-lands of Scotland, we cannot expect to find, in the same manner,[n] even a smith,[o] a carpenter, or a mason within less than twenty or thirty miles of another smith,[p] carpenter, or mason. The scattered families who live at ten or fifteen miles distance from the nearest of any[q] of those three[r] artisans, must learn to perform themselves a great number of little pieces of work for which, in more populous countries, they would readily have recourse to one or other of them,[s] whom they now can afford to send for[t] only upon very extraordinary occasions.[u] In a savage tribe of North Americans, who are generally hunters, the greatest number who can subsist easily together seldom exceeds one hundred or[v] one hundred and fifty persons.[w] Each village is at so great a distance from every other, and it is so very difficult and dangerous to travel the country, that there is scarce any intercourse between the different[x] villages[y] even of the same nation except what war and mutual defence give occasion to. In such a country it is impossible that any one employment should be entirely separated from every other. One man, etc:[z] One man may excel all his companions in some particular piece of dexterity, but it is impossible that he can be wholly employed in it, for want of a market to take off and exchange for other commodities the greater part of the goods which he would, in this case, necessarily produce. Hence the poverty which must necessarily take place in such a society. In a tribe of Tartars, or wild Arabs, who are generally shepherds, a greater number can live conveniently in one place. They do not depend upon the precarious accidents of the chace for subsistence, but upon the milk and flesh of their herds and flocks, who graze in the fields adjoining to the village.[a] The Hottentots near the Cape of Good-hope are the most barbarous nation of shepherds that is known in the world.[b] One of their villages or Kraals, however, is said generally to consist of upwards of five hundred persons. A Hord of Tartars frequently consists of five, six, or even ten times that number. As among such nations, therefore, tho' they have scarce any foreign commerce, the home market is somewhat[c] more extensive, we may expect to find something like the beginning of the division of labour.[d] Even in each village of Hottentots, therefore, according to Mr. Kolben,[e] there are[f] such[g] trades as those of a smith, a taylor, and even a phisician, and the persons who exercise them, tho' they[h] are not entirely, are principally supported by those respective employments, by which too they are greatly distinguished from the rest of their fellow citizens. Among the Tartars and Arabs we find the faint commencements[i] of a still[j] greater variety of employments. The Hottentots, therefore, may be regarded as a richer nation than the North Americans, and the Tartars and Arabs as[k] richer than the Hottentots. The compleat division of labour, however, is posteriour to the invention even of agriculture. By means of agriculture the same quantity of ground[l] not only produces corn but is made capable of supporting a much greater number of cattle than before. A much greater number of people, therefore, may easily subsist in the same place. The home market, in consequence,[m] becomes much more extensive. The smith, the mason, the carpenter, the weaver, and the taylor soon find it for their interest not to trouble themselves with cultivating the ground, but to exchange with the farmer the produces of their several employments[n] for the corn and cattle which they have occasion for. The farmer too very[o] soon comes to find it equally for his interest not to interrupt his own business with[p] making cloaths for his family, with building or repairing his own house, with mending or making the different instruments of his trade, or the different parts of his houshold furniture, but to call in the assistance of other workmen for each of those purposes whom he rewards with corn and with cattle.[q]

---

[a] 'would' deleted. [b] 'bartering and' deleted. [c] 'which one thing for another' deleted. [d] 'originally' deleted. [e] 'The lar greater the market, the larger the commerce' deleted. [f] Replaces 'into according to'. [g] The last two words replace 'into'. [h] End of p. 1 of MS. [i] 'buss' deleted. [j] 'there' deleted. [k] 'being obliged upon this account, not only frequently' deleted. [l] 'on this account' deleted. [m] 'in the same manner' deleted. [n] The last four words replace 'such as'. [o] 'or' deleted. [p] 'or another' deleted. [q] Replaces 'either'. [r] Replaces 'two'. [s] Replaces 'those workmen'. [t] 'at much trouble and expence' deleted. [u] 'It is the same thing with the mason' deleted. P. 2 of the MS. ends with 'same'. [v] 'one hundred and fifty men two hundred' deleted.

[w] 'They live' deleted. In the *Wealth of Nations* (edited by R. H. Campbell and A. S. Skinner, Oxford University Press, 1976), Vol. II, pp. 689–91, Smith refers to the hunting stage of the North American Indians as 'the lowest and rudest state of society', and adds that 'An army of hunters can seldom exceed two or three hundred men. The precarious subsistence which the chace affords could seldom allow a greater number . . .' Cf. *Lectures on Justice, etc.*, p. 20.

[x] The last two words replace 'one'. [y] 'and another' deleted.

[z] The words 'one man, etc:' and the three sentences which precede them are written in the margin. Indicators show that the three sentences are intended to replace the following passage, which has been deleted: 'In a tribe of ['savage' deleted] hunters who perhaps do not among them make above a hundred or a hundred and fifty persons and who have no regular commerce or intercourse of any kind with any other tribe, except such as mutual hostility and war may give occasion to, it is scarce possible that any one employment of any kind should be completely separated from every other.'

[a] In the *Wealth of Nations*, Vol. II, p. 690, Smith describes 'nations of shepherds' (typified by the Tartars and Arabs) as 'a more advanced state of society'. The main use of the division into socio-historical stages in the *Wealth of Nations* is in the discussion of the expense of defence and justice in Book V.

[b] A similar point is made in the *Wealth of Nations*, Vol. II, p. 634. [c] Replaces 'a good deal'.
[d] 'We find' deleted.

[e] Peter Kolben (or Kolb), *The Present State of the Cape of Good Hope* (German edn., 1719; English edn., London, 1731). Smith's comments on the Hottentots in this section of the fragment were probably derived from p. 216 of Vol. I of the English edn. (population of kraals), Ch. XIX *passim* (the smith and the tailor), and Ch. XXV *passim* (the physician).

[f] Replaces 'is'. [g] 'a' deleted. [h] End of p. 3 of MS. [i] 'in the same manner' deleted. [j] Replaces 'much'. [k] Replaces 'much'. [l] 'is made to support far' deleted. [m] The last two words replace 'therefore'. [n] 'with' deleted. [o] The last two words replace 'too'. [p] Replaces 'in order to'. [q] The last thirteen words replace 'for each of these purposes'.

APPENDIX C

Fragment 'B'

or ten men, and sailing from the port of Leith, will frequently in three days, generally in six days, carry two hundred tuns of goods to the same market. Eight or ten men, therefore, by the help of water carriage, can transport, in a much shorter time, a greater quantity of goods from Edinburgh to London than sixty six narrow wheeled waggons drawn by three hundred and ninety six horses and attended by a hundred and thirty two men: or than forty broad wheeled waggons drawn by three hundred and twenty horses and attended by eighty men. Upon two hundred tuns of goods, therefore, which are carried by the cheapest land carriage from Edinburgh to London there must be charged the maintenance of eighty men for three weeks, both the maintenance and what, tho' less than the maintenance, is however of very great value, the tear and wear of three hundred and twenty horses as well as of forty waggons. Whereas upon two hundred tuns of goods carried between the same markets by water carriages, there is to be charged only the maintenance of eight or ten men for about a fortnight and the tear and wear of a ship of two hundred tuns burden. If there was no other communication, therefore, between Edinburgh and London but by land, as no goods could be transported from the one place to the other except such whose price was very high in proportion to their weight,[a] there could not be the hundredth part of the commerce which is at present carried on between them, nor, in consequence, the hundredth part of the encouragement which they at present mutually give to each other's industry. There could be very little[b] commerce of any kind between the distant parts of the world. How few goods are so precious as to bear the expence of land carriage between London and Canton in China,[c] which at present carry on so extensive a commerce with one another and give consequently so much mutual encouragement to each other's industry? The first improvements, therefore, in arts and industry are always made in those places where the conveniency of water carriage affords the most extensive market to the produce of every sort of[d] labour. In our North American colonies the plantations have constantly followed either the sea coast or the banks of the navigable rivers, and have scarce any where extended themselves to any considerable distance from both. What James the sixth of Scotland said of the county of Fife, of which the inland parts were at that time very ill while the sea coast was extremely well cultivated, that it was like a coarse woollen coat edged with gold lace, might[e] still be said[f] of the greater part of our North American colonies.[g] The countries in the world which appear to have been first civilised are those which ly round the coast of the Mediterranean Sea. That sea,[h] by far the greatest inlet that is known in the world, having no tides nor consequently any waves except such as are caused by the wind only, was by the smoothness of its surface as well as by the multitude of its islands and the proximity of its opposite coasts[i] extremely favourable to the infant navigation of the world, when from the[j] want of the compass men were[k] afraid to quit the coast, and from the imperfection of the art of shipbuilding to abandon themselves to the boisterous waves of the ocean. Egypt, of all the countries upon the coast of the Mediterranean, seems to have been the first[l] in which either agriculture or manufactures were[m] cultivated or improved to any considerable degree.[n] Upper Egypt scarce extends[o] itself any where above five or six miles from the Nile; and in lower Egypt that great river, etc:[p] breaks itself into a great many different canals which with the assistance of a little art afforded, as in Holland at present, a communication by water carriage not only between all the great towns but between all the considerable villages and between almost all the farm houses in the country. The greatness and easiness of their inland navigation and commerce, therefore, seem to have been evidently the causes of the early improvement of Egypt.[q] Agriculture and manufactures too seem to have been of very great antiquity in some of the maritime provinces of China and in the province of Bengal in the East Indies. All[r] these are countries very much of the same nature with Egypt, cut by innumerable canals which afford them an immense inland navigation.

---

[a] The last twenty-five words are written in the margin. [b] The last two words replace 'scarce any'. [c] End of p. 1 of MS. [d] 'industry' deleted. [e] Replaces 'is'. [f] The last two words replace 'true'. [g] 'the most favoured by nature perhaps of any country in the world the countries in the world perhaps the most favoured by nature' deleted. [h] 'the gre' deleted. [i] 'was' deleted. [j] The last two words replace 'men for'. [k] The last two words replace 'were' and an indecipherable word which is deleted above the line. [l] End of p. 2 of MS. [m] Replaces 'seem to have been'. [n] 'In lower Egypt the Nile' deleted. [o] The first few words of this sentence originally read 'In the upper Egypt the

country scarce extends'. 'In' and 'the country' have been deleted, and 'upper' emended to 'Upper'. *p* This sentence is written in the margin.

q 'They seem to have been the only people in the world who never ventured from', followed by eight or nine indecipherable words, deleted. Possibly the indecipherable words referred to the fact that the Egyptians did not venture beyond their own shores because of an alleged 'superstitious antipathy to the sea' (*Wealth of Nations*, Vol. I, p. 367). *r* Replaces 'both'.

APPENDIX D

Extract from the 'Early Draft' [a]

A porter is of use to a philosopher, not only by sometimes carrying a burden for him, but by facilitating almost every trade and manufacture whose productions the philosopher can have occasion for. Whatever we buy from any shop or ware-house comes cheaper to us by means of those poor despised labourers, who in all great towns have set themselves aside for the particular occupation of carrying goods from one place to another, of packing and unpacking them, and who in consequence have acquired extraordinary strength, dexterity, and readiness in this sort of business. Every thing would be dearer if before it was exposed to sale it had been carried, packt, and unpackt by hands less able and less dexterous, [b] who for an equal quantity of work would have taken more time, and must [c] consequently have required more wages, which must have been charged upon the goods. The philosopher on the other hand is of use to the porter, not only by being sometimes an occasional customer, as well as [d] any other man who is not a porter, but in many other respects. If the speculations of the philosopher have been turned towards the improvement of the mechanic arts, the benefit of them may evidently descend to the meanest of the people. Whoever burns coals has them at a better bargain by means of the inventor of the fire engine. Whoever eats bread receives a much greater advantage of the same kind from the inventors and improvers of wind and water mills. Even the speculations of those who neither invent nor improve any thing are not altogether useless. They serve at least to keep alive and deliver down to posterity the inventions and improvements which had been made before them. They explain the grounds and reasons upon which those discoveries were founded, and do not allow [e] the quantity of usefull knowledge [f] to diminish. [g] In opulent and commercial societies, besides, to think or [h] to reason comes to be, like every other employment, a particular business, which is carried on by a very few people, who furnish the public with all the thought and reason possessed by the vast multitudes that labour. Let any ordinary person make a fair review of all the knowledge which he possesses concerning any subject that does not fall within the limits of his particular occupation, and he will find that almost every thing he knows has been acquired at second hand, from books, from the literary instructions which he may have received in his youth, or from the occasional conversations which he may have had with men of learning. A very small part of it only, he will find, has been the produce of his own observations or reflections. All the rest has been purchased, in the same manner as his shoes or his stockings, from those whose business it is to make up and prepare for the market that particular species of goods. It is in this manner that he has acquired all his general ideas concerning[i] the great subjects of religion, morals, and government, concerning his own happiness or that of his country. His whole system concerning each of those important objects will almost always be found to have been originally the produce of the industry of other people, from whom either he himself or those who have had the care of his education have procured it in the same manner as any other commodity, by barter and exchange for some part of the produce of their own labour.

[a] The extract reproduced here begins on the first page of folio 8 of the MS., and finishes about one-quarter of the way down the third page, at the end of the section on the division of labour. [b] The counterpart of the first paragraph of FA begins here. The only substantive differences between the two passages are indicated in [c–f]. [c] FA omits 'must'. [d] FA has 'like' instead of 'as well as'. [e] FA has 'suffer' instead of 'allow'. [f] FA has 'science' instead of 'knowledge'. [g] The counterpart of the first paragraph of FA ends here. [h] 'or' is written over an erasure. [i] 'concerning' is written over an erasure.

New Light on Adam Smith's Glasgow Lectures on Jurisprudence[1]

I

We now possess two separate sets of student's notes of Adam Smith's lectures on Jurisprudence at Glasgow University: the set published by Cannan in 1896[2] which, as now appears probable, relates to the course delivered in the 1763–4 session;[3] and the recently discovered set, soon to be published, which specifically relates to the course delivered in the 1762–3 session.[4] From these two sets of notes, taken together, we are now able to obtain a fairly accurate picture of what the Jurisprudence section of Smith's lectures to his Moral Philosophy class must have been like during his last two years at Glasgow.

But Smith's appointment as a professor at Glasgow dated from 1751 – eleven years before the delivery of the earlier of the two courses in respect of which we possess student's notes. What were his Jurisprudence lectures like, then, in the first years of his teaching career at Glasgow? The information about this which has come down to us – most of it contained in Dugald Stewart's *Biographical Memoir* of Smith[5] – has so far been distressingly meagre and vague. We have the famous account of 'Mr. Smith's lectures while a Professor at Glasgow' with which John Millar supplied Stewart in the early 1790s.[6] We have the intriguing extract quoted by Stewart from 'a short manuscript drawn up by Mr. Smith in the year 1755'.[7] We have Stewart's statement about the 'considerable change'

---

[1] This essay was originally published in *History of Political Economy*, **8**, 1976, pp. 439–77. No amendments of substance have been made.

[2] *Lectures on Justice, Police, Revenue and Arms* (edited by E. Cannan, Oxford University Press, 1896).

[3] See above, p. 36.

[4] The new notes are being edited by Professor D. D. Raphael, Professor P. G. Stein, and myself, for publication in Glasgow University's bicentennial edition of Smith's *Works and Correspondence*.

[5] Dugald Stewart, *Biographical Memoir of Adam Smith* (Kelley reprint, 1966). The original version of this *Memoir* was read by Stewart at the Royal Society of Edinburgh on 21 January and 18 March 1793.

[6] *Ibid.*, pp. 10–13.

[7] *Ibid.*, pp. 67–8; and see above, pp. 25–6.

which the plan of Smith's lectures underwent during his last four years at Glasgow, after the publication of *The Theory of Moral Sentiments* in 1759.[8] And that is just about all. The rest is virtually silence. This awkward gap in our knowledge about the early development of Smith's ideas has had to be filled by speculation and conjecture, and a number of crucial questions have remained unsolved. For example, to what extent did Smith, at the outset, base his Moral Philosophy course on Francis Hutcheson's? What role, in the early years, did 'economics' play in his course, and at what point exactly was it brought in? Did he use the four stages theory in his early lectures, or was this theory a later importation, derivative rather than original? We have all tried to make educated guesses about such questions as these, but only the boldest of us have dared to lay any claim to certainty.

It is the main purpose of this essay to present a new document which enables us, I think, to be a little more certain about these issues than has hitherto been possible. The document consists of a set of notes, discovered in the Commonplace Book of a professorial colleague of Smith's, which appear to me to be selective extracts from a student's notes of a relatively early version of Smith's Jurisprudence lectures. When read together with the 1762–3 and Cannan notes, these extracts cast a certain amount of new light on the development of Smith's thought during his Glasgow period, and, in particular, on the three specific questions mentioned in the previous paragraph.

The professorial colleague concerned was the celebrated John Anderson;[9] and the discovery of this set of notes in his Commonplace Book was made in July 1970 by Mr A. H. Brown, now of St Antony's College, Oxford. Mr Brown was at that time working on Semyon Desnitsky, the noted Russian jurist and social thinker, who came to Glasgow University as a student in 1761 and who upon his return to Russia made good use of what he had learned at Glasgow from Smith and Millar.[10] During his period of study at Glasgow Desnitsky had an altercation with John Anderson,[11] and Mr Brown therefore spent some time going through the Anderson papers at

---

[8] *Ibid.*, p. 42. 'After the publication of the *Theory of Moral Sentiments*', says Stewart, 'Mr. Smith remained four years at Glasgow. . . During that time, the plan of his lectures underwent a considerable change. His ethical doctrines, of which he had now published so valuable a part, occupied a much smaller portion of the course than formerly; and accordingly, his attention was naturally directed to a more complete illustration of the principles of Jurisprudence and of Political Economy.'

[9] On Anderson, see J. Muir, *John Anderson and the College He Founded* (John Smith and Son, Glasgow, 1950), and D. Murray, *Memories of the Old College of Glasgow* (Jackson, Wylie and Co., Glasgow, 1927), pp. 113–19 and 379–93.

[10] On Desnitsky, see W. R. Scott, *Adam Smith as Student and Professor* (Jackson, Son and Co., Glasgow, 1937), pp. 158 n. and 424 ff.; A. H. Brown, 'S. E. Desnitsky, Adam Smith and the *Nakaz* of Catherine II', in *Oxford Slavonic Papers*, New Series, Vol. VII, 1974; and A. H. Brown, 'Adam Smith's First Russian Followers', in A. S. Skinner and T. Wilson (editors), *Essays on Adam Smith* (Oxford University Press, 1975), pp. 247–73.

[11] Mr. Brown tells the story in his article 'Adam Smith's First Russian Followers', *ibid.*

Strathclyde University to see whether there was anything in them which might throw light on this incident. It was then that he found a set of notes in Anderson's Commonplace Book which seemed to him to bear an interesting resemblance to Adam Smith's lectures on Jurisprudence as reported in the 1762–3 and Cannan notes. My own initial reaction, when Mr Brown told me of this discovery, was one of scepticism; and it was only some time later, after I had become rather more familiar with the 1762–3 notes and had studied the Anderson notes more carefully,[12] that I came round to the view that Mr Brown's original intuition was well founded.

Anderson's Commonplace Book is bound in three octavo volumes. Each volume contains approximately 370 pages, numbered in pencil, the great majority of which are completely unused. The entries include (in addition to the set of notes with which we are mainly concerned here) a number of remarks on scientific subjects, comments on several recently published books, 'pensées' on assorted topics, and (in Volume III) a number of observations on France written on the occasion of a visit to that country. The question of the dating of these entries will be considered in more detail below, in the second section of the present article: all that needs to be said at this juncture is that the last item in Volume III is specifically dated 1755, and that one's general impression is that the majority of the shorter comments, 'pensées', etc. in Volumes I and II were probably written between 1753 and 1755. The set of notes in which we are interested appears at the back of Volume I on pp. 292–368, *starting on p. 368* (i.e., the notes are written, as it were, upside down).

The notes are reproduced in full at the end of this article, prefaced by an explanation of the conventions which I have adopted in editing them. There seems to be nothing in the form or presentation of the notes which is inconsistent with the hypothesis that they were selective extracts made by Anderson from a student's notes of *some* course of lectures (leaving aside for a moment the question of *which* course). There are indeed certain indications which could reasonably be regarded as positively suggesting this. The mis-spellings 'Colvin' for 'Kolben' (p. 30),[13,14] and 'course' for

---

[12] I am extremely grateful to Mr C. G. Wood, librarian of the Andersonian Library, University of Strathclyde, and to Mrs E. Frame, sub-librarian, who gave me facilities for studying the notes and have been generous in providing me with other relevant material and information about Anderson.

[13] This page reference and the similar ones which follow are to the pages of the Anderson manuscript, renumbered in accordance with a scheme described in the note which precedes the reproduction of the manuscript at the end of this essay. The point where a new page of the manuscript (as so numbered) begins is indicated in the reproduction by an appropriate arabic italic numeral in square brackets.

[14] The supposed 'History of Africa' by 'Colvin' mentioned on p. 30 of the notes would seem almost certainly to have been in fact a then very well-known book on the Cape of Good Hope by Peter Kolben (or Kolb), of which an English translation (*The Present State of the Cape of Good-Hope*) appeared in 1731. The peculiar custom which is referred to in the notes appears to be that described by Kolben on pp. 119–24 of Vol. I of the translation. The beating (and/or

'courts' (p. 10), for example, look very much as if they may have had their origin in lecture room mishearings. In a number of places the corrections made by Anderson (e.g., the deletion of repetitions on pp. 5, 11, 22, and 28) seem to suggest that he is copying from another document. In other places (more particularly in the first few pages) they seem to suggest that he is making an effort to improve the language and style of an imperfect original. Occasionally, it would appear, Anderson adds his own comments – as on p. 5 (where he makes this clear by his use of the words 'My own'); on p. 12 (where the reference to 'Mr. Hume's Essay' may possibly he his); and on p. 36 (where the reference to 'Mr. Wallace' is very probably his).[15]

Let us now try to test the hypothesis that the notes had their origin in an early version of Smith's Jurisprudence lectures. For fairly obvious reasons this hypothesis is not at all an easy one to test. The basic comparison which it would seem most useful to make in this connection, at any rate in the first instance, is between the Anderson notes and the 1762–3 notes. Now the latter consist of a very long and reliable set of student's notes of the major part of Smith's Jurisprudence lectures in the 1762–3 session, based in all probability on shorthand notes taken down by the student in class and subsequently transcribed; whereas the former, if the hypothesis is correct, consist of a very short set of summarized extracts made by Anderson some time in the early or middle 1750s from notes of Smith's lectures taken down by a student about whose note-taking ability and methods very little can be surmised. In view of this appreciable difference in the probable nature, origin, and date of the two documents, we could hardly expect to find – and in fact we do not find – a high degree of conformity between individual words and expressions, the construction of individual sentences, etc. We must therefore seek mainly for other types of conformity, asking ourselves, for example, whether the sequence of points in a significant number of chains of reasoning is more or less the same in both documents; whether the same unusual or idiosyncratic arguments and illustrations are employed at key points in both; and whether the order of treatment of the different topics is more or less the same in both documents taken as a whole. And of these types of conformity, it is clear, we would have to be able to find a relatively large number before we could regard our hypothesis as confirmed. By a stroke of luck of the kind which is rarely vouchsafed to Smith-scholars, this condition can in fact be fulfilled. For the hypothesis *not* to be correct, I believe, it would be necessary to postulate either the existence of some common literary source which has managed to escape the attention of all workers in this field, or the accumulation of a quite unbelievable number of coincidences.

---

abuse) of the mother by the son, it is true, occurs according to Kolben not after the father's death, as stated in the notes, but after the son's ceremonial induction into the society of men. The use by Kolben of the word 'milk-sop' (p. 122), however, would seem to establish the connection pretty decisively.

[15] Cf. pp. 71–2 below.

As an example, let us take the long passage in the Anderson notes headed 'Of Slaves', which begins half-way down p. 30 of the manuscript and ends at the foot of p. 35. A paragraph-by-paragraph comparison of this passage with corresponding parts of the section on slavery in Volume III of the 1762–3 lecture-notes[16] yields the following results:[17]

| *Anderson notes* | *1762–3   Lecture notes* |

Of Slaves.

Many causes of slavery – by way of punishment – in order to pay debt – but above all by war. – No humanity to prisoners of war, of old. If they did not kill them they thought them their property, and this the greatest origin of slavery. – Slavery could not be introduced in a polished age, and all countries were at first rude. – In the heroick ages slaves were happy; in polished ages not so. In the first state, the slave eat and wrought with his master, and there subsisted an intimacy between them. In the last state, they were removed from the sight of their masters and therefore cruelly used. At present there is more sympathy between a farmer and his servant, than between a duke and his footman. And as the blacks seem not from their skin {to partake of the same nature with the whites, the imagination of a barbarous white supposes him not to be of the same nature with himself, and therefore uses him ill with less scruple}. (Aristotle spends some ⟨?time⟩ in proving that a slave can have no virtue.) To be a slave in a despotic government is no worse than to be a freeman – see Montesquiou.

(Volume III)

I shall now observe the different methods in which slaves might be acquired in those countries where it has been in use. – The 1st, captives taken in war . . . When the conqueror has got his enemy into his power there is then no one to protect him; his life and all he has he owes to the mercy of his conqueror if he inclines to spare him. He is reckoned to belong intirely to the conqueror, in recompence for his delivery . . . This seems to have been the originall introduction of slaves, and was universally received amongs⟨t⟩ all the early nations . . . 3d method is when criminalls are adjudged to slavery. Slavery is a punishment often inflicted on criminalls . . . 4th is that by which insolvent debtors were adjudged or given over to their creditors (pp. 144–6). We may observe here that the state of slavery is a much more tollerable one in a [a] poor and barbarous people than in a rich and polished one . . . In a poor country there can be no great difference betwixt the master and the slave in any respect. They will eat at the same table, work together, and be cloathed in the same manner, and will be alike in every other particular. In a

[16] In the Cannan notes, the relevant passages (with which a similar comparison may be made) appear on pp. 94–104 of the published version.
[17] The extracts from the Anderson notes are printed exactly as they appear in the reproduction of the whole document at the end of this essay, but with page numbers and textual notes omitted. The extracts from the 1762–3 lecture notes are printed more or less as they will appear in the published version, with page numbers inserted at appropriate intervals, but with textual and editorial notes omitted. In both cases the punctuation and capitalization have been improved, but otherwise the reproductions are as close as possible to the original manuscripts. For an explanation of what the different kinds of brackets and braces mean, see the note on p. 81 below.

rich country the disproportion betwixt
them will be prodigious in all these
respects. This dis⟨pro⟩portion will
make the rich men much more
sev⟨e⟩r⟨e⟩ to their slaves than the
poorer ones. A man of great fortune, a
nobleman, is much farther removed
from the condition of his servant than
a farmer. The farmer generally works
along with his servant; they eat together, and are little different. The disproportion betwixt them, the condition
of the nobleman and his servant, is so
great that he will hardly look on him
as being of the same kind; he thinks
he has little title even to the ordinary
enjoyments of life, and feels but little
for his misfortunes ... The more
arbitrary the government is in like
manner the slaves are in the better
condition, and the freer the people the
more miserable are the slaves ... (pp.
105–10).

A slave in Rome had no religion,
i.e., he did not share in the publick
worship; he was considered in the
same light with the cattle of his
proprietor. Hence of old, see Tacitus,
etc., it was common for the slaves to
become Jews, as they held there was
an universal deity, whereas in the
heathen religion every deity had a
particular province and there was no
deity allotted for the slaves.

Slaves were admitted to no religious
society and were reckond profane ...
Each city had its peculiar deities.
Minerva presided over Athens; Rome
was under the protection of Mars and
Jupiter who dwelt in the Capitoll.
These were supposed to favour only
their particular people. What had
Jupiter who dwelt in the Capitoll to do
with a slave who came from Syria or
Cappadocia ... Their masters prayed
for their thriving and multiplying in the
same manner as for their cattle ... This
it was which made all religions which
taught the being of one supreme and
universall god, who presided over all,
be so greedily receivd by this order of
men. Even the Jewish religion, which
is of all others least adapted to make
conquests, was greedily received by
them ... Tacitus and [blank in MS.]
tell us that a great part hominum servilis
et libertinae conditionis were greatly
addicted to the Jewish religion (pp.
96–9).

We never hear of the insurrection of slaves in Persia, etc.

In Tyre, Carthage, and Lacedaemon the people lived well ⟨?compared⟩ to their slaves. – The Germans armed their slaves.

Corruptions bring on their own remedies. – The common law and not Christianity suppressed slavery – it was not abolished by humanity or the improvement of manners – but as the slaves were armed by their lords and so dangerous to the king, the king abolished slavery. – Slavery subsisted under the emperours after Christianity was the popular religion. – The cannon law supposes slavery. – Slavery still subsists in Muscovy which is a Christian country.

Our salters and colliers differ much from slaves. They can have property and consequently families; they can buy their liberty; the price of their labour is fixed by law; they are punished by law – that is, they are only confined to one trade and one master, the first of which was the state of the antient Egyptians.

We see accordingly that no absolute monarch was ever in danger from the ⟨?slaves⟩, neither the Mogulls country, Persia modern or ancient, nor Turky, etc. ever were (pp. 104–5).

In the same manner Carthage, Tyre, Lacedemon, etc. were all in danger from their slaves (p. 104). Amongst the old Germans and others, as Tacitus tells, they were used with the greatest possible humanity (p. 106).

The circumstances which have made slavery be abolished in the corner of Europe in which it now is are peculiar to it, and which happening to concurr at the same time have brought about that change ... The clergy ... promoted greatly the emancipation of the villains. The slaves ... made the chief body of the soldier⟨s⟩ in these times, and in them the power of their superiors consisted. The kings interest also led him on this account to lessen the authority of the nobles and their vassalls over their villains (pp. 117–19). But we are not to imagine the temper of the Christian religion is necessarily contrary to slavery. The masters in our colonies are Christians, and yet slavery is allowed amongst them. The Constan⟨t⟩inopolitan emperors were very jealous Christians, and yet never thought of abolishing slavery. There are also many Christian countries where slavery is tollerated at this time (pp. 127–8). The Zars of Muscovy have very great power, yet slavery is still in use ... (p. 122).

The colliers in this manner have a great many of the priviledges of free men; their lives are under the protection of the laws as others; their property is also insured to them; and their liberty is not alltogether taken away. They have the benefit of marriage and the exercise of religion. So that they are no way restricted more than other men, excepting that they are bound to exercise a certain business and in a certain place. And this has been the case with many other persons who thought themselves free . . . The old Aegyptians, who never thought themselves in any respect slaves, were after the time of Sesostris obliged in like manner to adhere to ⟨the⟩ exercise of their forefathers business (p. 128).

Were our salters and colliers put upon the same footing with other labourers, it would be much better for their masters. – When men are constrained to work for another they will not work so hard as if at liberty – this is manifest in quarrying and other mines. In the Newcastle mines work is done cheaper than in this country. In this country a collier and salter can earn more than a quarrier or any other labourer who works as hard. – In the mines of Silesia, the miners go voluntary below ground and live there for years.

This immoderate price of labour in these works would soon fall if the masters of them would set their colliers and salters at liberty, and open the work to all free men . . . (p. 129). This work indeed, being somewhat more dissagreable and more hazardous than others of the same sort, they might perhaps require wages somewhat higher, but this would not come above 8^d or 9^d; so that a collier has now about 4 times the wages he would have were the work open to all men. But notwithstanding of this high wages we see the colliers frequently run off from the works in this country to those about Newcastle, where they will not earn above 13^d or 14^d a day as the work is open; but we never saw any come from Newcastle here (p. 130).

Attempts to introduce agrarian laws, and the abolition of debts, were the sources of constant disorder in antient states, and are quite unknown in the modern. – The cause of this slavery – for as in every great town the inhabitants are either gentlemen or work hard, a man that has no land can get subsistence only by his labour; but of old the slaves were mechanicks and not freemen, and therefore the freemen who had no lands in Rome, Athens, etc. were entirely dependent on the great for their living – and the great were liberal, as the people had the disposal of all places.

We are told by Aristotle and Cicero that the two sources of all seditions at Athens and at Rome were the demands of the people for an agrarian law or an abolition of debts. This was no doubt a demand of the taking away so much of ones property and giving it to those to whom it did not belong. We never hear of any such demands as these at this time . . . The poor people now who have neither a land estate nor any fortune in money, can gain a livelyhood by working as a servant to a farmer in the country, or by working to any tradesman whose business they understand. But at Rome the whole business was engrossed by the slaves, and the poor citizens who had neither an estate in land nor a fortune in money were in a very miserable condition; there was no business to which they could apply themselves with any hopes of success. The only means of support they had was either from the generall largesses which were made to them, or by the money they got for their votes at elections (pp. 141–2).

It will be seen that almost every point made in this relatively long section of the Anderson notes has its direct counterpart in the 1762–3 notes; that the language in which the points are expressed, although never exactly the same, is often much more similar than we might reasonably have expected; and that after the first paragraph of the Anderson notes the order of treatment of the different topics is more or less the same in both documents. Given the probability that Smith when delivering his lectures trusted at any rate to some extent to 'extemporary elocution',[18] and remembering that we are comparing a very full set of lecture notes with what is at the best a collection of summarized extracts from another (and probably much earlier) set of lecture notes, the degree of conformity revealed by this comparison must surely be regarded as very high indeed.

As another example, let us take the two references to Montesquieu on p. 26 of the Anderson notes. The first of these, which relates to Montesquieu's argument that since in hot climates women are married very young and are old at twenty it is natural that in such places polygamy should be introduced, reads as follows:

See Montesquiou, B xvi, ch 2ᵈ – et que la polygamie s'introduise. Suppose the fact true, it will only follow that he ought to take another but not that polygamy ought to be established – But the fact is not true. – Intemperance in love indeed makes the easterns fond of very young women, as rapes are committed in London upon children five years old – but Cleopatra had a child at 40. –

The corresponding passage in the 1762–3 lecture notes is the following:

It is ascerted also as an argument in favours of polygamy that in the warmer climates the women loose there beauty much sooner than they do in this country, and that at the time when their beauty [and] would render them fit to be the object of affection their weakness and youth render them all together unfit for being the objects of his confidence and proper to be put on an equall ⟨?footing⟩, as this time is past before the other comes. And on the other hand when their sense and experience would render ⟨them⟩ fit for this, their want of beauty and incapacity

---

[18] John Millar reported to Dugald Stewart that Smith, in delivering his lectures, 'trusted almost entirely to extemporary elocution' (Dugald Stewart, *Biographical Memoir of Adam Smith*, p. 13). Other accounts, however, are not entirely consistent with this.

of bearing children counterballance it. They tell us that the women in those countries ripen much sooner than in the northern ones, that they are fit for marriage by 7 or 8 and leave bearing children in 20th or thereabouts. Now this fact is not better ascertained than the former. We are told indeed that they have children by 11 or 12 years of age, and so would many women in this country as well as in the southern ones. It is said that Mahomet married his wife [blank in MS.] at 5 and lived with her at 8. But this has probably been no more than the rape of an infant, which are but too common in more northern climates. On the other hand there is no certainty that they cease to bear children nearly as soon as is alledged. We find that Cleopatra, an Aegyptian, at the age of 36 when the women are past the prime of their beauty even in this country, had charms enough to retain Antony, a man generally very fickle, so as to bring on a separation with Octavia and his ruin; and about a year before this she had born a child . . . But altho it was realy the case that the time in which a woman was capable of bearing children and being a proper companion for a man was limited to betwixt twelve and 20, this would not at all require the establishment of polygamy. It might indeed require voluntary divorce, that the husband, after the woman was incapable of being a proper companion for him, should have it in his power to put her away and take another, but it could never require that he should have more than one who were fit wives at the same time.[19]

It will be seen that in this passage all the arguments and illustrations that are briefly summarized in Anderson's extract duly appear and take their proper place. Remembering once again the very different nature of the two documents which we are comparing, the degree of conformity revealed in this comparison must be regarded as high.

The same is true in the case of the second reference to Montesquieu on p. 26, which relates to the latter's argument that if in a particular country there is a large surplus of women over men (as, allegedly, at Bantam in Java) this might be taken as justifying polygamy. Anderson's short summary reads as follows:

B. xvi, ch. 4. This opinion seems to be ill founded, for the births are not kept regularly in Asia. – Meaco is a capital. – It is filled with saraglios. – In Scotland if the people were numbered there wd be found more males in the kingdom than females.–

The corresponding passage in the 1762–3 lecture notes is the following:

It is advanced indeed in favours of polygamy by Montesquieu on the authority of [blank in MS.] that at Bantam, the capitall of the island Java, there are 10 women born for one man; and a Dutch author tells us that on the coast of Guinea there are 50 women for one man. In Europe

[19] 1762–3 notes, Vol. III, pp. 37–40. Cf. the Cannan notes, published version, pp. 83–4.

we are certain that the proportion is very different. It is generally thought that ⟨there⟩ are about 12 women to 13 men, and others say that there are about 16 to 17, and that proportion appears certainly to be hereabouts from the bills of mortality which are kept in different parts of Europe . . . We are told that at Macao, the capitall of Japan, when the inhabitants were numbered there were found about 11 women to 9 men . . . This fact we are indeed pretty well assured of, as it was found so on a publick numbering of the people. But then it does not even establish that there was so great a disproportion as it appears to do. For we are to consider that as this was the capitall of the country, in which the head man of their religion resided who alone had 500 or 600 wives, and many other rich men who would no doubt have considerable numbers, there would be collected here a number of women who might well be supposed to make this disproportion, altho in the other parts of the country they were born in the same proportion as in Europe, which is very probable. This is the only fact which is well attested, for we have never heard of any bills of mortality being kept in those countries of which this is related.[20]

Then again, take the account on pp. 19–20 of the Anderson notes of *fur manifestus* and *fur non manifestus* (manifest and non-manifest thief) which involves yet another reference to Montesquieu – this time to his statement that 'Lycurgus, with a view of rendering the citizens dexterous and cunning, ordained that children should be practised in thieving, and that those who were caught in the act should be severely whipped'.[21] Anderson's extract reads as follows:

Fur manifestus and non manifestus. Vide L'Esprit des Loix, an ingenious account but it seems not to be just.

For it does not appear that the Lacedaemonians were allowed to steal any thing but provisions from the publick table. Vide Plutarch. – And there was this distinction between the fur man. and non man. among all nations which is owing to this, that there is a greater hatred against the criminal if taken immediately than if afterwards or if his punishment is delayed – rubra manu among the Romans, taken in the fang among the Scotch.–

The corresponding passage in the 1762–3 lecture notes is the following:

Amongst the Romans theft was punished with the restitution of double of the thing stolen, with this distinction, that if the thief was caught with the thing stolen about him he was to restore ⟨ ?four⟩ fo[u]ld, and two fold if he was not caught in the fact: in the fang or not in the fang (as it is expressed in the Scots law ⟨⟩) and in the Latin writers fur manifestus et nec manifestus. It will be proper to take the more notice

---

[20] 1762–3 notes, Vol. II, pp. 34–7. Cf. the Cannan notes, pp. 81–3.
[21] Montesquieu, *The Spirit of Laws* (Hafner edition, New York, 1949), Vol. II, p. 163.

of this, as the reason of it does not appear to be very evident, and that which is alledged by Montesquieu, tho very ingenious, does not appear to me to be the true one. He says that this law was borrowed from the Lacedemonians, who, as they traind their youth chiefly to the military art, encouraged them in theft, as it was imagined this might sharpen their wit and skill in the stratagems of war. Theft therefore was as they suppose not ⟨?at⟩ all discouraged amongst them, but rather honoured if it was not discovered before it was finished; but when the thief was discovered it was looked on as a disgrace, as being not cleverly performed . . . But this does not appear probable in any part. For in the 1st place there is no good ground for imagining that the Lacedemonians encouraged theft. This is conjectured from some passages of [blank in MS.] particularly one where he tells that there was a table kept at the publick charge for the old men of the city, but none for the younger men. They however were encouraged to pourloin for themselves what they could from the table, for the reason above assigned. This however is very different from what is properly denominated theft, which was not at all encouraged . . . Punishment is always adapted originally to the resentment of the injured person; now the resentment of a person against the thief when he is caught in the fact ⟨?is greater⟩ than when he is only discovered afterwards and the theft must be proved against him, which gives the persons resentment time to cooll. The satisfaction he requires is much greater in the former than in the latter case. We see too that there was the same odds made in the punishment of other crimes. The murderer who was caught *rubro manu* was punished much more severely than he against whom the murder was afterwards proven.[22]

Once again there is the same kind of parallel between the two passages, and the degree of conformity seems much too close to be merely accidental.

And so one may go through the Anderson notes picking out many other passages of which there are close parallels in the 1762–3 notes[23] – and also of course in the Cannan notes,[24] and (occasionally) in the *Wealth of Nations*.[25] Naturally there are not only resemblances but also differences:

[22] 1762–3 notes, Vol. II, p. 150. Cf. the Cannan notes, p. 147.

[23] Cf., e.g., the first paragraph on p. 4 of the Anderson notes with pp. 93–4 of Vol. I of the 1762–3 notes; the paragraph beginning 'Of mankind . . .' on p. 36 of the Anderson notes with pp. 132–3 of Vol. III of the 1762–3 notes; and the last paragraph on p. 38 of the Anderson notes with pp. 36–8 of Vol. IV of the 1762–3 notes.

[24] Cf., e.g., the first two sentences on p. 14 of the Anderson notes with the sentence beginning 'In the same manner . . .' on p. 252 of the Cannan notes; the last paragraph on p. 23 of the Anderson notes with p. 75 of the Cannan notes; p. 25 of the Anderson notes with pp. 80–1 of the Cannan notes; and the comment on the exposure of children on p. 28 of the Anderson notes with the similar comment at the foot of p. 104 of the Cannan notes.

[25] Cf., e.g., the statement on p. 12 of the Anderson notes that 'Locke, Montesquiou, and Law think that the lowness of interest is owing to the plenty of money' with the statement in Book II, Ch. IV of the *Wealth of Nations* that 'Mr. Locke, Mr. Law, and Mr. Montesquieu . . . seem to have imagined that the increase of the quantity of gold and silver, in consequence of the discovery of the Spanish West Indies, was the real cause of the lowering of the rate of interest through the greater part of Europe'.

and some of the latter (notably those discussed below) are of considerable interest and importance. But when one compares, for example, the sections in the Anderson notes on testaments, marriage and divorce, criminal law, and the origin of government with the corresponding sections in the 1762–3 and Cannan notes, the differences appear to be mainly in detail, ordering, and illustration rather than in fundamental approach. And even when the differences are major rather than minor – as, most notably, in the analysis of prices and money – a greater number of echoes of the Anderson version are in fact to be found in the 1762–3 and Cannan notes than might appear at first sight.[26]

For reasons of space, I shall not document any more of these parallels at this juncture, but proceed immediately to a comparison of the *order* in which the different individual subjects are treated in the Anderson notes (taking them as a whole) and in the 1762–3 notes. One preliminary point that has to be appreciated here is that the order of the main topics in the 1762–3 notes is radically different from their order in the Cannan notes. Near the beginning of the latter, it will be remembered, the student reports Smith as saying:

> The civilians begin with considering government and then treat of property and other rights. Others who have written on this subject begin with the latter and then consider family and civil government. There are several advantages peculiar to each of these methods, though that of the civil law seems upon the whole preferable.[27]

In what follows in the Cannan notes – which, as I have already said, probably relate to the course delivered in the 1763–4 session – Smith duly adopts the method of 'the civil law'. In his 1762–3 course, however, it is clear from the recently discovered notes that he had adopted the alternative method, beginning with 'property and other rights' and then going on to consider 'family and civil government'.

The sequence in which the different individual subjects are treated (within this broad framework) in the 1762–3 notes is set out in the following table, side by side with a list of the pages on which the corresponding subjects are dealt with in the Anderson notes:

Sequence of topics in 1762–3 lecture notes	*Pages in Anderson notes on which corresponding subjects are dealt with*
1. General	p. 1
2. Property (including testaments)	pp. 1–6
3. Contract	pp. 7–14

[26] Cf., e.g., pp. 7–8 of the Anderson notes with some of the comments on pp. 79–84 of Vol. II and pp. 71–5 and 119–24 of Vol. VI of the 1762–3 notes, and pp. 134, 176–7, and 188–9 of the Cannan notes.
[27] Cannan notes, p. 8.

It will be seen that the sequence of the subjects in the two documents is almost exactly the same.[28] There are of course considerable differences in the relative amounts of space devoted to the different subjects in the two documents – notably in the case of 'Police', where Anderson has extracted only two sentences from the student's notes. And there is another difference of much greater significance – namely, that in the Anderson notes the 'economic' sections dealing with prices, money, interest, etc. are located round about the middle of the first half of the document, sandwiched between the sections dealing with testaments and those dealing with injuries, whereas in the 1762–3 notes almost all of the corresponding 'economic' subjects are dealt with under the heading 'Police' in the final part of the document.[29] This difference will be further discussed below: in the meantime, let us simply note that the close correspondence in the order in which the different subjects are treated in the two documents, when coupled with the high degree of conformity in the content of many passages, strongly suggests that the Anderson notes, like the 1762–3 notes, had their origin in lectures on Jurisprudence given by Adam Smith.

II

The next question to be discussed is that of the *dating* of the particular course of lectures to which the Anderson notes relate.

Smith was elected to the chair of Logic at Glasgow University on 9 January 1751 and admitted on 16 January, but he did not start teaching at the University until the beginning of the next academic session, in October 1751. In the 1751–2 session he not only lectured to his Logic class (mainly, it appears, on Rhetoric and Belles Lettres), but also gave some lectures on 'natural jurisprudence and politics' to the Moral Philosophy class, the work of which (because of the illness of the then professor of Moral Philosophy, Thomas Craigie) was in that session shared out among 'several masters'. In November 1751 Craigie died, and a few months later

[28] It will be observed that in Table I have juxtaposed pp. 7–14 of the Anderson notes (containing the main 'economic' passages) with the 'Contract' section of the 1762–3 notes. This procedure will be more fully justified in the third section of this essay, on pp. 78–9 below.

[29] It is probable, of course, that in the lectures from which the Anderson notes were derived various other 'economic' matters were discussed under the heading 'Police'. But if we can assume that the order of the different subjects in the Anderson notes reflects their order in these lectures (which there seems no reason to doubt), it remains true – and very important – that prices, money, and interest were discussed *not* under the heading 'Police' but under some other and earlier heading.

Smith was translated from his chair of Logic to the now-vacant chair of Moral Philosophy, being elected on 22 April 1752 and admitted on 29 April. His first *full* course of lectures to the Moral Philosophy class, therefore, was delivered in the 1752–3 session.[30]

For a number of reasons, most of which will become apparent later, it seems highly improbable that the Anderson notes relate to the courses which Smith gave in 1762–3 or 1763–4 – the two sessions in respect of which we possess fairly full and reliable student's notes of his Jurisprudence lectures. Nor does it really seem at all likely that the Anderson notes relate to the lectures which Smith gave at Edinburgh before coming to Glasgow. It is at least possible, however, that they may relate to the lectures on 'natural jurisprudence and politics' which he gave to Craigie's class in the 1751–2 session.[31] Thus the range of possible dates is quite a wide one: the relevant lectures *could* have been given in any one of the sessions during the period from 1751–2 to 1761–2. And when one tries to identify the particular session concerned one soon comes face to face with a number of difficulties of an extraordinarily frustrating character.

Let us consider first the internal evidence in the Anderson notes themselves. These notes contain, as we have seen, a number of references to Montesquieu's *The Spirit of Laws*, which appeared in 1748. There is a mention of 'Mr. Hume's Essay', in a context which suggests that it is the essay *Of Interest* – first published in 1752 – which is being referred to.[32] There is also a mention of 'Mr. Wallace', in a context which suggests that it is Robert Wallace's *Dissertation on the Numbers of Mankind in Antient*

---

[30] The facts in this paragraph have been derived from W. R. Scott, *op. cit.*, pp. 66–7 and 137–40; John Rae, *Life of Adam Smith* (Macmillan, London, 1895), pp. 42–6; and the minutes of University Meetings in the Glasgow University Archives. Special attention should be drawn to the minutes of the University Meeting held on 11 September 1751, which to my knowledge have not been previously noticed, and which cast a certain amount of additional light on the content of Smith's lectures to the Moral Philosophy class in the 1751–2 session. The Meeting decided that in Craigie's absence the teaching should be shared out as follows: 'The Professor [of Divinity] undertakes to teach the Theologia Naturalis, and the first book of Mr. Hutchesons Ethicks, *and Mr. Smith the other two books de Jurisprudentia Naturali et Politicis*, and Mr. Rosse and Mr. Moor to teach the hour allotted for the private classe'. (My italics.)

[31] Smith's lectures to Craigie's class (in which he no doubt used much of his Edinburgh material) did not include natural theology or ethics, whereas the full course which he began delivering in 1752–3 in his new capacity as professor of Moral Philosophy *did* include these subjects. The fact that the Anderson notes contain nothing on natural theology or ethics, therefore, may perhaps be regarded as a reason for considering the 1751–2 lectures as at least a *possible* source. But nothing can safely be deduced from the *absence* of anything in a set of notes like these; and there are other arguments, involving too many minutiae to be canvassed here, which tell in favour of a slightly later date than 1751–2.

[32] The reference appears on p. 12 of the notes. Hume's essay *Of Interest* first appeared in a volume entitled *Political Discourses*, the publication date of which is given on the title page as 1752. If this volume did appear in 1752 it was probably very early in that year, and there is some evidence which suggests that it may in fact have appeared at the end of 1751. (See on this question Jacob Viner, *Guide to John Rae's 'Life of Adam Smith'* (Kelley, New York, 1965), pp. 53–8.) The comment in the notes which includes the reference to Hume's essay may well have been Anderson's own – in which case the only thing that necessarily follows is that *Anderson made his summary of the student's notes* after the appearance of Hume's essay.

and Modern Times – first published in 1753 – which is being referred to.[33] Rather more interesting, perhaps, is the fact that there are two specific page references in the notes,[34] which turn out to be to the first (English) edition of Francis Hutcheson's *Short Introduction to Moral Philosophy*, which appeared in 1747.[35] The interest arises because a second edition of this work, *in which the relevant pagination is different*, was published in 1753.[36] If this new edition had in fact been available at the time when the lectures were delivered, one might perhaps have expected Smith to have referred his students to it rather than to the earlier – and by then presumably rather scarce – edition. But this piece of evidence, although quite suggestive, is not of course by any means conclusive.

We must now go on to consider the other items in Anderson's Commonplace Book – at the back of Volume I of which, it will be recalled, the notes in which we are interested are to be found – to see whether dates can be attached to any of them. So far as Volume III is concerned there is no problem: all the entries consist of comments on France, evidently written during a period of residence in that country; and to a number of these entries Anderson himself has fixed specific dates, ranging from the middle of 1754[37] to December (*sic*) 1755.[38] In Volumes I and II, however, none of

[33] The reference appears on the left-hand page facing p. 36 of the notes, and the comment which includes it was very probably Anderson's own. At first sight it might seem rather unlikely that the 'Mr. Wallace' referred to was Robert Wallace, since the statement in the text on p. 36 immediately opposite the comment refers to 'the want of inhabitants in ancient nations, and where polygamy takes place', and Robert Wallace, as is well known, argues strongly in his *Dissertation* that there was *not* in fact any 'want of inhabitants' in ancient nations. Wallace does recognize, however, that polygamy can have a deleterious effect on population; and he does endeavour to give reasons (including poverty and parental neglect, which are also mentioned on p. 36 of the Anderson notes) for what he regards as the relative scarcity of people in modern nations. Anderson's comment on the left-hand page, then, may plausibly be regarded as an attempt to put forward another reason, over and above those adduced by Wallace, for the lack of populousness in modern nations. It is perhaps worth noting that there is another reference to 'Wallace' on p. 4 of Vol. III of Anderson's Commonplace Book, where a note reads 'See Wallace's Answer to L. Dun's Advices'. This turns out to be a reference to a pamphlet by Robert Wallace entitled *The Doctrine of Passive Obedience and Non-resistance* which was published in Edinburgh in 1754. The only other point which needs to be added here is that there is no evidence to suggest that Smith himself, at this point in his lectures, made any reference to Wallace's *Dissertation*. Thus although Anderson could probably not have written his comment until after the appearance of the *Dissertation*, it is at least conceivable that Smith could have given the relevant lecture before its appearance.

[34] They appear on pp. 3 and 5 of the notes.

[35] The *Short Introduction* was an English translation of a work which Hutcheson originally published (in 1742) in Latin.

[36] The passages quoted by Smith from pp. 156 and 172 of the first edition appear on pp. 147 and 162 respectively of the second edition.

[37] The earliest specific date – 15 August 1754 – appears on p. 13 of Vol. III.

[38] The date 'December 1755' appears in the final entry in Vol. III, which is written on the inside back cover. I am not quite sure, however, whether this entry was in fact written as late as December 1755, even though Anderson was very probably still in France at that time (see below, p. 75. It would seem at least possible from the context that the word 'December', which is interpolated, was inserted at this point in error, and that the note was actually written (at Toulouse) at the beginning rather than the end of 1755. Since nothing hangs on this I shall not elaborate the point.

the entries is specifically dated, and it is rather difficult to ascribe even provisional dates to most of them. In Volume I there is a reference to Montesquieu in one of the entries,[39] which presumably shows that this entry could not have been written before 1748; and there are also some comments on Vernet's *Dialogues*, an English translation of which appeared in 1753.[40] The other items in Volume I – some miscellaneous comments on scientific subjects, and a note on the respective merits of different editions of Livy – do not seem to me to be datable with any degree of precision. Volume II begins with some observations on Anson's *A Voyage Round the World*, the edition concerned being described by Anderson as '2^d Edit: London. 1748';[41] and the only other item in Volume II is a detailed scheme for the distribution of certain funds to Scottish ministers. One of the provisions of this scheme, however, is of some interest from the point of view of our present inquiry. After 1758, Anderson proposed, an individual who had not by then spent three years studying certain subjects at a university should not be eligible for a particular benefit. Read in its context, this statement would seem to indicate that the entry concerned was probably written round about 1753, or 1754 at the latest.

So far as these other items in the Commonplace Book are concerned, then, the three most important points which emerge are, first, that one of the entries in Volume I could not have been written before 1753; second, that one of the entries in Volume II was probably written not later than 1754; and third, that all the entries in Volume III were probably written between the middle of 1754 and some date in 1755. The general feeling one gets is that the period covered by these entries might well have been a relatively short one of not more than two or three years from, say, 1753 to 1755. But even if this were so it would not of course *necessarily* follow that the particular set of notes in Volume I in which we are interested belonged to the same period: there are very many blank pages in the Commonplace Book, and it would have been quite possible for this set of notes to have been inserted much later. All one can really say about this is that there are no other entries in the Commonplace Book which are definitely ascribable to a later date, and that the internal evidence in the notes themselves

---

[39] It appears on p. 15 of Vol. I.
[40] The comments appear on pp. 11–14 of Vol. I. There is apparently some doubt about the date of publication of the first (French) edition of Jean Jacob Vernet's *Dialogues Socratiques*. One of the French biographical dictionaries which I have consulted states that the book was published in Paris in 1745, and with additions in 1755. Another, however, substitutes 1746 and 1756 for 1745 and 1755. The British Museum and the Bibliothèque Nationale hold only one edition, the title page of which states that it was published in Paris in 1754, but gives no indication of the number of the edition. However, the page references and actual quotations in Anderson's comments show clearly enough that he was in fact referring to an English translation of Vernet's book, entitled *Dialogues on Some Important Subjects*, which according to the title page was published in London in 1753.
[41] The first edition of Anson's *A Voyage Round the World* was published in 1748. Copies of a second and third edition, both also dated 1748, are held by the British Museum.

(such as it is) is at least *consistent* with their having been written between 1753 and 1755.

In view of all this, it seems worth while to ask some questions about the *motives* which might have impelled Anderson to make selective extracts from a student's notes of Smith's lectures, and about the *opportunities* which he might have had to do this. So far as his motives are concerned, I do not think that one need look much further than genuine interest.[42] When Smith came to Glasgow, his reputation had preceded him; and Anderson himself, in a letter of December 1750, told a correspondent that he was glad to hear that there were 'two such able candidates for the Logic Chair in Glasgow, as Smith and Muirhead'.[43] Later, of course, Anderson quarrelled with Smith (and indeed with most of his other professorial colleagues), and this can perhaps be taken as another indication that the notes are more likely to be of an earlier than a later date.[44]

On the question of Anderson's opportunities, it can of course be said immediately that *after his arrival at Glasgow to take up his chair* (in October 1756, apparently) they would have been virtually unlimited. But in view of the fact that most of the evidence, uncertain though it is, would seem to point to the likelihood of a date for the notes rather earlier than this, we have to ask whether he might also have had an opportunity before 1756.

We know that in 1750 Anderson was appointed as tutor to Lord Doune, the son of the Earl of Moray, and that at that time his provisional plan was to 'go to Scotland next summer, to Glasgow or St. Andrew's in winter, and abroad, after a stay of some years at one of these Universities'.[45] This plan, however, was evidently altered: the accounts relating to Lord Doune's education, kept in the Moray Muniments, indicate that the boy remained at Harrow School for virtually the whole period of Anderson's tutorship – from August 1750 to August 1753, when Anderson took him back to the family seat at Donibristle.[46]

The next thing we know for certain about Anderson's movements at this period is that he went to France shortly after the middle of 1754 with

---

[42] There is nothing at all in the notes to suggest that Anderson might have compiled them in order to catch Smith out in some way.

[43] Letter of 27 December 1750 from Anderson to Gilbert Lang (original held by the Andersonian Library, University of Strathclyde).

[44] It is interesting – and perhaps significant in the present context – that Anderson's antipathy towards Smith revealed itself rather earlier than is usually assumed. In a letter to Gilbert Lang dated 16 January 1755 (original held by the Andersonian Library, University of Strathclyde), Anderson tells his correspondent about his appointment to the chair of Oriental Languages at Glasgow. He had hoped, he says, to be appointed to the chair of Latin, but, as he puts it, 'Doctor Cullen and Mr. Smith, in a manner that I need not relate, jockied me out of it'.

[45] Letter of 27 December 1750 to Gilbert Lang.

[46] I have not myself inspected the relevant documents in the Moray Muniments. Mr Wood, however, obtained photocopies of them some time ago, and according to information about them with which Mrs Frame has kindly supplied me they show that Lord Doune remained at Harrow for the whole period of Anderson's tutorship – apart from vacations, when Anderson rented lodgings in London for the two of them and does not seem to have travelled very far from that city.

a 'Mr Campbell' (presumably in some kind of tutorial capacity), apparently sailing from Dublin to Bordeaux.[47] While he was in France, on 17 December 1754, he was elected to the chair of Oriental Languages at Glasgow University. The Clerk was instructed to write to Anderson in France, telling him of his election and signifying to him 'that the University desires in case of his acceptance, that he come hither against the sitting down of the College next session, that he may be ready to begin teaching the first of November'.[48]

At a University Meeting on 13 February 1755, however,

> a letter was read from the Primate of Ireland directed to the Principal by which he in a very civil but earnest manner makes application to the Principal and other members that they would allow Mr. Anderson to stay another winter with Mr. Campbell in France, providing his office can be supplied by one of the Masters during his absence . . .[49]

The Meeting – not, it would appear, without some misgivings – resolved 'to allow Mr. Anderson to be absent another winter'. He returned to Scotland, however, in June 1755, and was formally admitted to his chair at a University Meeting on 25 June.[50] But this seems to have been only a relatively brief visit: his name appears among those present at a University Meeting on 26 June 1755, but not again until 25 October 1756. It seems very probable, therefore, that he took advantage of the privilege the University had afforded him, and stayed another winter with 'Mr Campbell' in France.

This visit in June 1755 is the only one which we know for certain that Anderson paid to Glasgow University before he began teaching there in October 1756. But there is a gap of a whole year in our knowledge of Anderson's movements at this period – from August 1753, when he took Lord Doune back to Donibristle, to the middle of 1754, when he went to France with 'Mr Campbell'. During that period he *could* quite possibly have been in Glasgow, either as the tutor of 'Mr Campbell' or in some other capacity. And whether this was so or not, *if* 'Mr Campbell' had

[47] In Anderson's letter of 16 January 1755 to Gilbert Lang, which is written from Toulouse, Anderson speaks specifically of having arrived at Bordeaux from Dublin. 'Mr Campbell' is mentioned by name in the minutes of the University Meeting of 13 February 1755, to be quoted shortly in the text, and he is also mentioned in Vol. III of Anderson's Commonplace Book.
[48] Minutes of University Meeting of 17 December 1754 (Glasgow University Archives).
[49] Minutes of University Meeting of 13 February 1755 (Glasgow University Archives). Leechman, Simson, and Smith were appointed as a committee 'to draw up a civil letter to the Primate and acquaint him that the University has granted his desires, to be signed by the Clerk in name of the University, and sent off next post. . .'
[50] In a letter from Edinburgh dated 10 June 1755 (Glasgow University Archives, no. 26854), Anderson wrote to an unnamed person at Glasgow University informing him of his movements and asking 'what day will be most convenient for my admission'. At a University Meeting on 19 June 1755 Anderson 'read the critical discertation he had been appointed to make as his tryal', and it was agreed to admit him 'upon Wednesday next at twelve of the clock, after he has signed the Confession of Faith'. Anderson duly signed this at a Meeting on 25 June, and 'thereafter he was solemnly received by all the members'.

been a student at Glasgow before he went to France with Anderson, and *if* he had attended Smith's lectures, our mystery might be well on the way to being solved: Anderson, out of interest, might very possibly have made selective extracts from the notes of Smith's lectures taken by 'Mr Campbell'. Unfortunately luck deserts us at this crucial point: we are not sure who this 'Mr Campbell' actually was. Why, we may ask, did no less a personage than the Primate of Ireland intervene on his behalf in February 1755?[51] Rae, in his *Life of Adam Smith*, states in passing that 'Mr Campbell' was in fact the Primate of Ireland's son, but I have been unable to find any evidence which would support this.[52] Nor have I been able to find any trace in the University of Glasgow Matriculation Albums, in the relevant period, of any student called 'Campbell' with Irish connections – although this, of course, is not at all decisive on the point.

To sum up on the dating issue, then, the internal evidence in the notes themselves, together with that in the other entries in the Commonplace Book, is at the very least fully *consistent* with a date between 1753 and 1755 for the entry of the notes. Anderson's motive would possibly have been stronger then than later; and he could very well have had the necessary opportunity at some time during that period. One is obliged to admit, however, that the evidence is also *consistent* with a date after 1755. But the general feeling one gets, looking at the evidence as a whole – and looking, too, at the important *differences* between the Anderson notes and the 1762–3 notes, which we have still to consider – is that the balance of probability lies in favour of an earlier date rather than a later one. My own tentative guess would be that the relevant lectures were delivered in one of the three sessions 1751–2, 1752–3, or 1753–4.

---

[51] The letter from the Primate referred to in the minutes of the University Meeting of 13 February 1755 is extant (Glasgow University Archives, no. 26853). It does not throw very much more light on the identity of 'Mr Campbell', but it does at least clear up the doubt which existed in Scott's mind (*op. cit.*, p. 188, footnote) as to which of the two possible holders of the office of 'Primate of Ireland' was the one concerned: it was in fact George Stone, the Archbishop of Armagh. He states that he is making the request on behalf of 'a gentleman of very great worth and fortune in this kingdom' whom he seems to imply (but does not actually state) is the father of 'Mr Campbell'. There is also extant in the Glasgow University Archives (no. 15626) a draft letter to the Primate prepared by Smith, in which it is stated (*inter alia*) that before the Primate's letter was received the University had already been solicited to the same effect by 'several persons of the greatest distinction in this country particularly by the Earl of Glasgow the present Rector of the University'. A letter from the Primate dated 8 March 1755 thanking the University for granting his request (Glasgow University Archives, no. 266339) does not add anything further. There is a distinct air of mystery about the whole affair: one detects throughout the presence of undercurrents which never come to the surface.

[52] John Rae, *op. cit.*, p. 85. Scott, *op. cit.*, p. 188, footnote, states that 'Mr Campbell' has not been identified. If he was in fact Archbishop Stone's son this might help to explain the mystery, since Stone was unmarried but was frequently accused of immorality by his political opponents. Not enough hangs on this, however, to make any further investigation – or speculation – profitable.

III

The last question to be asked is the most interesting of all: what light, if any, do the Anderson notes throw on the development of Smith's thought during his Glasgow period? The best starting-point here, I suggest, is a consideration of the question of the connection between Smith's work and that of his teacher Francis Hutcheson.

After the discovery of the Cannan lecture notes, a number of scholars – notably Cannan himself[53] and Scott[54] – drew attention to certain interesting parallels between the way in which Smith dealt with Moral Philosophy in his lectures on the subject (as reported in the Cannan notes) and the way in which Hutcheson dealt with it in his *Short Introduction to Moral Philosophy* (1747) and *System of Moral Philosophy* (1755).[55] If we compare these works of Hutcheson's with the 1762–3 notes rather than with the Cannan notes, the parallels become more striking, since the order of treatment of the main subjects in the 1762–3 notes is much closer to Hutcheson's than the order of treatment in the Cannan notes. In the Cannan notes, as we have already seen,[56] Smith adopted the method of 'the civilians', beginning with government and then treating of property and other rights. In the 1762–3 notes, however, Smith used a different method, beginning with property and other rights and then treating of family and civil government – and this, basically, was the method which Hutcheson had adopted.

If we now compare these works of Hutcheson's with the Anderson notes, the parallels become more striking still. It is not simply that – as we would expect from what has been said above – the order in which the main topics are treated is very close to Hutcheson's. There are also certain other indications which make the connection with Hutcheson much more manifest. For example, as I have already pointed out,[57] the notes contain two specific page references to Hutcheson's *Short Introduction*. The heading to the section on prices, 'De Pretio Rerum' (p. 7), is a fairly clear echo of the title of the chapter on prices ('De Rerum Pretio') in the Latin work of Hutcheson's of which his *Short Introduction* was an English translation. The comments on oaths and vows on p. 22 of the Anderson notes, which appear to have no very definite counterpart in the 1762–3 or Cannan notes,

[53] See, e.g., the 'Editor's Introduction' to the Cannan notes, pp. xxiv–vi.
[54] See in particular W. R. Scott, *Francis Hutcheson* (Cambridge University Press, 1900), *passim*.
[55] The *Short Introduction*, as we have already seen, was an English translation of a work which Hutcheson originally published (in 1742) in Latin. The *System*, a much longer work, was a printed version of Hutcheson's lectures (presumably in their final form of the 1740s), published posthumously. From these two books, which are very similar in structure, we may readily reconstruct the elements of the Moral Philosophy course which Smith attended when he was a student at Glasgow. The references to the books in the text below are to the facsimile edition of Hutcheson's *Collected Works* (Georg Olms Verlagsbuchhandlung, Hildesheim, 1969).
[56] See above, p. 69.
[57] See above, p. 72.

probably owe their origin to a chapter on this subject in the *Short Intro-duction*.[58] And the comment on Plato on p. 23, of which once again there seems to be no counterpart in the 1762–3 or Cannan notes, may well have been derived from Hutcheson.[59] Most important of all, however, is another consideration which will take a little more time to develop.

It relates to the location, in both the *Short Introduction* and the *System*, of the famous 'economic' chapters in which prices, money, and interest are dealt with.[60] As is well known, Hutcheson in both books introduced these 'economic' chapters in the course of a general discussion of *contract*. This procedure of his was by no means as arbitrary as has sometimes been suggested.[61] In Book II of both the *Short Introduction* and the *System* he embarks upon a study of what he calls 'adventitious rights', which he classifies into 'real' and 'personal'.[62] The principal real right is *property*, which is either 'original' or 'derived'.[63] Derived property can be alienated or transferred in various ways – most notably by *contract* and by *testament* (or intestate succession).[64] In the *System*, at the beginning of his chapter on the transfer of property, he draws attention to 'the necessity and use of frequent contracts and translations of property';[65] and at the end of this chapter, after discussing (*inter alia*) testamentary and intestate succession, he points out that personal rights too very often arise from contracts. A consideration of these rights, he says, 'leads to the subject of contracts or covenants, the main engine of constituting either personal rights or real'.[66] In the *Short Introduction* the reasons for the transition to a separate consideration of contracts are not quite so clearly spelt out: in this much shorter book, Hutcheson contents himself with saying at the beginning of the relevant chapter that property may be transferred 'either *gratuitously* in donations; or for *valuable consideration* in commerce', and with promis-ing to 'treat of contracts and commerce hereafter'.[67]

The next six chapters, then, in both the *Short Introduction* and the *System*, deal with contract and quasi-contract, in general and in particular. In this broad context, the famous chapter on prices and money takes its place quite naturally. It is related to what has gone before, since (as Hutcheson puts it in the *Short Introduction*) 'to maintain any commerce among men in interchanging of goods or services, the values of them must

[58] Book II, Ch. XI (*Collected Works*, Vol. IV, pp. 203–8). The corresponding chapter in the *System* will be found in the *Collected Works*, Vol. VI, pp. 44–53.
[59] See *Collected Works*, Vol. VI, p. 185.
[60] Book II, Chaps. XII and XIII of the *Short Introduction* (*Collected Works*, Vol. IV, pp. 209–22); and Book II, Chaps. 12 and 13 of the *System* (*Collected Works*, Vol. VI, pp. 53–77).
[61] E.g., by W. L. Taylor, *Francis Hutcheson and David Hume as Predecessors of Adam Smith* (Duke University Press, Durham, North Carolina, 1965), pp. 22–4.
[62] *Collected Works*, Vol. IV, p. 147, and Vol. V, p. 309.
[63] *Ibid.*, Vol. IV, p. 152, and Vol. V, p. 324.
[64] *Ibid.*, Vol. IV, pp. 171 ff., and Vol. V, pp. 340 ff.
[65] *Ibid.*, Vol. V, p. 340.
[66] *Ibid.*, Vol. V, p. 358.
[67] *Ibid.*, Vol. IV, p. 171.

be some way estimated';[68] and it is also related to what comes after, since in the following chapter Hutcheson deals with (*inter alia*) 'onerous contracts', in which 'the parties profess to transfer mutually things of equal value'.[69]

After the chapters on contract, Hutcheson proceeds directly to a discussion of 'rights arising from injuries and damages done by others'.[70] Thus the analysis of prices, money, and interest, in the embryo form in which it appears in Hutcheson, enters into the picture under the general heading of contract, which is dealt with immediately after the discussion of testaments and immediately before that of injuries. *And this, it would appear, is exactly how and where the analysis of prices, money, and interest entered into the course of Smith's lectures from which the Anderson notes were derived.* The *location* of the relevant sections in the Anderson notes is certainly the same: as we have already seen, they are sandwiched between the sections dealing with testaments and those dealing with injuries.[71] And the suggestion that Smith was at that time including his 'economic' analysis under the general heading of contract is strengthened by the passage on p. 14 of the Anderson notes, which occurs immediately after the last of the 'economic' sections and which clearly deals with an aspect of contracts in general.

It would seem very likely, then, that at the outset Smith's Moral Philosophy course (in certain respects at least) was rather closer to Hutcheson's than has generally been supposed; that in particular Smith's analysis of prices, money, and interest was at first presented under the general heading of contract, as it had been with Hutcheson; and that it was only later that this 'economic' material, having no doubt been greatly expanded and developed, was transferred from 'Contract' to 'Police' – i.e., to the place in which it is found in the 1762–3 notes.[72]

But it is also clear from the Anderson notes that in certain other respects Smith had, at the time of the course to which these notes relate, already departed quite considerably from the lines laid down by Hutcheson. One obvious point here is that there was clearly much more straight *law* in Smith's course than there had been in Hutcheson's. Another is that the content of the 'De Pretio Rerum' section has been expanded appreciably beyond that of the corresponding sections in Hutcheson, so as to include a discussion of (for example) bills of exchange, paper money, and stocks, together with an updated analysis of interest apparently based on Hume's

---

[68] *Ibid.*, Vol. IV, p. 209.
[69] *Ibid.*, Vol. IV, p. 214. Cf. Vol. VI, p. 64.
[70] *Ibid.*, Vol. VI, p. 86. Cf. Vol. IV, p. 228.
[71] Cf. above, p. 70.
[72] When one knows what one is looking for, one can see vestigial traces of its former inclusion under the 'Contract' heading in the 1762–3 notes, Vol. II, pp. 79–84, and (correspondingly) in the Cannan notes, p. 134.

essay on the subject.[73] Finally, and perhaps most important of all, Smith has evidently in many places added a *historical* dimension to the argument, which in most contexts is much more pronounced than it ever was in Hutcheson. Perhaps we can surmise from the large number of direct and indirect references to Montesquieu in the Anderson notes[74] that *The Spirit of Laws* was one of the main literary influences leading Smith towards this historicization of the analysis.

In this connection, the use in the Anderson notes (on pp. 1–3 and 37) of a *stadial* theory (or theories) of socio-economic development is of considerable interest. When we compare these passages with the corresponding ones in the 1762–3 and Cannan notes,[75] we can detect both resemblances and differences. The resemblances are sufficiently great to suggest that Smith had indeed, as some of us have recently ventured to conjecture,[76] developed the elements of at any rate *a* four stages theory by the early or middle 1750s. The differences, however, seem to suggest that, at the time of the course to which the notes relate, he may still have had some little way to go before he arrived at the mature four stages theory which is so clearly expounded and so ubiquitously applied in the 1762–3 and Cannan notes. In the Anderson notes, the first stage is characterized by 'hunting and fishing'; the second stage appears to be characterized by the acquisition of 'property in common' by a clan or a nation; and the third stage is characterized by the emergence of agriculture, permanent settlements, and private property in land. In the 1762–3 and Cannan notes, all the stages are defined unambiguously in terms of different modes of subsistence – the first three being hunting, pasturage, and agriculture – and changes in the state of property are regarded as *consequences* of changes from one of these modes of subsistence to the next.

It is of course possible that at the time of the Anderson notes Smith was closer to the mature four stages theory than these notes would at first sight seem to suggest. For example, in his discussion of the second stage he *may* in the relevant lecture have specifically associated 'property in common' with pasturage (as he apparently did in the corresponding lecture in 1762–3),[77] but the student – or Anderson – may simply have failed to note this association. It seems rather more probable, however, that at

[73] It *may*, of course, have included much more than this: Anderson's extracts are not necessarily all-inclusive, or even representative, and as I have said above nothing can safely be deduced from the *absence* of anything in the Anderson notes.
[74] There are direct references to Montesquieu on pp. 9, 12, 19, 26 (two references), 31, and 39 of the Anderson notes. There is also an indirect reference on p. 9: the opinion that the Jews were the inventors of bills of exchange, which Smith here refutes, was in fact Montesquieu's (*The Spirit of Laws*, Book XXI, Ch. 20). It is possible, of course, that Anderson, who thought highly of Montesquieu, paid special attention to the references to him in the lecture-notes.
[75] In the case of the 1762–3 notes, the comparison can most usefully be made with Vol. I, pp. 47–53 and 66–8, and Vol. IV, pp. 36–8; and in the case of the Cannan notes with pp. 108–10, and p. 20. These references, however, are by no means exhaustive.
[76] Cf. above pp. 24–8.
[77] 1762–3 notes, Vol. 1, pp. 48–9.

the time of the Anderson notes Smith was still using his stadial theory more or less exclusively in connection with the problem of changes in the state of property, and had not yet fully succeeded in separating the mode-of-subsistence 'basis' from the state-of-property 'superstructure'. As his ideas developed, we may perhaps surmise, this distinction was more clearly made, and the theory applied in a number of other spheres – and also, incidentally, emancipated from its connection with the two 'principles' described at the beginning of the Anderson notes.

THE ANDERSON NOTES

The notes which follow appear at the back of Volume I of Anderson's Commonplace Book, on pp. 292–368, *starting on p. 368*. Anderson evidently turned the book upside down and commenced writing on p. 368, which was now (the book being upside down) the first right-hand facing page. When he had filled this page he turned it over and continued on the next right-hand page (p. 366), and so on for a total of 39 right-hand pages until the notes concluded on p. 292. On seven occasions he wrote additional notes on the left-hand facing page. In the reproduction of the notes which follows, I have renumbered the relevant right-hand facing pages from 1 to 39, indicating by an appropriate arabic italic numeral in square brackets [ ] the point at which each new right-hand page begins. Braces { } are used to indicate the additional notes which are written on left-hand facing pages. In most cases the appropriate place for the insertion of this material in the main text is not specifically indicated by Anderson and has had to be guessed at. In editing the text of the manuscript for publication, I have ignored Anderson's capitalization, and up to a point his punctuation, in the interests of readability. Common contractions for 'the,' that,' 'which,' 'and,' etc., are spelt out, together with words containing a raised letter; but most of the other contractions are reproduced exactly as they appear in the manuscript. Most of the deletions, replacements, doubtful readings, etc., are listed in the textual notes set at the end of the text, referred to by letter superscripts. Straight interlineations which do not involve deletions, etc., are not specifically noted at all. Angle brackets ⟨ ⟩ are used to indicate words, letters, etc., which have been omitted from the text but which ought properly to be there; square brackets [ ] are used to indicate words, letters, etc., which are there but which ought properly to have been omitted. The spelling of the original has been retained, and so far as possible the dividing lines, dashes, etc., used by Anderson have been reproduced.

[*1*] 1 Principle

To deprive a man of life or limbs or to give him pain is shocking to the rudest of our species when no enmity or grudge subsists, i.e., where no punishment is due or danger apprehended.

2 Principle

We acquire a liking for those creatures or^a things^b which we are much conversant with, and thus^c to deprive us of them must give us pain.

Hunting and fishing are all the arts that^d prevail in the first states of society. To deprive a man of the beast or fish he has caught, or of the fruit he has gathered, is depriving him of what cost him labour and so giving him pain, and is contrary to the laws of the rudest society.

By the second principle when a clan or nation hunt and fish [2] long (i.e., have lived long) in one tract of country they acquire an exclusive property and it is considered as theirs, i.e., they acquire property in common (vide the histories of America and Caesar and Tacitus), which is the second state of perfection in society.

When confined to one country their arable ground and crops are in common. {Tho contrary to^e Act of Parliament, all unenclosed fields in this country, after the gathering in of the harvest, are in common. In such a state are the lands in Arabia and many parts of N. America all the year round, i.e., they have a common right to the fruits, and the land is considered as the property of no individual.} When their numbers encrease, when instruments of husbandry are invented (vide Hesiod^f), and when they have built huts and towns, they will begin to labour little spots about their houses and^g the *publick* fields [3] will be neglected, and hence will arise private property in lands founded both upon the first and second principle; which is^h the third state of society advancing towards perfection. {By the Gothic holdings the prince was considered as the proprietor of the ground, and the land-holders had no right to accessions, etc. unless^i expressly named in the charter. Hence^j in Scotland the land holder had originally^k no right to fishing, lime stone, coal, gold and silver mines, etc.^{l} But^m as^n these rights were very inconvenient to the land holders^o they were all given away^p in the charter except the right to gold and silver mines.}

P.156^q one head of a family, by his first arriving in a vast island must not pretend to property in the whole, etc.

This will hold when the inhabitants are pushed for room and the common necessaries of life, as was the case in antient Greece. But where they fit out fleets in order to encrease their wealth, etc. they are deemed to have a property in^r the whole no more than they can ever reasonably hope^s to cultivate. Thus Brasil, Mexico, etc. are thought by all nations to be the property of the Spaniards.

[4] Children succeed to the goods of their *intestate* father, not on account of the *parental relation*, but on account of their connection with his^t goods, etc., i.e., they succeed by the 2d^u principle. For^v in barbarous nations the children who had^w left the family did not succeed at all, and

the distant relations and servants who lived in the family succeeded equally to the children in it.–

Where there are no manufactures and where agriculture is little minded, the country must soon be overstocked with inhabitants; hence the Teutones, etc. made their invasions. Feu, the German word, signifies pay (as fee in English ⟨⟩). As the conquests were made by armies and by^x generals who were not able to [5] maintain them, they were put in possession of the lands, instead of receiving pay, and were obliged to military service, etc.

P.172.^{y} It is absurd that men, etc.

1. Whatever is said or done by a dying person makes the greatest impression on his surviving friends and acquaintances. {(My own) We remember triffling circumstances when^z connected to an event that makes a strong impression upon us. And^a when a dying person gives us his advice he is supposed to be perfectly disinterested, which is another cause of our regard.}

2. We have a sympathy to the dying person and place ourselves[s] in his stead.

3. It is for the interest of society that wills should be observed.

Among the antient Romans (vide Au. Gellius) and the patriarchs (vide the History of Abraham) the heir seemed to have^b succeeded by the favour of the people and not by any established right.

Gap of three lines in MS.

[6] As the feudal law had mil⟨i⟩tary service principally in view, and as a man at 16 was able to bear arms, 16 was the age of majority till the 12th century when such heavy armour came in fashion that a youth at that age could not bear it, and this produced the^c change of the age of majority from 16 to one and twenty where it now continues.

Gap of half a page in MS.

[7] De Pretio Rerum

The value of any commodity is equal to the sum of what^d the majority of all the persons who want that commodity are willing to do or give for it.^{e}

If all that the Europeans are willing to give for all the cinnamon imported this year is £50,00,^{f} if double that quantity is imported next year, a pound of cin. which is sold this^g year for 10 shs will next^h year be sold for 5. Hence together with the additional expence the Dutch burn their spices.

Suppose 100 men want the same commodity, that[i] 99 are willing to give 10 shs for the pound, but that 1 is willing to give 20. The seller however will never think of asking more than 10 from that single person; and hence the value of the commodity must be regulated by the majority of the buyers. [8] Suppose a crown this year contains one oun. of silver and next year only half an oz.; it will then pass not for the half which it ought naturally to do but for[j] something more (perhaps 3 or 4 shs), and that on account of the ignorance of the people who receive it and of their debts. 1, on acct of their ignorance. As soldiers (etc.) are accustomed to receive 3 and 6[d] and still receive the same number of pieces (for the coin is only supposed to be debased) they would be equally well pleased since they get as much drink, etc. for it as formerly. 2[ly], on acct of their debts. As to the person to whom they owe 10 shs this[k] year they will only pay 10 shs next year of a baser coin.

[9] Montesquieou's acct of money refuted – as to the aliquot parts of gold.–

The Jews not the inventors of bills of exchange.

1. There are letters equivalent to b. of ex. mentioned in Demosthenes orations.

2. The ordering[l] a distant[m] person by a letter to pay the debt he owes me, to the bearer of my letter must have been a very natural and antient thing. But this does not come up to a bill of exchange. The great advantage attending a bill of ex. is that it is simple and admits of none of the delays attending prosecutions before common courts of justice. But, by an Act of the legislature in all commercial [10] states, the prosecutions for none acceptance, etc. are free from all the delays in the common course of justice. – The Jews therefore could not be the cause of this as they were so far from being a governing people that they[n] were persecuted in all countries.

About the end of the [the] 13th centy some of the trading towns saw the necessity of making quick dispatch in all prosecutions about bills of exchange; they established consuls, etc.[o] Other towns saw the necessity of the same laws in order to encourage commerce, and hence are all bills of exch.

Gap of four lines in MS.

[11] {By law a man cannot be punished for coining medals, or pieces of silver and gold to his own arms, etc. – He is only punished for counterfeiting the coin and arms of the state. – }

I. Paper money by private banks.

II. Do by established banks, e.g. the banks of England and Amsterdam.

III. Do stocks such as the African Company.

IV. Credit upon governt security.

[p]The two first depend chiefly on their credit. –

The two last may be guilty of great frauds. The managers of the stocks may give out their dividend is doubly of what it is tho they expect more ships home that year. Upon the which many will buy very high and so may be greatly cheated. And

The^q governt of any country may reduce the legal interest, or they may be obliged to stop payment by an invasion or civil war. –

[*12*] Locke, Montesquiou, and Law think that the lowness of interest is owing to the plenty of money. But, etc. – – as in Mr. Hume's Essay the^r general^s doctrine.–

No enclosures in England till the Reformation. The Spaniards were possessed of Peru, and thought that only miners were necessary to make them rich. The English knew they could reap no benefit from their mines but by selling them such goods as they wanted. Hence the flourishing of commerce in the reins^t of Q El., K Jam., and the first 15 of K Ch the 1$^{st.}$ – Corn can be easily exported; but hay or the feeding of cattle is unprofitable un[*13*]less the country is populous (or unless there is an easy export, e.g. Cork and Scotland). Hence tho^u the country of England grew populous by large towns, villages, etc. of manufactures, there was no great demand for cattle, and as enclosures are necessary in grass farms hence England was unenclosed (as Scotland is at present) till the establishment of commerce.

Tho accumulated interest seems in itself to be very reasonable – yet it has been forbidden in all countries. 1. Because it may easily give room for the greatest oppressions. 2^{ly}, because it is the creditors fault if he wants his interest at the end of the^v year as he may use diligence, etc.

[*14*] In general. Where there are penal laws against any action that very circumstance makes contracts in that case the better observed. Hence debts of honour are religiously kept by cheating gamesters. – And the smugglers in England when a boat comes off to them, they sell their goods and receive payment by the buyers throwing the money put up in bag into the smugglers ship. The⟨y⟩ have not time to count this money and can have no redress in case of a fraud.

[*15*] In order to judge of the reasonableness and origin of different punishments we must call to mind what^w a private person feels when injured.

Our aversion to a murderer, etc. is principally fear and terror. Our aversion to a thief, contempt and disregard. Hence murderers have always suffered the last punishment. And theives have been fined, ducked, or punished with infamy.

It is true that in many countries theft is punished with death, but this is owing to its frequency, [*16*] and one may be tempted to mutilate or put to death by repeated provocations. It is true likewise that in this and most Gothic countries demembration and murder seemed to have been punished by fines, which was probably owing to these reasons. In the infancy of governments the magistrate commonly judges only in smaller differences. Two Indians, e.g., may wound or pursue the same deer and a difference about the property may easily arise. They appeal to a third person and if his judgement is thought right, his [17] neighbours make him their umpire likewise: vide Hesiod's account of the origin of government. But a person who had lost a limb or a brother by murder would not have patience to appeal to an arbitrator but would take vengeance at his own hand (among the Jews the relations of a murdered person could slay the murderer unless he fled to a city of refuge). Taking revenge in this way threw rude governments into convulsions, and was likewise attended with great danger to the avenger. Hence the magistrate and the avenger and the murder⟨er⟩ for the sake of mutual safety agreed to take money as a punishment.

[18] In all rude countries the laws cannot give sufficient protection to the innocent, for which reason the inhabitants are obliged to enter into small associations for their own safety. And as those of the same name and family are[x] connected together by blood, and by their situation (for in[y] countries where there is no commerce people seldom go far from home), hence the origin of clanship among[z] all unpolished[a] nations.

The Lex Talionis among all nations, vide the [19] Jewish laws, and the 12 Tables – at last abolished as too cruel a punishment, for if a man who had broke his neighbour's arm in a fit of passion were brought to the scaffold he must feel more than the injured person, who had no previous knowledge of what was to befall him.

Fur manifestus and non manifestus. Vide L'Esprit des Loix, an ingenious account but it seems not to be just.

For it does not appear that the Lacedaemonians were allowed to steal any [20] thing but provisions from the publick table. Vide Plutarch. – And there was this distinction between the fur man. and non man. among all nations which is owing to this, that there is a greater hatred against the criminal if taken immediately than if afterwards or if his punishment is delayed – rubra manu among the Romans, taken in the fang among the Scotch.–

Robberies punished with death because of their frequency. Forgery punished with, at present uni[21]versally, death. Because of the ease in forging, and the hurt it does to commerce. Among the antients not punished with death because few could write and many forms[b] were required.

There seems to have been no policy of insurance among the antients.

The civil law is in the right concerning its[c] determinations as to the advisers and employers of those who perpetrate crimes, and cannon law almost always in the wrong.

For such is the temper of mankind that they will [22] advise to crimes and propose things in a passion which they could not execute.[d]

The punishment of crimes committed 20 years before the criminal[e] was taken was not inflicted by the Roman[f] law, provided that sentence was not passed against him.

The force of oaths arises from the mind's attending, at that time, to all the motives which can induce the swearer to veracity.

A vow a promise to God, and[g] sometimes a promise to men or a man – i.e., there are two branches in a vow.–

[23] ———————————

In the most rude countries divorce is reckoned a hardship – or a thing extraordinary – and therefore a constant union between the husband and wife must be natural to men.

Plato is unjustly blamed for encouraging libidinous desires, since by his plan they would be under greater restraints than in the present state of society.

In barbarous ages the wife is not punished for infidelity, as in polished ages, because of her low state, she being considered as a slave (vid Homer's acct of Helen). For the same reason the infidelity of the husband is little minded in barbarous nations.–

[24] In polite ages adultery severely punished. 1st, because the inter-course between the sexes[h] is general. 2, marriage is a vow. Not so severely punished always in the man, because the dignity of the wife depends upon the dignity of the husband. And the men are the makers of the laws.–

Of Divorces

1. Liberty to divorce allowed to the husband and to him only, in the first ages of Rome and in all barbarous nations. – By the early Roman law the husband could judge his wife like his slave.

2. The second state of divorces is when the wife is allowed to divorce as well as the husband.

3. The 3 state is when the liberty of both is restrained within certain limits.

[25] Against Polygamy.

1. The inclinations,[i] in degree, of both sexes are proportioned to each other when uncorrupted.

Where polygamy takes place, many of the wives must be neglected – and there must be constant jealousies – for education cannot alter the natural effects of love entirely.

There is a melancholy among the women[j] of the east, and so the half of the species are miserable.

Unnatural lusts prevailed in antient Greece and Rome because there was a sort of polygamy by the multitude of female slaves, likewise at Algiers and likewise in Italy and London because whores are common in Italy and London.–

Where polygamy takes place there is such a multitude of children, that the estate cannot be divided among them.

[26] See Montesquiou, B xvi, ch 2^{d} – et que la polygamie s'introduise. Suppose the fact true, it will only follow that he ought to take another but not that polygamy ought to be established. – But the fact is not true. – Intemperance in love indeed makes the easterns fond of very young women, as rapes are committed in London upon children five years old – but Cleopatra had a child at 40. –

B. xvi, ch. 4. This opinion seems to be ill founded, for the births are not kept regularly in Asia. – [k]Meaco is a capital. It is filled with saraglios. – In Scotland if the people were numbered there wd be found more males in the kingdom than females. –

[27] The sentiment of love fixes upon one, and as polygamy is contrary to this sentiment it is contrary to nature.

The taking care of children natural in the highest degree. –

It arises too from the childs always being with, and being caressed by, its parent – where this does not take place the sentiment of the child goes along with the sentiments of all others, and he conforms to the general rule.

Exposing of Children

To do no good to our fellow creatures is not reckoned so criminal, as to do them direct hurt. And thus the exposition of children was considered as an imperfect [28] obligation. – It took place among the Greeks and Romans, but if the child lived several weeks the father had no right to expose it. – Miscarriage or abortion little minded in modern times, and the women who are guilty of the last think it less criminal to procure it in the first quarter of their pregnancy than in the last. Aristotle B.III recommends it. In rude societies, the government[l] was cautious of intermedling in private affairs and so of correcting this abuse.

Of Bastard

The mother is reckoned the proprietor of the bastard.

Mistresses much respected in barbarous ages, almost as much as the wife. – Teucer almost on a level with Ajax. – In this country bas[29]tards were highly respected.

Patria Potestas

This subsists among all barbarous nations – in full force in the times of the greatest liberty in Rome and little abused – taken away in the decline of the Empire when abused. – The helplesness of the child puts it in the power of the father. – Among the Romans, the son could be sold, scurged, or put to death by the father – the negroes sold by their fathers.

As in rude countries the wife is in a state of slavery, and the son inherits his father's absolute power, in all barbarous nations the mother is treated as a slave. – Telemachus is insolent to his mother thro' the [*30*] whole of the Odyssey. – Upon the death of his father, says Colvin in the History of Africa, the son goes home and beats his mother, and he is reckoned a milk-sop who does otherwise.

Of Slaves

Many causes of slavery – by way of punishment – in order to pay debt – but above all by war. – No humanity to prisoners of war, of old. If they did not kill them they thought them their property, and this the greatest origin of slavery. – Slavery could not be introduced in a polished age, and all countries were at first rude. – In [*31*] the heroick ages slaves were happy; in polished ages not so. In the first state, the slave eat and wrought with*m* his master, and there subsisted an intimacy between them. In the last state, they were removed from the sight of their masters and therefore cruelly used. At present there is more sympathy between a farmer and his servant, than between a duke and his footman. And as the blacks seem not from their skin {to partake of the same nature with the whites, the imagination of a barbarous white supposes him not to be of the same nature with himself, and therefore uses him ill with less scruple.} (Aristotle spends some ⟨?time⟩ in proving that a slave can have no virtue.) To be a slave in a despotic government is no worse than to be a freeman – see Montesquiou.

A slave in Rome had no religion, i.e., he did not share in the publick [*32*] worship; he was considered in the same light with the cattle of his proprietor. Hence of old, see Tacitus, etc., it was common for the slaves to become Jews, as they held there was an universal deity, whereas in the heathen religion every deity had a particular province and there was no deity allotted for the slaves.

We never hear of the insurrection of slaves in Persia, etc.

In Tyre, Carthage, and Lacedaemon the people lived well ⟨?compared⟩ to their slaves. – The Germans armed their slaves.

Corruptions bring on their own remedies. – The common law and not Christianity suppressed slavery – it was not abolished by humanity or the [*33*] improvement of manners – but as the slaves were armed by their lords and so dangerous to the king, the king abolished slavery. – Slavery subsisted under the emperours after Christianity was the popular religion. – The cannon law supposes slavery. – Slavery still subsists in Muscovy which is a Christian country.

Our salters and colliers differ much from slaves. They can have property and consequently families; they can buy their liberty; the price of their labour is fixed by law; they are punished by law – that is, they are only confined to one trade and one master,^{n} the first of which [34] was the state of the antient Egyptians.

Were our salters and colliers put upon the same footing with other labourers, it would be much better for their masters. – When men are constrained to work for another they will not work so hard as if at liberty – this is manifest in quarrying and other mines. In the Newcastle mines work is done cheaper than in this country. In this country a collier and salter can earn more than a quarrier or any other labourer who works as hard. – In the mines of Silesia, the miners go voluntary below ground and live there for years.

[35] Attempts to introduce agrarian laws, and the abolition of debts, were the sources of constant disorder in antient states, and are quite unknown in the modern. – The cause of this slavery – for as in every great town the inhabitants are either gentlemen or work hard, a man that has no land can get subsistence only by his labour; but of old the slaves were mechanicks and not freemen, and therefore the freemen who had no lands in Rome, Athens, etc. were entirely dependent on the great for their living – and the great were liberal, as the people had the disposal of all places.

[36] (Plato and Aristotle – their great aim in their Republicks is to prevent disorders from agrarians and the abolition of debts – a modern legislator never thinks of this.)

Of mankind the half die under 7, and of these the children of the vulgar most commonly. It is not unusual in Wales, Ireland, and the Highlands to see women without a child who have born above a dozen, which is owing to their poverty which renders them unfit to bring up the most tender of all animals, viz infants.

This then must be one cause of the want of inhabitants in ancient nations, and where polygamy takes place. {There is a cause not mentioned by Mr. Wallace, viz the drinking of spiritous liquors.}

[37] Nothing has appeared more surprizing than the government of nations because the few govern the many.

In barbarous ages the 1st state of society is that of seperate families. The 2^d the union of families for safety and the decis⟨i⟩on of differences; and familiarity and common interest unites them firmly together. 3^{ly}, the wisdom and wealth of one procures him authority, and there is a common governour or chief but without any expressed prerogative. – In this state the older the wiser a good maxim in the choice of magistrates, because there are no means of acquiring knowledge by books, etc. Hence the governours or chiefs in Africa are old men [38] – Nestor celebrated for his age and wisdom. – Two chiefs may be often found in such a state, and as they have no power independent of wisdom, etc. it is not inconvenient, tho in polished nations, when each are supported by courts, attendants, etc. the most miserable of all institutions.

In this state governing often becomes hereditary in one family, because it is natural to transplant our love or dislike to the representative of the deceast person.

As in the first state families united for deciding differences and defending each other, so in the second villages, and so in the^o third nations with their chiefs or kings {and in that state a king may become like Agammemnon in Homer, the king of kings.}

[39] Montesquiou's division of the powers in a state very just.

1. In the rude state of society, no laws passed unless every member is consulted, and a dissenter must leave that^p society.

The laws of police are longer of being executed, and more difficult⟨l⟩y executed, in a free than in an absolute government. The laws of police are stricter and better executed in France than in England, and in Japan than in France. –

a. Replaces 'of' *b.* '2 Principle' interlined above 'things' and deleted *c.* Reading doubtful *d.* Replaces 'which' *e.* Replaces 'by' *f.* The words 'Descrip of a plow' are interlined above 'vide Hesiod' *g.* The words '(besides the fields which belong to the society)' are deleted at this point *h.* The last two words replace 'and this will be' *i.* 'na' deleted *j.* Replaces an illegible word *k.* The last four words replace 'proprietor had' *l.* Several illegible words interlined and deleted *m.* Replaces 'But as these were' *n.* 'some' deleted *o.* 'and' deleted *p.* Two or three illegible words deleted *q.* The words 'in Hutcheson', followed by an illegible word, are interlined above 'P.156' *r.* Replaces 'to' *s.* 'perhaps' deleted *t.* Replaces 'the' *u.* Replaces 'first' *v.* Reading doubtful; replaces an illegible word *w.* Replaces 'have' *x.* Illegible word deleted *y.* 'it' deleted *z.* Replaces 'in'.

a. 'at death' deleted. The word 'on', written above 'at', is also deleted *b.* Illegible word deleted *c.* The last five words replace four illegible words *d.* 'all' deleted *e.* 'Thus' deleted *f. Sic g.* Replaces 'last' *h.* Replaces 'this' *i.* Replaces 'and' *j.* The last sixteen words replace 'the value then would not be half but' *k.* Replaces 'last' *l.* Reading doubtful *m.* The last two words replace 'another' *n.* 'are' deleted *o.* 'and' deleted *p.* Illegible word deleted *q.* 'the' deleted *r.* Reading doubtful *s.* The last two words replace 'pretty much' *t.* Reading doubtful *u.* Reading doubtful *v.* Reading doubtful *w.* 'we' deleted *x.* 'more naturally' deleted *y.* Illegible word deleted *z.* Replaces 'in'.

a. Replaces 'uncivilised'; 'countries' deleted *b.* Reading doubtful *c.* Replaces 'that' *d.* 'and they will propose things in a passion' deleted *e.* Replaces 'prisoner' *f.* Replaces an illegible word *g.* Illegible word deleted *h.* The last three words replace 'with women' *i.* 'of' interlined and deleted *j.* Replaces an illegible word *k.* Illegible word deleted *l.* '(the government)' deleted *m.* Replaces an illegible word *n.* 'which' deleted *o.* 'second' deleted *p.* Reading doubtful.

PART TWO

MARX

V

A Plain Person's Guide to the Transformation Problem[1]

I

As everyone nowadays knows, in Volume I of *Capital* Marx began by defining the 'value' of a commodity as the total quantity of labour which was normally required from first to last to produce it, and proceeded with his analysis on the provisional assumption that commodities would actually tend to sell on the market 'at their values' – i.e., at prices which were directly proportionate to the quantities of labour required to produce them. In particular, he retained this assumption in his famous analysis of surplus value in Parts III and IV of Volume I, in which he laid the theoretical foundations for his explanation of the origin, persistence, and level of capitalist profit.

'The labour of a manufacturer', Adam Smith had said many years before, 'adds, generally, to the value of the materials which he works upon, that of his own maintenance, and of his master's profit'.[2] Marx's analysis of the origin of surplus value was based on a notion bearing a distinct family resemblance to this. Raw materials and elements of fixed capital, Marx argued, to the extent that they are used up in the production of a particular commodity, contribute no more than their own 'value' (measured by the amount of past or dead labour embodied in them, and hereafter printed without quotation marks) to the total value of that commodity. The remainder of the commodity's value is added through, and to the extent of, the present or living labour of the wage-workers who are employed by the capitalist in the process of production. And this living labour, in a normal working day, will generally add enough value not only to compensate the capitalist for the wages he has to pay the workers concerned, but also to provide, over and above this, a *surplus* value, which is realized if and when the capitalist sells the commodity at its value on the market, and which constitutes the unique source of his profit.

---

[1] This essay is essentially new, and embodies certain changes in my previously expressed views, although in some places it draws on material which I have already published elsewhere.

[2] Adam Smith, *Wealth of Nations* (edited by R. H. Campbell and A. S. Skinner, Oxford University Press, 1976), Vol. I, p. 330.

If we now assume, as Marx also did in Volume I of *Capital*, that the length of the working day and the level of the real wage per head are the same in all industries, it follows logically that the ratio of realized surplus value to expenditure on wages will also be the same in all industries. But it does *not* follow, of course, that the ratio of surplus value to the value of the total capital employed – i.e., roughly, the rate of profit – will be the same in all industries. For the total capital employed normally consists not only of funds for expenditure on wages (Marx's 'variable' capital), but also of machinery and raw materials (Marx's 'constant' capital); and the proportion in which capital is divided between these two constituent parts will obviously differ greatly from one industry to another. Assuming, then, as we are still doing, that all commodities are sold at their values in the Marxian sense, so that the whole of the surplus value generated in a particular industry accrues directly to the capitalists in that industry in the form of a net gain, it appears to follow from Marx's analysis that industries which employ a relatively large amount of machinery and raw materials and a relatively small amount of labour will earn a lower rate of profit on their capital than industries which employ a relatively small amount of machinery and raw materials and a relatively large amount of labour. Yet such a state of affairs is obviously inconsistent with the facts of the real world: at any rate in a modern capitalist system, and under reasonably competitive conditions, the rate of profit will tend to be more or less the same in all industries, notwithstanding manifest differences in the way in which the capitals concerned are divided between their two constituent parts.

Something obviously has to give, and it is fairly clear what it must be. If we postulate the simultaneous existence both of a uniform rate of profit on capital and of differences in the constitution of capital, and if we are unwilling to relinquish the fundamental Marxian notion that surplus value is the unique source of profit, the only thing that *can* give, on Marx's premises, is the assumption that commodities are sold at their values. Marx himself realized this from the beginning, of course, but in his published work he did not formally drop the assumption that commodities are sold at their values until Part II of Volume III of *Capital*. Under modern competitive capitalism, he then said, surplus value was 'transformed' into profit, which was earnable at a more or less uniform rate on all capitals, however they were constituted. What happened, essentially, according to his account, was that as a result of the migration of capital from one industry to another in search of the highest rate of profit, the aggregate mass of surplus value generated over the economy as a whole was redistributed among the capitalists in different industries so that each came to share in it, not in accordance with the amount of *labour* he employed, but in accordance with the proportion which the *total capital* he employed bore to the aggregate capital in the economy as a whole. Inter-industry competition, in other words, redistributed aggregate surplus value in such a way as to equalize the rate of profit on capital in different industries. And, as a necessary consequence of this, the equilibrium prices of the great majority of commodities would come to diverge quite appreciably from their values. The transformation of surplus value into profit necessarily implied the transformation of values into 'prices of production' which were equal to paid-out costs plus profit on capital at the average rate. Marx argued, however, for reasons which will be discussed later, that his Volume III analysis in terms of prices of production should properly be regarded as a modification, and not as a contradiction, of his initial Volume I analysis in terms of values.

What I have tried to do in the four preceding paragraphs is to give a short account, as simple and non-technical as possible, of the analytical content of that part of Marx's economic theory to which what later came to be known as the 'transformation problem' relates. The nature of the 'transformation problem' will be clarified in this and the two following essays: all we need to note at this juncture is that the term has meant rather different things at different times. When it first appeared in the literature it had a relatively narrow connotation, referring as it usually did to a particular technical problem which arose out of the fact that Marx's method of transforming values into prices (as reflected at any rate in his arithmetical illustrations) operated only on outputs, leaving the values of inputs untransformed. In more recent times, however, particularly during the last two decades, the meaning of the term has often been broadened to include not only this technical problem but also a number of others – some of them of a much more fundamental nature – relating to Marx's transformation procedure in general. What *sense* did it make for Marx to 'start with values' when he knew very well that commodities hardly ever actually sold at their values under capitalism? Does the Volume III analysis really do no more than modify the Volume I analysis, as Marx claimed, or should it actually be regarded as contradicting it? In what sense, if any, did Marx's method of transformation possess a 'historical' dimension? Questions such as these – some new, some old – are more and more being viewed today as aspects of the 'transformation problem' in the much broader sense which that term has now come to assume. Most of the contemporary debates which profess to be about the 'transformation problem' are in fact little less than debates about the general validity of Marx's theory of value and distribution as a whole.

In the remainder of the present essay, and in the two essays which follow it, various aspects of the 'transformation problem' in both its narrower and its broader senses are discussed. Each of the essays is more or less self-contained, and each concentrates on a separate aspect of the problem, but their themes are of course interconnected. In the present essay I discuss the development of Marx's own ideas about the transformation procedure from *The Poverty of Philosophy* to Volume III of *Capital*, and then go on to deal with what might be called the arithmetic of the problem – i.e., the arithmetical illustrations of the transformation of values into prices which were employed by Marx himself, and the rather more complex algebraic formulations which were put forward by later economists in an endeavour to solve the 'transformation problem' in the original, narrower meaning of the term. In the next essay I touch briefly upon some of the contemporary debates, and go on to deal with two of the central questions which have recently come to the forefront of the discussions – the question of why Marx 'started with values', and the question of whether his job could today be done more effectively with the aid of Sraffa-type commodity production models. In the third essay I try to tackle the important problem of whether Marx's transformation analysis does or does not possess a meaningful 'historical' dimension.

II

Anyone who attempts to test, or to justify, the proposition that the prices of commodities are determined by the quantities of labour required to produce them is bound sooner or later, and in one way or another, to come face to face with the fact that in a competitive capitalist society equilibrium price ratios are not normally equal to embodied labour ratios.

Adam Smith, for example, having begun by proclaiming that price ratios and embodied labour ratios *would* be equal in a pre-capitalist society where the whole produce of labour still belonged to the labourers, then went on to argue that when capitalism came on to the historical scene, so that profits as well as wages had to be paid, the sweet simplicity of this pre-capitalist mode of price determination was disturbed – and disturbed to such an extent, Smith believed, that there was no longer any real sense in which prices could be said to be determined by embodied labour.[3]

Ricardo, criticizing Smith's attitude to this problem some forty years later, did not seek to deny that there would in fact be a divergence between price ratios and embodied labour ratios under capitalism. He claimed merely that the particular reason which Smith had given for the appearance of this divergence was not an adequate one. A mere redivision of the product between wages and profits, he argued, would not *in itself* be sufficient to bring about such a divergence. The crucial point as Ricardo saw it was that under capitalism there were big differences in the constitution of capitals (or, as he often put it, in the 'durability' of capitals) as between different industries. Under such conditions, it could be readily shown that a re-division of the product between wages and profits could (and normally would) lead to a change in the relative equilibrium prices of commodities, even though nothing whatever had happened to the quantities of labour required to produce them. Ricardo argued, however, that although this certainly meant that the rule according to which prices were determined in pre-capitalist society was 'considerably modified' when capitalism came on

---

[3] *Wealth of Nations*, Vol. I, pp. 65–7.

to the historical scene, it did *not* mean (as Smith had thought) that this rule then had to be replaced by an entirely different one.[4]

These analyses by Smith and Ricardo constituted Marx's starting-point when he began thinking seriously about the problem of the divergence. As early as 1847, in *The Poverty of Philosophy*, Marx spoke about Ricardo's discussion of 'the influence that the accumulation of capital and its different aspects (fixed capital and circulating capital), as also the rate of wages, can have on the proportional value of products'.[5] In 1859, again, in his comments on Smith and Ricardo in the *Critique of Political Economy*, he noted that the idea of the determination of value by labour time, which Smith 'regards as true when considering simple commodities', becomes confused as soon as he 'examines the higher and more complex forms of capital, wage-labour, rent, etc.'; whereas Ricardo, by way of contrast, 'neatly sets forth the determination of the value of commodities by labour-time, and demonstrates that this law governs even those bourgeois relations of production which apparently contradict it most decisively'.[6] And near the end of this section of the *Critique*, speaking of the argument (often raised against Ricardo by later economists) to the effect that it is 'demand and supply' rather than embodied labour which determines exchange value, Marx says that in fact

> this strange conclusion only raises the question how on the basis of exchange-value a market-price differing from this exchange-value comes into being, or rather, how the law of exchange-value asserts itself only in its antithesis.

This problem, Marx promises, will be solved (in his forthcoming work) in the section dealing with 'the theory of competition'.[7]

The fact that Marx by this time had already given a certain amount of attention to the way in which he was going to solve this problem is clear from a passage in Notebook IV of the *Grundrisse* (written, apparently, round about the end of December 1857 or the beginning of January 1858), which is noteworthy as the first clearly recognizable formulation by Marx of the basic ideas lying behind the procedure for the transformation of values into prices which he was later to put forward in Volume III of *Capital*.[8] The passage concerned deserves full quotation:

> With that, we come to another point. A *general rate of profit* as such is

[4] *Works of David Ricardo*, edited by P. Sraffa, Vol. I (Cambridge University Press, 1951), pp. 30–43.
[5] Karl Marx, *The Poverty of Philosophy* (Martin Lawrence, London, n.d.), p. 41. These, Marx continues, are 'the chief problems with which Ricardo is concerned'.
[6] Karl Marx, *A Contribution to the Critique of Political Economy* (Lawrence and Wishart, London, 1971), pp. 59–60.
[7] *Ibid.*, p. 62.
[8] Or, rather, the first recognizable formulation of these ideas which I have so far been able to find. It is at least possible that Marx's notebooks of the early 1850s, which I have not read, may contain something relevant.

possible only if the rate of profit in one branch of business is too high and
in another too low; i.e. that a part of the surplus value – which corresponds to surplus labour – is transferred from one capitalist to the other.
If in 5 branches of business, for example, the respective rate of profit is

$$\begin{array}{ccccc} A & B & C & D & E \\ 15\%, & 12\%, & 10\%, & 8\%, & 5\% \end{array}$$

then the average rate is 10%; but, in order for this to exist in reality,
capitalist A and B have to give up 7% to D and E – more particularly, 2
to D and 5 to E – while C remains as it was. It is impossible for rates of
profit on the same capital of 100 to be equal, since the relations of surplus
labour are altogether different, depending on the productivity of labour
and on the relation between raw material, machinery and wages, and on
the overall volume in which production takes place. But suppose that a
given branch of business, E, is necessary, say, the bakery trade, then the
average 10% has to be paid to it. But this can happen only if A and B
credit E with a part of their surplus labour. The capitalist class thus to a
certain extent distributes the total surplus value so that, to a certain
degree, it [shares in it] evenly in accordance with the *size* of its capital,
instead of in accordance with the surplus values actually created by the
capitals in the various branches of business. The larger profit – arising
from the real surplus labour within a branch of production, the really
created surplus value – is pushed down to the average level by competition,
and the deficit of surplus value in the other branch of business raised up
to the average level by withdrawal of capitals from it, i.e. a favourable
relation of demand and supply. Competition cannot lower this level
itself, but merely has the tendency to create such a level. Further developments belong in the section on competition. This is realized [*realisiert*] by
means of the relation of prices in the different branches of business, which
fall *below* the *value* in some, rise *above* it in others. This makes it seem as
if an equal sum of capital in unequal branches of business created *equal
surplus labour or surplus value*.[9]

Some of the propositions in this passage are evidently inexact, and the
terminology is different in some respects from that which Marx was later
to adopt in this connection, but the underlying ideas are essentially the same.
The general or average rate of profit characteristic of modern capitalism,
Marx is saying, is achieved through a competitive redistribution of the
total surplus value generated over the economy as a whole; and this process
of redistribution necessarily implies that the equilibrium prices of some

[9] Karl Marx, *Grundrisse* (translated by M. Nicolaus, Penguin Books, London, 1973), pp. 435–6.
The same ideas seem to be implied, although they are never very clearly expressed, at various
points in a later section of the *Grundrisse* entitled 'Capital as Fructiferous. Transformation of
Surplus Value into Profit' (pp. 745–78). See in particular p. 767, where Marx says that 'the
profit of the capitalist class, concretely expressed, *can never be greater than the sum of the
surplus value*'.

commodities will fall below their value and that those of others will rise above it.

The next important landmark in the development of Marx's ideas on this subject is a letter which he wrote to Engels on 2 August 1862,[10] giving him (apparently for the first time) fairly full details of the nature of the solution to the problem which he had now decided to put forward in Volume III of *Capital*.[11] Let us assume, says Marx, that the length of the working day is given and uniform; that the ratio of 'surplus' to 'necessary' labour[12] is everywhere given as $1:2$; and that '£1 = 1 working day' (i.e., that any commodity which has taken x working days to produce will be bought and sold for £x). Let us also assume that there are four industries in the economy, in each of which the ratio of machinery and raw materials – i.e. 'constant' capital (c) – to capital laid out in wages – i.e. 'variable' capital (v) – is different. Taking the average capital of 100 employed in each industry, let us suppose that the situation is as follows:[13]

	c		v		Surplus value		Total value
(1)	80	+	20	+	10	=	110
(2)	50	+	50	+	25	=	125
(3)	70	+	30	+	15	=	115
(4)	90	+	10	+	5	=	105
					55		

If these commodities were sold at their (Marxian) values, the four outputs would obviously sell at £110, £125, £115, and £105 respectively, and the rates of profit realized on each capital of 100 would be 10%, 25%, 15%, and 5% respectively. But such a situation would evidently be impossible under competitive capitalism. What actually happens, Marx claims, is that competition equalizes the rate of profit by redistributing the total of 55 (= £55) surplus value among the four capitals so that each receives one-quarter of it – i.e. $13\frac{3}{4}$. To make this possible, each commodity must obviously sell at £$113\frac{3}{4}$ – i.e., commodities (1) and (4) will be sold at prices higher than their values, and commodities (2) and (3) at prices lower than their values.

---

[10] *Correspondence of Marx and Engels* (translated by D. Torr, Lawrence and Wishart, London, 1936), pp. 129–33.

[11] See the 'Draft Plans for Parts I and III of *Capital*' in *Theories of Surplus Value*, Part I (Foreign Languages Publishing House, Moscow, n.d.), pp. 401–3.

[12] 'Necessary' labour is the labour required to cover the worker's wages; 'surplus' labour is the labour he performs over and above this. The ratio of 'surplus' to 'necessary' labour is frequently described by Marx as the 'rate of surplus value', or the 'rate of exploitation'.

[13] The figures in the table are those used by Marx, but I have slightly altered their order, and the headings under which they appear, for the sake of clarity. The quantities are expressed in terms of (Marxian) values, the unit being the labour-day.

Competition, in other words, reduces commodities to prices which are
'*above, below* or *equal* to their *value*, according to the organic composition
of the respective capitals'.[14]

In the simplified form in which Marx presents the analysis in this letter,
it is evident that one question of some importance is glossed over. Where do
the elements of c and v, which enter as inputs into the production of the four
commodities, actually come from? If they are produced within the system
covered by the model, so that they appear in it not only as inputs but also as
outputs, should not their values be transformed into prices on *both* sides of
the relevant equations? It is here that the transformation problem in the
narrower of the two senses distinguished above comes into the picture. It
will cause us much trouble a little later on: in the meantime, let us note
simply that Marx had probably already given some thought to it at the time
when he wrote his letter to Engels of 2 August 1862. Certainly, at any rate,
there is a significant passage in *Theories of Surplus Value*[15] in which Marx
explains that the conversion of value into price 'works in two ways'. First,
he says, 'the profit which is added to the capital advanced may be either above
or below the *surplus-value* which is contained in the commodity itself'. But
second, and quite apart from this,

> the cost-price of constant capital – or of the commodities which enter into
> the value of the newly produced commodity as raw materials, auxiliary
> materials and machinery [or] labour conditions – may likewise be either
> above or below its value.

The reason why this is important, Marx goes on to explain, is that

> every commodity which enters into another commodity as constant
> capital, itself emerges as the result, the product, of another production
> process. And so the commodity appears alternately as a pre-condition for
> the production of other commodities and as the result of a process in
> which the existence of other commodities is the pre-condition for its own
> production.

But he does not consider in any detail the implications which this might have
for his transformation procedure, contenting himself with a bald statement

---

[14] The way in which Marx brings money into the picture here is especially to be noted, since
in later formulations he quite often takes this aspect of the matter for granted. It is also
interesting to find that there is no reference whatever in this letter to the question of whether,
after the transformation, one can say that the 'law of value' still remains operative.
[15] *Theories of Surplus Value*, Part III (Lawrence and Wishart, London, 1972), pp. 167–8. The
main text of *Theories of Surplus Value* was written by Marx between January 1862 and January 1863. The passage in question takes the form of a commentary on a statement by Samuel
Bailey to the effect that the prices of finished commodities cannot be said to be determined by the
quality of labour embodied in them because some of the inputs may be purchased at monopoly
prices. There are a number of other passages in *Theories of Surplus Value* containing interesting
comments on the 'transformation problem', but for reasons which will become clear later it will
be convenient to postpone consideration of these until the next essay in this volume.

to the effect that 'this important deviation of cost-prices from values brought about by capitalist production does not alter the fact that cost-prices continue to be determined by values'.

III

If we are prepared to pass over *Value, Price and Profit* – in which Marx side-steps the transformation issue by saying merely that commodities sell at their values 'on the average', that values 'ultimately' regulate market prices, etc. – we may now skip to 1867, the year of the publication of Volume I of *Capital*. An interesting exchange of letters between Marx and Engels in the months preceding its publication reveals Marx resolutely refusing, as a matter of principle, to contemplate saying anything concrete whatever in Volume I about the question of the transformation of values into prices. This question cannot possibly be dealt with, Marx explains,[16] until 'the *transformation* of *surplus value* into *profit*, of *profit* into *average profit*, etc. has been demonstrated'. This in its turn ('since the turnover of capital, etc., plays a role here') takes for granted 'a prior demonstration of the *circulation process of capital*' – which Marx was planning as the subject of Volume II of *Capital*. Thus in order not to spoil (as he put it) 'the whole method of dialectical exposition', it was necessary to delay the discussion of the transformation of values into prices until Volume III. And Marx adheres to this self-denying ordinance throughout Volume I, where it is only in three or four rather vague premonitory statements in footnotes,[17] and in one short formulation of the problem (as distinct from its solution) in the text,[18] that the coming events are permitted to cast their shadows before.

The question continued to be very much in Marx's mind, however, as he went on with the preparation of Volumes II and III. This is strikingly shown by a long letter he wrote to Engels on 30 April 1868,[19] in which he explained with some care 'the method by which the rate of profit is developed' and gave a full description of the appropriate transformation procedure as he had by that time come to envisage it. Although the essence of this description was the same as it had been from the beginning (aggregate surplus value is redistributed among the different capitals in proportion to their size, and this necessarily involves a divergence of prices from values in the case of the products of all capitals except those with an organic composition equal to the social average), one or two of the relevant points were elaborated or clarified, and an indication was given of the way in which Marx intended to link up the Volume III transformation analysis with the Volume II analysis

---

[16] In a letter to Engels dated 27 June 1867. This letter is not included in the edition of the *Correspondence* referred to in [10], but will be found in *Selected Correspondence of Marx and Engels* (Foreign Languages Publishing House, Moscow, n.d.), pp. 229–31.

[17] See, e.g., *Capital*, Vol. I (Foreign Languages Publishing House, Moscow, 1954), pp. 166, 216, and 220.

[18] *Ibid.*, p. 307.

[19] *Correspondence of Marx and Engels* (translated by D. Torr), pp. 240–5.

of the circulation of capital.[20] In Volume II itself (which did not appear until 1885, two years after Marx's death), however, the self-denying ordinance is still adhered to: Marx consistently assumes throughout that commodities are exchanged at their values. One can certainly find, it is true, the odd reference to the divergence of prices from values;[21] and there is one passage – which Engels as editor of Marx's manuscripts should really not have allowed to slip through – in which the Volume III transformation analysis is very explicitly anticipated:

> In the distribution of the social surplus-value among the various capitals invested in different branches of industry, the differences in the different periods of time for which capital is advanced (for instance the various degrees of durability of fixed capital) and the different organic compositions of capital (and therefore also the different circulations of constant and variable capital) contribute equally toward an equalization of the general rate of profit and the conversion of values into prices of production.[22]

But it is Engels's preface to Volume II, rather than anything in the actual text itself, which is of importance in the history of the transformation problem. For it was in this preface that Engels issued his curious challenge to 'those economists who claim to have discovered in Rodbertus the secret source and a superior predecessor of Marx'. Let them now demonstrate what Rodbertian economics can accomplish, Engels says, by solving (prior to the publication of Volume III of *Capital*, in which the correct solution will be revealed) the apparent contradiction between the Ricardian law of value and the reality of modern competitive capitalism:

> If they can show in which way an equal average rate of profit can and must come about, not only without a violation of the law of value, but on the very basis of it, I am willing to discuss the matter further with them.[23]

Thus was inaugurated the famous Marxian Prize Essay Competition, upon the results of which Engels reported nine years later in his preface to Volume III of *Capital*.

Some of the competitors were very wide of the mark, but two of them, Wilhelm Lexis and Peter Fireman, came remarkably near it. The *essence* of Marx's Volume III solution conformed fairly closely to their anticipations, but his exposition was of course much more elaborate. Volume III opens with a long section (Part I) entitled 'The Conversion of Surplus-Value into

---

[20] There is no *discussion* in this letter of the question of whether the 'law of value' can be said to remain operative after the transformation; but in one place Marx does refer, in passing, to 'the previously developed and *still valid* laws of value and of surplus value' (my italics).

[21] See, e.g., *Capital*, Vol. II (Foreign Languages Publishing House, Moscow, 1957), pp. 91 and 393.

[22] *Ibid.*, p. 216. The passage occurs in a chapter dealing with Ricardo's theories of fixed and circulating capital.

[23] *Ibid.*, p. 18.

Profit and of the Rate of Surplus-Value into the Rate of Profit'.[24] The basic idea put forward here (and throughout Volume III) is that profit on capital is 'a converted form of surplus-value, a form in which its origin and the secret of its existence are obscured and extinguished'.[25] Suppose, then, that we put a new label, 'profit', on the entity which we have up to now been calling 'surplus value', and that we assume that 'the amount of profit falling to a given capital' is 'equal to the total amount of surplus-value produced by means of this capital during a certain period of circulation'. If we also assume that commodities sell at their values, then the amount and the rate of profit will be 'determined by ratios of simple figures given or ascertainable in every individual case'.[26] Marx's exposition remains for some time in this 'mathematical field', as he calls it, showing (*inter alia*) how 'different lines of industry have different rates of profit, which correspond to differences in the organic composition of their capitals and, within indicated limits, also to their different periods of turnover'.[27] It is not until Part II of Volume III (entitled 'Conversion of Profit into Average Profit'), and indeed not until the end of the first chapter of Part II, that he explicitly poses the question of the apparent contradiction between the model he has been using and the real world of competitive capitalism. These statements he has been making about differences in the rate of profit, he now says,

> hold good on the assumption which has been the basis of all our analyses so far, namely that the commodities are sold at their values. There is no doubt, on the other hand, that aside from unessential, incidental and mutually compensating distinctions, differences in the average rate of profit in the various branches of industry do not exist in reality, and could not exist without abolishing the entire system of capitalist production. It would seem, therefore, that here the theory of value is incompatible with the actual process, incompatible with the real phenomena of production, and that for this reason any attempt to understand these phenomena should be given up.[28]

The four remaining chapters of Part II are devoted to the resolution of this apparent contradiction.

The arithmetical tables which Marx uses in Part II to illustrate his argument do not differ essentially from those he had previously used, although they are a little more elaborate. The following summary table incorporates all the essential data which they contain:[29]

---

[24] *Capital*, Vol. III (Foreign Languages Publishing House, Moscow, 1954), pp. 25–139.
[25] *Ibid.*, p. 47.
[26] *Ibid.*, p. 49.
[27] *Ibid.*, p. 151.
[28] *Ibid.*, p. 151.
[29] It is in effect an amalgamation of the tables on pp. 153–5 of Vol. III of *Capital*, with some of the figures rearranged.

1	2	3	4	5	6	7	8
Capitals	Used-up c	Cost price	Surplus value	Value	Profit	Price of production	Deviation of price from value
I $80c+20v$	50	70	20	90	22	92	+2
II $70c+30v$	51	81	30	111	22	103	−8
III $60c+40v$	51	91	40	131	22	113	−18
IV $85c+15v$	40	55	15	70	22	77	+7
V $95c+5v$	10	15	5	20	22	37	+17
			110	422	110	422	

Here we have five different spheres of production, in each of which the total value of the capital employed is the same ($=100$). The organic composition of this capital, however, is different in each case. Marx assumes, in the interests of greater realism, that only a portion (shown in column 2) of the value of the constant capital is transferred to the commodity in the period we are considering. The 'cost price' of the commodity (i.e., the sum of v and used-up c, both reckoned in value terms) is shown in column 3. It is assumed that the rate of surplus value is everywhere equal to unity, so that surplus value in absolute terms (shown in column 4) is in each case equal to v. The total value of each of the outputs being considered (shown in column 5) is given by the sum of the cost price and the surplus value.

Now it is evident that the sale of these commodities at their values would result in very unequal rates of profit being earned on each of the capitals. Therefore, at any rate under competitive capitalism, the commodities clearly *cannot* sell at their values. What happens, according to Marx's account in Volume III (which in this respect is basically the same as his earlier accounts), is that the total pool of surplus value generated over the economy as a whole, amounting in the present case to 110, is redistributed (by means of the competitive transfer of capital from industry to industry in search of the highest profit) among the individual capitals in proportion to the total size of each – in this case uniformly, so that each receives a profit of 22 (column 6). The 'price of production' (column 7) – i.e., the long-run equilibrium price at which each output actually tends to sell – is the sum of the cost price and the profit, and this sum will necessarily differ in each case from the value.

Under competitive capitalism, then, according to this account, the capitalists in the different spheres of production 'do not secure the surplus-value, and consequently the profit, created in their own sphere by the production of these commodities'. What they in fact secure

is only as much surplus-value, and hence profit, as falls, when uniformly distributed, to the share of every aliquot part of the total social capital from the total social surplus-value, or profit, produced in a given time by the social capital in all spheres of production.[30]

And in order to make this redistribution of the total social surplus value and the formation of an average rate of profit possible, the prices of most of the commodities concerned must necessarily diverge from their values. The prices of commodities produced with capitals of higher organic composition than the social average will be higher than their values; the prices of commodities produced with capitals of lower organic composition than the social average will be lower than their values; and only in those spheres, if any, where the organic composition of capital happens to be equal to the social average will prices be equal to values.[31]

But if this is so, in what sense can it be said that the average rate of profit comes about (as Engels put it in his challenge to the Rodbertians) 'not only without a violation of the law of value, but on the very basis of it'?[32] This is of course the crucial question, and Marx answers it in rather different ways in different contexts. His most usual answer is that the average rate of profit (which is added to the given cost prices to form the final prices of production) has to be 'deduced out of the values of the commodities',[33] which means that the 'law of value' can still be regarded ('in the last instance')[34] as the regulator of the prices of production. As he puts it in a key passage in Chapter X,

> Since the total value of the commodities regulates the total surplus-value, and this in turn regulates the level of average profit and thereby the general rate of profit – as a general law or a law governing fluctuations – it follows that the law of value regulates the prices of production.[35]

This is the system of determination which Marx evidently has in mind when he states or implies, as he does so often, that the reason why prices of production can still be said to be ultimately determined by values is that 'the sum of the profits is equal to the sum of the surplus values'.[36]

Now in Marx's method of transformation as we have just described it, the prices of production are calculated by adding a proportionate share of the given sum of the surplus values to each of the cost prices, *the magnitudes of the latter being reckoned in value terms and assumed to remain unaffected by the transformation*. In other words, while the values of the commodities comprising the *output* of the system are duly transformed into prices of

---

[30] *Ibid.*, p. 156.
[31] *Ibid.*, p. 161.
[32] Above, p. 104.
[33] *Capital*, Vol. III, p. 155.
[34] *Ibid.*, p. 205.
[35] *Ibid.*, p. 177. Cf. *ibid.*, p. 838: 'The level of the rate of profit is likewise a magnitude held within certain specific limits determined by the value of commodities.'
[36] See, e.g., *ibid.*, p. 170, 171, and 838–9.

production as a result of the redistribution of the given sum of the surplus values, the values of the commodities comprising the *input* of the system are left untransformed. This method would only make proper sense if all the inputs whose values make up the cost prices were produced by capitals of average organic composition, or if they were produced outside the system and for some reason or other purchased at their values. In reality, of course, many of these inputs will be produced within the system and purchased at prices of production which diverge from their values. What we have to do, therefore, is to amend Marx's model by building into it a set of specific assumptions concerning the interdependence of inputs and outputs in the system, and then, on this new basis, to work out what happens to prices when we redistribute the given sum of surplus values in a way which equalizes the rate of profit. And this is not as easy as it may perhaps sound. For one thing, there are a number of alternative postulates which may be made about the input/output relationships, and it is by no means obvious which of these ought to be chosen. And for another thing, to work out what happens to prices may not be at all straightforward. The ratio of the final price of each commodity must bear the same ratio to its value when it appears as an input as it does when it appears as an output. The equal rate of profit must be calculated in relation to the prices, and not the values, of the elements of capital. And in the end all the sums must add up – i.e., in the case of each commodity the final (transformed) prices of the inputs used to produce it, plus profit on capital at the average rate, must come out equal to the final (transformed) price of the commodity itself.

Marx was of course aware of the existence of this problem,[37] and there are three separate references to it in Volume III of *Capital*. In the first of these he writes as follows:

Aside from the fact that the price of a particular product, let us say that of capital B, differs from its value because the surplus-value realized in B may be greater or smaller than the profit added to the price of the products of B, the same circumstance applies also to those commodities which form the constant part of capital B, and indirectly also its variable part, as the labourers' necessities of life.

The prices of inputs, in other words, just like those of outputs, may diverge from their values. Marx does not, however, explore the implications of this in any depth: he states merely that

this always resolves itself to one commodity receiving too little of the surplus-value while another receives too much, so that the deviations from the value which are embodied in the prices of production compensate one another.[38] Under capitalist production, the general law acts as

[37] Cf. above, p. 102.
[38] The notion that 'the deviations from the value which are embodied in the prices of production compensate one another' is not very often to be found in Marx's work prior to Vol. III of *Capital*. In Vol. III, it first appears on p. 155, immediately following the arithmetical tables

the prevailing tendency only in a very complicated and approximate manner, as a never ascertainable average of ceaseless fluctuations.[39]

Nor are the second and third references any more helpful. In the second, he says merely that when we are thinking about the cost price we should bear in mind that 'there is always the possibility of an error if the cost-price of a commodity in any particular sphere is identified with the value of the means of production consumed by it', and then dismisses the matter by saying that 'our present analysis does not necessitate a closer examination of this point'.[40] In the third reference, which occurs during a discussion of the prices of production of commodities of average organic composition, he points out that the cost price of such commodities may differ from the sum of the values of the elements which make up this component of their price of production, but that it will still remain true that 'the quantity of profit falling to these commodities is equal to the quantity of surplus-value contained in them'.[41]

How would Marx have gone about solving the problem, then, if he had in fact addressed himself to it in a less perfunctory manner? In one respect, at any rate, he would really have had no option: in order to satisfy all the conditions, the model must of necessity be given the form of a set of equations in which the unknowns of the system – the average rate of profit and the prices of production (or price–value ratios) of the different commodities – are mutually and simultaneously determined. Such an approach would surely not have been regarded by him as in any way alien or 'un-Marxian': he was by no means averse to the use of algebraic formulae in economic analysis,[42] and prided himself (rather incautiously) on having given a 'mathematically precise proof' in the case of the transformation exercise.[43] He also explicitly recognized that 'the price of production is not determined by the value of any one commodity alone, but by the aggregate value of all commodities'[44] – a statement which, when read in its context, comes very close to a recognition of the fact that prices are *mutually* determined within a kind of general equilibrium framework. If confronted with the issue we are now discussing,

---

which Marx uses to illustrate his argument. From these tables, Marx says, it will be seen that one of the consequences of the redistribution of the sum of the surplus values is that the deviations of prices from values (shown in column 8 of the table in my text) will cancel one another out, or, what amounts to the same thing, that the sum of the prices will be equal to the sum of the values. In three or four later passages in Vol. III (pp. 163, 170, 197–8, and 740), the latter notion takes on something of a life of its own: its causal link with the redistribution of the sum of the surplus values tends to be obscured, and it is formulated in terms which suggest that Marx believed it to have a general significance, quite independent of the particular method of transformation illustrated in his tables.

[39] *Capital*, Vol. III, p. 159.
[40] *Ibid.*, p. 162.
[41] *Ibid.*, p. 203.
[42] Cf., e.g., *Correspondence of Marx and Engels* (translated by D. Torr), p. 242.
[43] *Capital*, Vol. III, p. 194.
[44] *Ibid.*, p. 202.

Marx might indeed have claimed that even his own, rather crude, transformation procedure in Volume III *in effect* amounted to the setting up and solution of a system of simultaneous equations, of the following form:

$$(c_1 + v_1)(1 + r) = a_1 p_1 \tag{1}$$
$$(c_2 + v_2)(1 + r) = a_2 p_2 \tag{2}$$
$$(c_3 + v_3)(1 + r) = a_3 p_3 \tag{3}$$
$$r[\Sigma(c + v)] = \Sigma s \tag{4}$$

Here the subscripts 1, 2, and 3 relate to three industries I, II, and III respectively;[45] p_1, p_2, and p_3 are the price–value ratios, or coefficients; and r is the average rate of profit. Equations (1), (2), and (3) represent the original value schema in its 'transformed' price form; and Equation (4) expresses the condition that the sum of the profits should be equal to the sum of the surplus values. Given the cs, the vs, and the as, and therefore also the ss, the four independent equations are sufficient to determine the four unknowns p_1, p_2, p_3, and r. If you now want to build the interdependence of inputs and outputs into the model, Marx might have said, simply postulate that (for example) one of the industries produces the elements of c and another produces the elements of v, and attach the appropriate price–value coefficients to these inputs on the left-hand side of the equations. Provided that the resulting system of equations is in fact soluble, Marx might have concluded, the statements in Volume III about the ultimate dependence of prices upon values still stand, since the transformation will have been effected on the basis of the redistribution of a predetermined sum of surplus values which has had of necessity to be 'deduced out of the values of the commodities'.[46]

But Marx did not, of course, say any of these things: we are here fathering upon him certain views about the appropriate method of solving the problem which in actual fact took many years to be explicitly formulated. It is now time to have a look at some of the more important of the major post-Marx contributions, with particular reference (in the present essay) to the transformation problem in the narrower of the two senses distinguished above.[47]

IV

Neither Böhm-Bawerk's famous *Karl Marx and the Close of his System* (1896), nor Hilferding's now equally famous reply to it (1904), made any

[45] Marx's arithmetical illustration in Vol. III in fact comprehended *five* industries. I have reduced the number to three here partly for the sake of simplicity and partly in order to pave the way for my consideration below of the three-sector models employed by Bortkiewicz and Winternitz.

[46] Above, p. 107.

[47] In this brief survey of Marx's transformation procedure in Part II of Vol. III, I have made little reference either to Chapter X (in which Marx discusses, *inter alia*, the question of the 'historical' dimension of the transformation problem), or to Chapter XI (in which he discusses the problem of the divergence between values and prices in the particular form in which it was tackled by Ricardo). I shall be coming back to these questions in the two following essays.

reference to the transformation problem in this narrower sense. It was not until 1907 that the problem was specifically formulated, and a solution attempted, by the German economist Ladislaus von Bortkiewicz,[48] who had apparently been stimulated by an attempt made by Tugan-Baranowsky to solve something like what we would call today the inverse transformation problem.[49] Bortkiewicz's treatment was the starting-point for most of the subsequent discussions, and deserves detailed consideration.

Bortkiewicz uses a three-industry schema, and builds the interdependence of inputs and outputs into his initial model by assuming that Department I produces means of production (i.e., the elements of c), Department II workers' consumption goods (i.e., the elements of v), and Department III capitalists' consumption goods (which do not enter anywhere as inputs). In addition, he announces that he is going to assume 'simple reproduction', the conditions of which may be expressed in the following system of equations:

$$\text{System } A^{50} \begin{cases} c_1 + v_1 + s_1 = c_1 + c_2 + c_3 & (1) \\ c_2 + v_2 + s_2 = v_1 + v_2 + v_3 & (2) \\ c_3 + v_3 + s_3 = s_1 + s_2 + s_3. & (3) \end{cases}$$

This schema is supposed to be set up in terms of money units, but the quantities are taken to reflect the (Marxian) values of the different items. If we call the average rate of profit r, and the price–value coefficient for means of production p_1, for workers' consumption goods p_2, and for capitalists' consumption goods p_3, the counterpart in price terms of Equations (1), (2), and (3) is the following system:

$$\text{System } B^{51} \begin{cases} (c_1 p_1 + v_1 p_2)(1+r) = (c_1 + c_2 + c_3)p_1 & (4) \\ (c_2 p_1 + v_2 p_2)(1+r) = (v_1 + v_2 + v_3)p_2 & (5) \\ (c_3 p_1 + v_3 p_2)(1+r) = (s_1 + s_2 + s_3)p_3. & (6) \end{cases}$$

Bortkiewicz's next step, which is a very curious one, is difficult to follow because of the mathematical verbiage in which it is disguised. What he does, in effect, is to use the equalities in System A in order to transform the price equations in System B into the following:

$$\text{System } C^{52} \begin{cases} (c_1 p_1 + v_1 p_2)(1+r) = a_1 p_1 & (7) \\ (c_2 p_1 + v_2 p_2)(1+r) = a_2 p_2 & (8) \\ (c_3 p_1 + v_3 p_2)(1+r) = a_3 p_3. & (9) \end{cases}$$

[48] A paper by Bortkiewicz entitled *On the Correction of Marx's Fundamental Theoretical Construction in the Third Volume of Capital*, in which he put forward his solution, appears in English translation as the appendix to a volume edited by Paul Sweezy (Kelley, New York, 1949), the chief contents of which consist of the two works by Böhm-Bawerk and Hilferding which have just been referred to in the text.

[49] Bortkiewicz, *op. cit.* (edited by Sweezy), p. 199.

[50] *Ibid.*, p. 200.

[51] These equations correspond to Bortkiewicz's Equations (11), (12), and (13) in *ibid.*, p. 202. For the sake of comparability, I have substituted my standard set of symbols for those used by Bortkiewicz.

[52] Although it may not be immediately obvious, these equations correspond to Bortkiewicz's Equations (19), (20), and (21) in *ibid.*, p. 203.

where $a_1 = c_1 + v_1 + s_1$; $a_2 = c_2 + v_2 + s_2$; and $a_3 = c_3 + v_3 + s_3$.[53] The effect of this procedure is to expunge completely from the equations in System C those conditions of simple reproduction which Bortkiewicz has carefully built into Systems A and B. All that the equations in System C really say is that the values of means of production and workers' consumption goods (which are assumed to be produced in Departments I and II respectively) must be multiplied by the same price–value coefficients when they appear as inputs as when they appear as outputs if the transformation is to be a valid one. Given that these equations can be solved, the solutions obtained for p_1, p_2, p_3, and r will clearly be valid for *any* value schema, whether it obeys the conditions of simple reproduction or not.

But it is evident that System C, at any rate as it stands, can *not* be solved, since there are four unknowns but only three equations. Bortkiewicz toys for a moment with the idea of adding an equation embodying the equality of total prices with total values, but decides instead to assume that 'the good which serves as the value and price unit' (e.g. gold) is produced in Department III, so that it is plausible to set

$$p_3 = 1$$

thereby reducing the number of unknowns to three and rendering the system of equations soluble.[54] Formulae emerge fairly readily for p_1, p_2, and r without the necessity of working out anything much more formidable than a quadratic equation.[55] Bortkeiwicz then proceeds to apply these formulae to the following specific set of figures (in 'value' terms):[56]

Table 1   Value calculation

Dept.	Constant capital	Variable capital	Surplus value	Value of product
I	225	90	60	375
II	100	120	80	300
III	50	90	60	200
Total	375	300	200	875

[53] Cf. pp. 109–10 above, where I suggested that Marx might have worked with a system of this type if he had been able (or willing) to give more attention to the problem.

[54] Bortkiewicz, *op. cit.*, p. 202.

[55] The simplest way to derive the solutions is to begin by obtaining from Equations (7) and (8) the equation
$$\frac{a_1 p_1}{c_1 p_1 + v_1 p_2} = \frac{a_2 p_2}{c_2 p_1 + v_2 p_2}$$
By multiplying out, collecting terms, and dividing through by $(p_2)^2$, one obtains a quadratic in p_1/p_2. Once we know what p_1/p_2 is we can easily determine r, since from Equation (7)
$$1 + r = \frac{a_1 p_1}{c_1 p_1 + v_1 p_2} = \frac{a_1 p_1/p_2}{c_1 p_1/p_2 + v_1}$$
By making use of Equation (9) and the postulated equality $p_3 = 1$, we can now easily obtain the absolute values of p_1 and p_2, as distinct from their ratio p_1/p_2.

[56] Bortkiewicz, *op. cit.*, pp. 204–5.

It will be noted that the corresponding row and column totals are equal – i.e., that the figures have been chosen so that (in value terms) conditions of simple reproduction prevail – and that a uniform rate of surplus value of $\frac{2}{3}$ is assumed. The application of the formulae derived from System C brings p_1 out at $\frac{32}{25}$, p_2 at $\frac{16}{15}$, and r at $\frac{1}{4}$, so that the price calculation is as follows:

Table 2   Price calculation

Dept.	Constant capital	Variable capital	Profit	Price of product
I	288	96	96	480
II	128	128	64	320
III	64	96	40	200
Total	480	320	200	1000

This is quite a spectacular result. Upon inspection, it will be seen that all the formal conditions laid down above[57] for a valid transformation of values into prices have apparently been satisfied; the sum of the profits comes out as equal to the sum of the surplus values, as it is plausible to assume that Marx would have wanted it to do; and in addition, for good measure, the corresponding row and column totals are still equal – i.e., the system in price terms still obeys the conditions of simple reproduction.

It may not be easy to see at first sight why the conditions of simple reproduction still prevail if, as I have claimed above,[58] the assumption that the system obeys these conditions has in fact been expunged from the equations in system C (from which the solutions for the unknowns are derived). The reason is simply that on the basis of these equations the price of the output of Department I will necessarily come out as equal to $a_1 p_1$ – i.e., by definition to $(c_1 + v_1 + s_1)p_1$; and since in the value scheme in Table 1 Bortkiewicz has chosen figures which make $c_1 + v_1 + s_1$ equal to $c_1 + c_2 + c_3$, it is hardly surprising that the row total $a_1 p_1$ should come out equal to the column total $(c_1 + c_2 + c_3)p_1$. The same also applies in the case of Department II; whence it follows, given that $p_3 = 1$, that the third row total (representing the price of the output of Department III) will also come out equal to the third column total (representing the sum of the profits).

Given that $p_3 = 1$, and that we start with a set of figures in value terms obeying the conditions of simple reproduction, it will also necessarily follow that the sum of the profits will come out equal to the sum of the surplus values. The equality of these two magnitudes in the present case has

[57] P. 108.
[58] P. 112.

in fact no more significance than the equally obvious *lack* of equality between the sum of the prices and the sum of the values.[59]

V

Winternitz, in his celebrated note in the June 1948 *Economic Journal*,[60] criticized Bortkiewicz's solution on three grounds. First, he said, it assumed that conditions of simple reproduction prevailed, whereas in actual fact these conditions were not relevant to the problem. Second, it involved the 'arbitrary and unjustified' assumption that the money commodity was produced in Department III, so that output prices in this Department were not affected by the changeover from values to prices. Third, Bortkiewicz's solution made the sum of the prices deviate from the sum of the values, which was un-Marxian.[61]

The system of equations which Winternitz himself proposed was as follows:[62]

$$(c_1p_1 + v_1p_2)(1+r) = a_1p_1$$
$$(c_2p_1 + v_2p_2)(1+r) = a_2p_2$$
$$(c_3p_1 + v_3p_2)(1+r) = a_3p_3$$
$$a_1p_1 + a_2p_2 + a_3p_3 = a_1 + a_2 + a_3.$$

Here the three Departments, as with Bortkiewicz, are assumed to produce respectively means of production, workers' consumption goods, and capitalists' consumption goods, but nothing at all is assumed about the nature of the conditions of reproduction. All that is postulated in the first three equations is that the price–value coefficients for the products of Departments I and II should be the same when these products appear as inputs as when they appear as outputs. Winternitz, it will be observed, did not appreciate that Bortkiewicz had in actual fact expunged the assumption of simple reproduction from the system of equations from which his solutions were derived, and that his own first three equations were therefore really precisely the same as Bortkiewicz's. The only difference, it is clear, lies in the fourth equation. Whereas Bortkiewicz made his system determinate by putting $p_3 = 1$, Winternitz makes his determinate by putting the sum

---

[59] Cf. Bortkiewicz, *op. cit.*, p. 205: 'That the total price exceeds the total value arises from the fact that Department III, from which the good serving as value and price measure is taken, has a relatively low organic composition of capital. But the fact that total profit is numerically identical with total surplus value is a consequence of the fact that the good used as value and price measure belongs to Department III.' If Bortkiewicz had chosen his figures so that the organic composition of capital in Department III was equal to the social average, both total profit and total surplus value *and* total price and total value would of course have come out equal.

[60] J. Winternitz, 'Values and Prices: A Solution of the So-called Transformation Problem', *Economic Journal*, **58**, 1948, pp. 276–80.

[61] *Ibid.*, p. 278.

[62] Once again, for the sake of comparability with the other models considered in this essay, I have substituted my standard set of symbols for those used by Winternitz.

of the prices equal to the sum of the values, believing this to be 'the obvious proposition in the spirit of the Marxian system'.[63]

Solutions emerge, of course. As in the Bortkiewicz system, one can easily formulate a quadratic in p_1/p_2 on the basis of the first two equations, thence readily deriving a solution for r. One can then proceed, with the aid of the other equations, to derive formulae for p_1, p_2, and p_3 in absolute terms. Winternitz's formula for r turns out (not unexpectedly) to be exactly the same as Bortkiewicz's, but because his fourth equation is different his solutions for the other unknowns are different.

The great virtue of Winternitz's contribution, as Kenneth May pointed out in another note in the *Economic Journal* a few months later,[64] was that it showed that the formal problem of linking values and prices was 'practically trivial mathematically'.[65] But there was still scope for further questions to be asked. For example, Winternitz complained that Bortkiewicz's solution made the sum of the prices deviate from the sum of the values, whereas 'the obvious proposition in the spirit of the Marxian system' was that these two magnitudes should come out equal. He said nothing, however, about the fact that his own solution made the sum of the profits deviate from the sum of the surplus values, which, it could reasonably be argued, was much more opposed to 'the spirit of the Marxian system' than the other deviation.[66] Then again, Winternitz complained that Bortkiewicz's assumption that the money commodity was produced in Department III (so that p_3 could be taken as equal to unity) was 'arbitrary and unjustified'. He said nothing, however, about the role (if any) which money played in his own system, whereas Marx had frequently brought money specifically into the picture (with the aid of the assumption that (for example) '£1 = 1 working day').[67] And finally, Winternitz did not appreciate an important characteristic of his own solution which Kenneth May was also to point out – that if it was independent of the conditions of simple reproduction, it was also independent (at any rate in principle) of 'the context of the division of the economy into three branches'.[68]

It was this last point which Francis Seton took up in his magistral article on the transformation problem in the *Review of Economic Studies* in 1957.[69] Most of the previous writers on this subject, said Seton, had assumed that the economy was subdivided into three Departments producing capital goods, wage goods, and luxury goods respectively, 'with the corollary that every physical commodity was not merely unequivocally identifiable as the product of one or other of these, but that its ultimate use in the economy was

[63] Winternitz, *op. cit.*, p. 279.
[64] K. May, 'Value and Price of Production: A Note on Winternitz' Solution', *Economic Journal*, **58**, 1948, pp. 596–9.
[65] *Ibid.*, p. 596.
[66] Cf. above, p. 107.
[67] Above, p. 101.
[68] K. May, *op. cit.*, p. 598.
[69] F. Seton, "The 'Transformation Problem'", *Review of Economic Studies*, **XXIV**, pp. 149–60.

equally invariable, and predetermined by its department of origin'. Seton's purpose was to show, as he put it, that 'the most general n-fold subdivision of the economy, in which each product may be distributed among *several* or *all* possible uses is equally acceptable – and easily handled – as a premiss for the required proof'.[70]

In Seton's n-industry model, k_{ij} represents the quantity of the product of industry j (reckoned in terms of embodied labour – i.e., of Marxian values) which enters as an input into the product of industry i;[71] $p_1, p_2, p_3, \ldots, p_n$ represent, as before, the price–value coefficients; and π represents the ratio of profit to total *output* (rather than, as in most of the models considered above, to total *cost*).[72] The relevant equations in price terms are then as follows:[73]

$$(k_{11}p_1 + k_{12}p_2 + k_{13}p_3 \ldots + k_{1n}p_n) + \pi(a_1 p_1) = a_1 p_1$$
$$(k_{21}p_1 + k_{22}p_2 + k_{23}p_3 \ldots + k_{2n}p_n) + \pi(a_2 p_2) = a_2 p_2$$
$$(k_{31}p_1 + k_{32}p_2 + k_{33}p_3 \ldots + k_{3n}p_n) + \pi(a_3 p_3) = a_3 p_3$$
$$\vdots \qquad \vdots \qquad \vdots \qquad \qquad \vdots \qquad \vdots \qquad \vdots$$
$$(k_{n1}p_1 + k_{n2}p_2 + k_{n3}p_3 \ldots + k_{nn}p_n) + \pi(a_n p_n) = a_n p_n.$$

From these n equations, it turns out,[74] one can derive solutions for π and for the *ratios* of the n prices (i.e., p_1/p_n, p_2/p_n, etc.), but in order to determine the *absolute* prices one must either reduce the number of unknowns by one (which can be done by postulating that one of the ps is equal to unity, thereby in effect using it, as Bortkiewicz did, as the *numéraire*), or provide an additional equation (which can be done by postulating, for example, that the sum of the prices is equal to the sum of the values, or that the sum of the profits is equal to the sum of the surplus values). Since all these postulates in effect involve 'the selection of a definite aggregate (or other characteristic) of the value system . . . *which is to remain invariant to the transformation into prices*', Seton nicknames them 'invariance postulates'.[75] His conclusion is that 'there does not seem to be an objective basis for choosing any particular invariance postulate in preference to all the others, *and to that extent the transformation problem may be said to fall short of complete determinacy*'.[76] It remains true, however, as Seton says, that his analysis has fully vindicated

[70] *Ibid.*, p. 150.
[71] The inputs are assumed (as later with Sraffa) to include not only means of production but also the wage-goods consumed by the workers.
[72] Cf. *ibid.*, p. 151, note 1: "For algebraic convenience we define the 'profit ratio' as the ratio of profit to *total value of output*. Obviously π will be equal in all industries if and only if the Marxian 'rate of profit' (profit ÷ total *cost*) is similarly equalized."
[73] I have made some slight alterations in the symbols and in the way in which the equations are formulated, once again for the sake of comparability.
[74] As one might intuitively have expected from the analyses of the three-industry case considered above, pp. 110–15.
[75] Seton, *op. cit.*, p. 152.
[76] *Ibid.*, p. 153.

'the internal consistency and determinacy of Marx's conception of the transformation process, and the formal inferences he drew from it'.[77]

VI

What can one say about the question, raised so sharply by Seton, of the proper choice of an 'invariance postulate'? Let us first note that for some writers the question of a choice does not arise at all: like Brand, they demand 'all or nothing'. M. C. Howard and J. E. King, for example,[78] claim that the important thing for Marx was that the 'rate of profit' should be identical in both the value and the price systems.[79] This will only be so, they argue, if the sum of the prices equals the sum of the values, *and* (at the same time) the sum of the profits equals the sum of the surplus values. In addition, the authors seem to suggest, the method of transformation must be such that when it is applied to a value schema obeying the rules of simple reproduction, the resulting price schema must also obey these rules. The authors then demonstrate that these conditions will be simultaneously fulfilled only in a very special case – that of a Bortkiewicz-type schema in which the organic composition of the capital in Department III is equal to the social average.[80] Since there is no *a priori* reason why the luxury goods industry in the real world should possess this characteristic, they argue, Marx's attempt to show that prices can be derived from values must be written off as a complete failure, and at any rate so far as the theory of price and profit is concerned we must desert Marx for Sraffa.

Maybe we must – but not for this particular reason. The important thing for Marx, surely, was not that the 'rate of profit' should remain invariant to the transformation,[81] but that the sum of the profits should be equal to, or in some meaningful sense derivable from, the predetermined sum of the surplus values.[82] It is true, of course, that in Marx's own rather crude method of transformation the redistribution of the sum of the surplus values resulted in a situation in which the sum of the prices did come out equal to the sum of the values. It is also true that Marx in one place suggested that even if inputs as well as outputs were transformed, the redistribution of the

---

[77] *Ibid.*, p. 160. Seton adds a *caveat* here to the effect that the same can certainly not be said of 'the body of the underlying doctrine, without which the whole problem loses much of its substance and *raison d'être*'.

[78] M. C. Howard and J. E. King, *The Political Economy of Marx* (Longman, Harlow, 1975), pp. 143–9. See also pp. 26–32 of the introduction by Howard and King to *The Economics of Marx* (Penguin Books, London, 1976), a volume of readings edited by them. The fact that I am critical of their attitude on the particular issue of the transformation problem does *not* mean that I am critical of these two books as a whole: on the contrary, I think very highly of them indeed.

[79] i.e., that the ratio of total surplus value to total capital in the value system should be equal to the ratio of total profit to total capital in the price system.

[80] Cf. above, p. 114, [59].

[81] I can find no textual evidence whatever, in Marx's own writings, to suggest that this was in fact the important thing for him.

[82] Cf. above, pp. 106–7.

sum of the surplus values would still result in a situation of this type.[83] He was in error here; but if this error had been pointed out to him he would, I think, have emphasized that the really essential thing he was trying to say was that the magnitude of profit was not determined by 'competition' or 'demand and supply'; that it was actually determined by the conditions of production, independently of and in a sense prior to prices; and that the only thing competition did was to redistribute this prior concrete magnitude in accordance with the capitalist rules of the game. The equality of the sum of the prices and the sum of the values, I think he would have admitted, was not in fact a necessary condition of the transformation, but merely a possible result of it in certain special cases.

The question of the proper choice of an 'invariance postulate', then, *pace* Howard and King, still remains on the agenda; and for the reasons just stated the equality of the sum of the prices and the sum of the values must probably be ruled out. The most likely-looking contender, therefore, would seem at first sight to be the equality of the sum of the profits and the sum of the surplus values. But it could I think be argued that the incorporation of this postulate in a Seton-type model, where the input/output relationships over the economy as a whole are fully specified, would in a sense be redundant, since the basic equations already imply the *kind* of relationship between total profits and total surplus values which Marx had in mind when he postulated their arithmetical equality in his crude model. For the sake of simplicity, let us take a three-sector model where the input/output relationships in value terms are as follows:[84]

$$k_{11}+k_{12}+k_{13}+s_1=a_1$$
$$k_{21}+k_{22}+k_{23}+s_2=a_2$$
$$k_{31}+k_{32}+k_{33}+s_3=a_3.$$
$$e_1 \quad e_2 \quad e_3$$

Here we show in each row not only the inputs into the industry concerned according to origin, but also, at the end, the residual surplus (or surplus value) *s* accruing to it. And in each column we show not only the outputs of the industry concerned according to destination, but also, at the bottom, the value of the remaining portion *e* of the industry's output which is available for consumption by the capitalists or (since we are not making any assumption about the conditions of reproduction) for investment by them. From the method of construction of the model it necessarily follows that

$$e_1+e_2+e_3=s_1+s_2+s_3.$$

When we transform the model from value terms into price terms, the basic equations become[85]

[83] See above, p. 109.
[84] This approach was suggested by the discussion in Seton, *op. cit.*, p. 150.
[85] I revert here – once again for the sake of comparability – to the symbol *r* for the average rate of profit, and to the method of presenting the equations with which we started.

$$(k_{11}p_1 + k_{12}p_2 + k_{13}p_3)(1+r) = a_1p_1$$
$$(k_{21}p_1 + k_{22}p_2 + k_{23}p_3)(1+r) = a_2p_2$$
$$(k_{31}p_1 + k_{32}p_2 + k_{33}p_3)(1+r) = a_3p_3.$$

Adding up these equations and cancelling out, we see that whatever the actual solutions for the unknowns are ultimately found to be, the sum of the profits will necessarily be equal to $e_1p_1 + e_2p_2 + e_3p_3$.

What one wonders is whether, for Marx, this might have been enough, given that $e_1 + e_2 + e_3 = s_1 + s_2 + s_3$, that a change in the magnitude of any of the ss will necessarily mean an equal change in the magnitude of the corresponding e, and that p_1, p_2, and p_3 are themselves functions of quantities specified in the value system. At these prices, the total profits received by the capitalists will just be sufficient to enable them to purchase the surplus product of the system, the total *value* of which will be equal to (and determined by) the total amount of surplus value which the system generates.

If one adopted this approach, one would of course still need an 'invariance postulate' in order to determine the *absolute* prices (as distinct from their ratios), but one would no longer be tempted to use the equality of the sum of the profits and the sum of the surplus values. The obvious procedure would be to postulate one of the ps as the *numéraire* and set it equal to unity, thus killing two birds with one stone – bringing 'money' into the picture (which has to be done at some stage, in one way or another), and making the system determinate.[86]

That is about as far as it seems to me to be worth while taking the transformation problem in the narrower sense – except, of course, that if we adopt the approach I have just outlined someone is bound to suggest that nothing would be lost, and perhaps a great deal gained, by reckoning the inputs and outputs not in *value* terms but in terms of physical units of the commodities themselves. But this leads us beyond our present bounds, and towards some of the debates on the transformation problem in the broader sense which are the subject of the next two essays.

[86] Mr David Laibman, in his article 'Values and Prices of Production: The Political Economy of the Transformation Problem' (*Science and Society*, Vol. XXXVII, 1973–4, pp. 404–36), has made a strong plea for accepting the rate of exploitation as the invariant linking the value and price systems. I have no ideological objection to this, but I cannot find an atom of evidence in Marx's own writings that this was what he himself had in mind.

VI

From Values to Prices:
Was Marx's Journey
Really Necessary?[1]

I

This essay is concerned with some of the issues which have been raised in the current controversies over the so-called 'transformation problem' – i.e., the problem of the conversion or transformation of Marx's Volume I 'values' and 'surplus values' into his Volume III 'prices of production' and 'profits'. During the last few years this seemingly rather esoteric problem has assumed a degree of importance which those of us who dabbled in it in the 1940s and 1950s never dreamed possible. For most of us in those innocent days the problem presented itself as a purely formal one, and once it had been shown to be technically soluble we breathed a sigh of relief and turned our attention to higher things. But with the recent revival of interest in Marxian economics the whole question of the 'transformation problem' has come on to the agenda again. Every other journal that one opens these days seems to contain an article on some aspect of the 'transformation problem'; symposia have been conducted on it in a number of countries; and there have been colloquia on it in publications as far apart from one another ideologically as the *Journal of Economic Literature* and the *Bulletin of the Conference of Socialist Economists*. The meaning of the term itself has been considerably broadened, and everyone now treats the issues involved as immensely serious: the particular attitude one takes towards them is widely supposed to be indicative of one's position on a whole number of other apparently quite unrelated questions. The debates have become inextricably mixed up with those on Sraffa's commodity production models, the 'capital controversy', and the so-called 'Ricardo–Marx tradition' in the history of economic thought, forming a witch's brew of considerable potency which Samuelson periodically emerges to sniff and stir.

[1] This essay owes its origin to a paper given at the 1975 conference of the Association of University Teachers of Economics at Sheffield University. It was published in amended form, under the title *Whatever Happened to the Labour Theory of Value?*, in the volume of the proceedings of the conference (*Essays in Economic Analysis*, edited by M. J. Artis and A. R. Nobay, Cambridge University Press, 1976). In the present version I have made a number of additional amendments, but some of the colloquial flavour of the original paper has been allowed to remain.

In this essay my aim is not to analyse these recent contributions, but rather to steer my way through them as quickly as possible in order to get around to one of the most important of the problems which the debates have brought into relief: the problem of why Marx thought it necessary to start with 'values'. Why did he think that *anything* had to be 'transformed' in order to arrive at the equilibrium prices characteristic of competitive capitalism? And if something *did* have to be 'transformed' in order to arrive at them, why did it have to be these mysterious, non-observable, Volume I 'values'?

The nature of Marx's transformation operation has been fully described in the previous essay, and a brief recapitulation is all that is necessary here. Marx started off in Volume I of *Capital* with a definition[2] of the 'value' of a commodity as the total quantity of labour which was 'socially necessary' in order to produce it, and proceeded with his analysis of the origin of 'surplus value' (the unique source of profit, as he envisaged it) on the assumption that the prices at which commodities sold on the market would normally be proportionate to their 'values' in this sense.[3] Then, much later, in Volume III of *Capital*, he endeavoured to bring his analysis into closer contact with reality by means of an operation which he described as the 'transformation' of surplus values into profits and (consequentially) of 'values' into prices of production. The essence of the matter, as Marx saw it, was that the total amount of surplus value generated over the economy as a whole was redistributed ('by competition') among the different industries in accordance with the ratio which the capital employed in each industry bore to the total capital employed in the economy, so that the *rate* of profit was equalized. To make this possible, the prices of all commodities (except those produced by capitals with an organic composition equal to the social average) had to adjust, diverging from 'values' to the extent necessary to equalize the rate of profit on capital over the economy as a whole. These divergences of prices from 'values', however, did not in Marx's view mean that the 'law of value' put forward in Volume I was no longer valid. For, as Marx put it in one place,[4]

if one did not take the definition of value as the basis, the *average profit*, and therefore also the [prices of production], would be purely imaginary and untenable. The equalisation of the surplus-values in different spheres of production does not affect the absolute size of this total surplus-value; but merely alters its *distribution* among the different spheres of production. The *determination of this surplus-value* itself, however, only arises out of

[2] To use the word 'definition' here is of course to beg a number of important interpretative questions. Marx himself, however, had no inhibitions about using the word. When he first introduced his notion of 'value' in Volume I of *Capital*, he went on immediately to speak of 'value as defined above'. See also his letters to Engels of 2 April 1858 and 8 January 1868.
[3] Once again this statement begs a number of questions, but it seems to correspond fairly closely to what Marx meant by the assumption, made explicitly several times in Volume I, that 'prices = values'.
[4] Marx, *Theories of Surplus Value*, Part II (Lawrence and Wishart, London, 1969), p. 190.

the determination of value by labour-time. Without this, the average profit is the average of *nothing*, pure fancy. And it could then equally well be 1000 per cent or 10 per cent.

The particular point about Marx's method of transformation upon which most attention has been concentrated is that in the arithmetical tables which he used to illustrate his argument he transformed only outputs, and not inputs, from values into prices. He recognized clearly enough the importance in the real world of the interdependence of inputs and outputs; he recognized, too, that the existence of this interdependence meant that his arithmetical illustrations were unrealistic; but he never got round to filling the consequent gap in his analysis with anything other than rather vague generalities. For a 'Marxian' transformation to be fully valid, obviously enough, the values of particular commodities must be transformed into prices not only when they appear on the output side of the equations but also when they appear on the input side – and transformed at the same rate, too, so that the price–value ratios are uniform in the case of each commodity. But if you in fact imposed this as a condition, would you or could you obtain a determinate solution for prices and the rate of profit? This was the form in which the 'transformation problem' usually presented itself to my generation. There was a certain amount of debate about it, but it was not too long before everyone was (or appeared to be) satisfied that the problem was really a very trivial one indeed. The three major landmarks in the process of discovery were the contributions by Bortkiewicz, Winternitz, and Seton, which have been surveyed in the previous essay.

At this point in the story, it may be appropriate if I introduce (with due apologies) an element of autobiography. In 1956 I published a modest piece on the transformation problem,[5] which took me a long time to write, but which turned out to contain two or three rather egregious errors. These errors were taken up by Seton and exposed (in the nicest possible way, of course) in his article – which seemed indeed to have been in part inspired by them. I comforted myself with the reflection that there were more ways than one of going down in history, and, since it seemed to me that Seton had solved the transformation problem once and for all, I turned my attention to other things. It was not until 1971 that I realized that the issue was by no means as dead as I had thought. In that year Samuelson published a very long and involved piece on the transformation problem,[6] in which he had the bad taste to resurrect this old article of mine and commend it to his readers. Worse than this, he had the temerity to fling out a challenge in one place in the article to 'Dobb and Meek' and in another to 'Marx and Meek'. To be placed *second* in each of these pairs was of course quite infuriating,

[5] It is reprinted in Ronald L. Meek, *Economics and Ideology and Other Essays* (Chapman and Hall, London, 1967), pp. 143 ff.
[6] P. A. Samuelson, 'Understanding the Marxian Notion of Exploitation: A Summary of the So-called Transformation Problem between Marxian Values and Competitive Prices', *Journal of Economic Literature*, **9**, 1971, pp. 399–431.

and I decided that I ought to give some attention to what had been and apparently still was going on in this field.

I found that a number of very curious things had been going on, and as the 1970s proceeded they became curiouser and curiouser. Seton, having already solved the transformation problem forwards, as it were, had joined with Morishima[7] to solve it backwards as well, just for good measure – an exercise which I could not help applauding, even if only as an acrobatic feat. Morishima then went on to demonstrate[8] that positive profits will be yielded if and only if there is positive surplus value in Marx's sense, and proclaimed this, with portentous capital letters, as the 'Fundamental Marxian Theorem', thereby implying (at any rate to one untutored and un-mathematical reader) that this was all that really mattered, and that attempts at the quantitative derivation of a specific rate of profit from a pool of surplus value of a determinate size were at the best merely of heuristic value. I was a little more worried about this, since it seemed to leave a great deal of Marxian economics, as I understood it, resting on a very slender pediment indeed – a pediment which I felt might collapse entirely if one were to drop two or three of Morishima's less realistic assumptions. But I was cheered by the fact that at about the same time a number of other writers were beginning to ask what Marx's reproduction schemes, and his law of the falling tendency of the rate of profit, would look like if one redid his analysis in terms of prices of production instead of in terms of values – which seemed to me a very useful question to ask.

During the last three or four years, the transformation problem seems to have become the focus of a rather bitter quarrel between two rival groups of radical economists – those who see Marx as having worked within a broad tradition or stream of thought with Ricardo at one end and Sraffa at the other, and those who see Marx as standing more or less outside this (and every other) stream of thought. Members of the latter group, so far as I can gather, usually tend to reject all the traditional methods of solving the transformation problem as being not only unacceptable but also un-necessary, and to anathematize them, along with Sraffa and all his wicked works, as 'neo-Ricardian'. In contrast, members of the former group usually tend to accept one or other of the traditional methods of solution (although for some of them a great deal seems to hang on choosing the *right* method from among the various alternatives), and to stress the strong analogy which they believe exists between Marx's work and Sraffa's in this respect. This debate has become very fierce, particularly when it impinges on the capital controversy (which of course it frequently does); and the word 'logical' is used so very often by the participants that one senses immediately that religion is heavily involved. Personally, although I have some sympathy for both points of view, and am no longer at all religious

[7] M. Morishima and F. Seton, 'Aggregation in Leontief Matrices and the Labour Theory of Value', *Econometrica*, **29**, 1961, pp. 203–20.
[8] M. Morishima, *Marx's Economics* (Cambridge University Press, 1973).

about such matters, I find myself leaning much more towards the 'neo-Ricardians' than towards their critics. I think that it *is* useful to talk in terms of a broad Ricardo–Marx–Sraffa tradition or stream of thought, in which the question of the relation between the social surplus and the rate of profit has always been (and still is) a central theme; and I shall be returning to this point in a later essay.

But having said all this, one still has an uneasy feeling that in this great whirlwind of debate the really essential question is in danger of being blown away. This question, as I have already said, is simply whether Marx's journey from Volume I to Volume III was really necessary. Why, to put the question in another way, did Marx start with the assumption that commodities sold 'at their values' when he was very well aware right from the beginning that in actual fact (at any rate under competitive capitalism) they sold at prices which in most cases diverged widely from their values? And why did he think it necessary, in his analysis of the determination of these real-world competitive prices, to *derive* them from values by means of this rather odd transformation process?

II

Let me first of all try to deal with some of the less convincing answers which are sometimes given to this question.[9] Some writers, particularly those who are anxious to 'sociologize' Marx, are apt to say that Marx was not really interested in prices, and that his theory of value was not intended to explain the level of prices at all: it was rather the embodiment or crystallization of a basic methodological principle. And there is of course something in this. It is probably true that Marx was not *very* interested in prices, or at any rate in the prices of individual commodities as distinct from those of broad groups of commodities. And it is also true, and in my opinion very important indeed, that his theory of value *did* embody or crystallize a basic methodological principle – the principle that conditions of exchange should properly be analysed in terms of conditions of production. But there is surely little doubt that he wanted his theory of value not only to embody this principle, but also to do another and more familiar job as well – the same job which theories of value had always been employed to do in economics, that is, to determine prices. The prices of production of commodities, Marx says, 'are not only determined by the values of the commodities and confirm the law of value instead of contradicting it', but, moreover, their very existence 'can be comprehended only on the basis of value and its laws, and becomes a meaningless absurdity without that premise'.[10] When one recalls the frequency of statements like this in *Theories of Surplus Value*, and when one recalls the strenuous efforts that Marx made in Volume III of *Capital* to

[9] Cf. W. J. Baumol, "The Transformation of Values: What Marx 'Really' Meant (An Interpretation)", *Journal of Economic Literature*, **12**, 1974, pp. 53–5.
[10] *Theories of Surplus Value*, Part III (Lawrence and Wishart, London, 1972), pp. 82–3.

show that prices of production, although they normally diverged from values, did so in an orderly, law-governed manner, and that they could in fact be said to be ultimately derived from or determined by values, one must surely come to the conclusion that this first attempt at an answer to our question simply will not stand up.

Other writers have argued that in Volume I, for the sake of simplifying his analysis and as a kind of first approximation to reality, Marx assumed that organic compositions of capital were equal in all industries – which, if it were true, would of course mean that under competitive conditions prices would tend to coincide exactly with values. Then in Volume III, they argue, he proceeded to a second approximation in which he dropped this initial simplifying assumption and demonstrated that the modifications which resulted were of a relatively minor character. But once again this just will not stand up to a scrutiny of the texts. Throughout Volume I Marx very carefully and repeatedly sets out the simplifying assumptions he is making; and so far as I can see there is not a single word anywhere which suggests that included among these was this alleged assumption about equal organic compositions of capital. There are, indeed, a number of positive statements to the contrary, as when he says very specifically:

On the basis of the same mode of social production, the division of capital into constant and variable differs in different branches of production, and within the same branch of production, too, this relation changes with changes in the technical conditions and in the social combinations of the processes of production.[11]

Nor does this interpretation seem to me to tally with Marx's insistence in Volume III that the analysis of prices must not simply be juxtaposed to, or compared with, the analysis of values, but rather in some meaningful sense derived from it.

In what other direction, then, should we look for an answer to our question? Joan Robinson says somewhere that if we want to understand what a theorist is really getting at we should look first at the doctrines he is seeking to oppose. And in the field of price theory Marx leaves us in no doubt at all about what he is seeking to oppose. He speaks again and again about the way in which bourgeois economists are 'blinded by competition'; how this blindness prevents them from penetrating through the external (competitive) disguise into the internal (exploitative) essence; and how for this reason they are deluded into propounding various apologetic theories of price which at the best are mere 'demand and supply' and/or 'adding-up' theories and at worst imply that profit and rent are in some way 'produced' by capital and land respectively. Even Smith and Ricardo, whom Marx always regarded as the 'best representatives' of classical political economy,[12] were in his opinion victims of this blindness, at any rate up to a point. Smith

---

[11] *Capital*, Vol. I (Foreign Languages Publishing House, Moscow, 1954), p. 306.
[12] *Ibid.*, p. 81, footnote.

starts off on the right foot by examining the value of commodities and deriving wages and profit from this value, but then 'takes the opposite course, and seeks on the contrary to deduce the value of commodities (from which he has deduced wages and profit) by adding together the natural prices of wages, profit and rent'.[13] Ricardo, too, although displaying nothing like the same naivety as Smith, is accused by Marx of postulating profit at the average rate as 'something pre-existent which, therefore, even plays a part in his determination of *value*'.[14] And the inadequacy of Smith and Ricardo on these issues in Marx's view was as nothing compared with that of their 'vulgar' successors.

The basic reason why Marx felt this kind of approach to be potentially apologetic was simply that profit on capital at the average rate is by definition related to the *total* capital employed, rather than to the part of that capital which is spent on the employment of labour. Thus if one *starts* with profit at the average rate (i.e., treats it as 'something pre-existent'), and then puts it forward as one of the constituent determinants of price, the crucial causal connection which Marx believed to exist between profit and the exploitation of labour is bound to be obscured.[15] If one is anxious not to obscure this connection but to reveal and emphasize it, Marx argued, one must begin by abstracting from those aspects of the competitive process which disguise the exploitative origin of profit. The best way of proceeding was to start by analysing the way in which, as a result of the class monopoly possessed by the capitalists, the work-force in each industry is compelled 'to do more work than the narrow round of its own life-wants prescribes',[16] thereby producing for the capitalists in the industry concerned a kind of free net gain, or surplus value, the magnitude of which will depend upon the *amount* of this extra work which the work-force is compelled to do. This process of the creation of surplus value was conceived by Marx as operating independently of, and in a sense prior to, the process of competition between capitalists in different industries which resulted in the formation of the final equilibrium prices of commodities.

Eventually, of course, the competitive disguise has to be put on again, and the process of the formation of these final equilibrium prices adequately explained. The essence of Marx's explanation, as we know, was that the total sum of the individual surplus values generated over the economy as a whole was redistributed among the capitalists in the different industries (through the mechanism of the competitive process) in such a way as to equalize the rate of profit – which meant that some capitalists would finish up with more surplus value than their own workers had produced and others would finish up with less.

[13] *Theories of Surplus Value*, Part I (Foreign Languages Publishing House, Moscow, n.d.), p. 95.
[14] *Ibid.*, Part II, p. 434.
[15] See the interesting discussion of this point in *Theories of Surplus Value*, Part III, pp. 482–3.
[16] *Capital*, Vol. I, p. 309.

It was vitally necessary, then, Marx believed, if the illusions created by competition were to be fully dispelled, to postulate the existence of a prior concrete magnitude – i.e., roughly, a magnitude which was independent of market prices – which could plausibly be regarded as constituting the ultimate source of profit and rent and as limiting the aggregate level of these revenues.[17] In his system, this prior concrete magnitude is compounded out of the *values* of commodities. The commodity-value, as he puts it, after deducting the value of used-up constant capital, is the 'original unit' which is divided up into wages, profit, and rent.[18] And after wages have been accounted for (at a rate which is conceived to be determined by social and physiological considerations), there remains the *surplus value*, that all-important magnitude which constitutes the ultimate source of profit and rent, and which is redistributed by competition in a way which at the same time equalizes the rate of profit and transforms the 'values' of commodities into the 'prices of production' at which they actually tend to sell. If one did not approach the problem in this way, Marx said, there was a grave danger that one would be misled into thinking that the levels of wages, profit, and rent (which of course assume 'mutually independent forms' as revenues) are each independently determined, and that 'the price of the commodities would then be formed by adding these three independent magnitudes together'.[19] This 'erroneous conception' completely obscures the exploitative origin of profit, which is of the very essence of capitalism; and the only way of avoiding this error, in Marx's opinion, was to start with *values*.

There is no doubt that this is part of the answer to our question, but in my view it is by no means the whole of it. *Given* the necessity, as Marx saw it, of postulating some kind of prior concrete magnitude which limited the aggregate level of class incomes, why exactly did he decide to constitute it of the 'values' of commodities – those 'values' at which he knew very well that commodities hardly ever in fact sold, at any rate in the economic system which he was primarily concerned to analyse? What *sense* does it make, to put the question in a more provocative way, to say that profit and rent are derived from, or paid out of, or limited by, the sum of those individual surplus values which Marx spoke of as being 'contained in the commodities',[20] but which (since the individual commodities were apparently never sold at their values, and the individual surplus values therefore never appropriated by their producers) can perhaps not too unfairly be described as abstract, unrealized, non-observable, or even imaginary quantities? And critics of Marx like Samuelson can give what they believe to be the turn of the screw at this point by arguing that Marx's procedure

[17] Marx's main discussion of this crucial point will be found in Chapter L of Vol. III of *Capital*, entitled 'Illusions Created by Competition'.
[18] *Capital*, Vol. III (Foreign Languages Publishing House, Moscow, 1959), p. 841.
[19] *Ibid.*, pp. 840–1.
[20] *Ibid.*, p. 839.

not only made no sense but was also quite unnecessary, since one can easily obtain the main results which Marx wanted to obtain – i.e., prices and the rate of profit uniquely determined, in a model in which it is assumed that profits are paid out of and limited by a pre-existent concrete social surplus – by using commodity production models *à la* Sraffa.

Why then was it that Marx, who was certainly no fool, believed firmly that 'starting with values' not only enabled one to emphasize the exploitative origin of profit, but also made perfectly good sense? This is a question for which a direct answer must be found. And now that we have permitted Samuelson to get his foot inside the door, as it were, we must also before we conclude try to answer another question: is it in fact possible to do Marx's job, and perhaps to do it better, on the basis of Sraffian commodity production models? Let us deal with these two questions – the first of which is in a sense very old and the second very new – in order.

III

The *main* reason why Marx thought that starting with values made good sense, I would suggest, has to be sought in certain features of his economic methodology. Marx's chief concern in his economic work, speaking very broadly, was with the analysis of what he called *the system of commodity production* – 'commodities' in his terminology being goods which were produced for sale or exchange on some kind of market by individual producers or groups of producers operating more or less independently of one another. The system of commodity production, as Marx conceived it, constituted the 'second great form' or 'second stage' in the development of society. It grew up within, and assisted in the eventual dissolution of, the 'first social forms', which were based (by way of contrast) on 'relations of personal dependence'. It underwent a process of internal development, assuming different forms and increasing in extent, and eventually reached its apogee under capitalism. And it was destined, sooner rather than later, to give way to the 'third stage' in the development of society, which would be based not on commodity relations but on socialist relations. This stadial scheme, which of course cuts across the other more familiar one of which Marx also made extensive use, is very clearly sketched out in the *Grundrisse*,[21] and there are many echoes of it in Marx's later economic work.

Now the particular type of economic organization upon which Marx concentrated most of his attention was of course *capitalism*. But, looking at capitalism as he did in the perspective of the broad stadial scheme just outlined, he believed that it was very important to visualize it first and foremost as a *particular form of the system of commodity production* – that form in which the great majority of products were commodities and the great majority of commodities were products of capital, and in which the direct aim of capital was the production of surplus value through the exploitation

---

[21] Marx, *Grundrisse* (translated by M. Nicolaus, Penguin Books, London, 1973), p. 158.

of labour power, which had itself become a commodity. 'Already implicit in the commodity', wrote Marx, 'and even more so in the commodity as a product of capital, is the materialization of the social features of production and the personification of the material foundations of production, which characterize the entire capitalist mode of production'.[22] Thus Marx believed that an analysis of *the commodity as such* was a necessary prerequisite of the analysis of capitalism. The logical starting-point, as he saw it, had to be an analysis of 'simple' (i.e. non-capitalist, or a-capitalist) commodity production and circulation; and the subsequent analysis of *capitalist* commodity production and circulation could not just be juxtaposed to this, but in some way or other had to be *developed out of it*. It was this methodological consideration, I think, which was in large part responsible for the way in which Marx posed the problem of the determination of prices. The great question here, Marx said in effect, was what happened to the 'law of value' appropriate to simple commodity exchange when one passed from this to capitalist commodity exchange. In other words, what kind of changes does the mode of price determination undergo when the simple commodity becomes capitalistically modified? It is important to note that there was nothing particularly 'metaphysical' or un-British about this way of posing the problem: up to a point, Marx was fairly obviously carrying on here in the tradition of Smith and Ricardo. And he was also carrying on in the same tradition when he 'started with values' – i.e., when he postulated that under simple commodity exchange prices would tend to be proportionate to quantities of embodied labour.

One must immediately add here, however, that in the case of Marx this procedure, although it assumed a logical form, also had a significant 'historical' dimension, which was present only in embryo (if indeed at all) in the work of Smith and Ricardo. It may or may not be useful to describe Marx's *general* economic method as 'logical–historical' in character (as I have myself ventured to do in the past); but there is surely little doubt that there was a 'historical' as well as a 'logical' side to his analysis of value, and in particular to his analysis of the transformation of values into prices of production. In other words, he regarded this transformation not simply as something which one worked out in one's mind, in the form of a chain of logical propositions, but also as something which, in a certain sense, had happened in history. There are several places in Marx's work in which this question is directly broached – for example Chapter X of Volume III of *Capital*, where, in the context of his treatment of the transformation problem, a very interesting and extended discussion includes the statement that 'it is quite appropriate to regard the values of commodities as not only theoretically but also historically *prius* to the prices of production'. This applies, Marx goes on to explain, to conditions in which the labourer owns his own means of production, and also to the guild organization of handicrafts, so long as the mobility of capital between different branches of production is low.[23] The fact that Engels, in his famous Supplement to Volume III, was somewhat incautious in commenting on this passage[24] should not lead us to underestimate its significance, particularly since there are at least half a dozen passages of similar import in Marx's work. Nor should it lead us to believe that Engels never said anything sensible on this issue. He did – and by no means least in his preface to Volume III, where he speaks as follows of Marx's economic method and its application to the analysis of values and prices:

> It is self-evident that where things and their interrelations are conceived, not as fixed, but as changing, their mental images, the ideas, are likewise subject to change and transformation; and they are not encapsulated in rigid definitions, but are developed in their historical or logical process of formation. This makes clear, of course, why in the beginning of his first book Marx proceeds from the simple production of commodities as the historical premise, ultimately to arrive from this basis to capital – why he proceeds from the simple commodity instead of a logically and historically secondary commodity – from an already capitalistically modified commodity.[25]

What Engels is saying here, to put it in a nutshell, is that Marx conceived the state of 'simple' commodity production with which he started not only as non-capitalist or a-capitalist, but also, in a certain sense, as *pre*-capitalist.

One has to be very careful here, of course. If one tries to justify Marx's procedure in 'starting with values' by saying that his analysis had a historical as well as a logical dimension, one runs the risk of getting the reply that this is really no justification at all, since there never in fact was an identifiable historical period characterized by the fact that commodities sold at their values. I think, however, that such a reply would embody a misunderstanding, if not a trivialization, of the rather sophisticated concept of historical stages which Marx employed. And I think, too, that such a reply would beg one of the most interesting questions of all – which is, what *kind* of conformity between logic and history would it be necessary to demonstrate in order to help justify Marx's proceeding from values to prices, rather than the other way round or not at all? These problems, which involve issues of considerable interest and importance, are the subject of the next essay in the present volume.

IV

The final question which I wish to discuss in this essay is that of whether it is in fact possible to do Marx's job, and perhaps even to do it better, on the

---

[23] *Ibid.*, Vol. III, p. 174.
[24] I am mainly referring here to Engels's statement, at the end of his discussion of this question in the *Supplement*, that 'the law of value . . . has prevailed during a period of from five to seven thousand years' (*Capital*, Vol. III, p. 876).
[25] *Capital*, Vol. III, pp. 13–14.

basis of Sraffian commodity production models. It is proper for me to declare an interest here, since I have already attempted to provide an affirmative answer with the aid of a set of five Marxian–Sraffian commodity production models.[26] Three of these models are in fact Sraffa's own: all that I personally have done is to add two other similar ones and to link the sequence of five together with a kind of logical–historical analysis similar to that employed by Marx. We begin with a pre-capitalist subsistence economy (model 1), which eventually becomes capable of producing, and does actually produce, a surplus product (model 2). A number of separate groups of capitalists now emerge, each taking over one of the industries in the economy and appropriating the whole of the surplus produced there as profit (model 3). We then assume that as a result of competition between the capitalists, and the consequent migration of capital from one industry to another in search of the highest profit, the rate of profit on capital is equalized over the economy as a whole (model 4). Finally, we assume that the workers combine and force the capitalists to return some of the surplus to them (model 5). Essentially, the models consist of a series of sets of input–output equations expressing the conditions of production in each industry in the economy, which determine mutually and simultaneously the prices of all the commodities concerned and also (where appropriate) the level of the average rate of profit.[27] Or, looking at the models from another point of view, we can say that they demonstrate the way in which the mode of price and income determination changes as we imagine ourselves proceeding upwards in five successive logical–historical stages from a pre-capitalist subsistence economy at the bottom to an advanced capitalist surplus economy at the top.

In Sraffian commodity production models, of course, the inputs and outputs are not expressed in terms of the values (in embodied labour units) of the commodities concerned, but rather in terms of the quantities (in physical units) of these commodities themselves. The use of these models may therefore worry some Marxists (and others) for whom the word 'labour' – and even more the words 'labour theory of value' – still have a kind of halo over them, and for whom the notion that profit 'resolves itself into a surplus value created by labour', or represents 'a deduction from the produce of labour', still appears as the whole essence of the matter. But certain grim realities have to be faced. First, if the technical difficulties standing in the way of the reduction of inputs to quantities of (dated) labour are really as great as Sraffa maintains,[28] then we just do not have any option: whether we like it or not, we simply *must* replace embodied labour models with

[26] Ronald L. Meek, *Studies in the Labour Theory of Value* (2nd edition, Lawrence and Wishart, London, 1973), pp. xxxii ff.
[27] Strictly speaking, 'profit' in the technical sense appears only in models 3, 4, and 5. In model 3 there are in effect different rates of profit in each industry; and in model 5 the rate of profit (and of course the prices) are indeterminate unless we postulate that the wage is known.
[28] P. Sraffa, *Production of Commodities by Means of Commodities* (Cambridge University Press, 1960), pp. 58–9 and 67–8.

commodity production models. Second, the notion that profit is produced exclusively by living labour, or that it is 'a deduction from the produce of labour', does not possess a great deal of scientific substance. If you *define* input and output as products of labour (or, to put it another way, if you decide to *measure* input and output in terms of labour), then obviously whenever there is a surplus of output over input its exclusive source will appear to be labour.[29] We should not worry too much, then, I suggest, if the models we use do not enable us to make statements of this rather unsatisfactory kind about exploitation.

But let us be careful not to concede too much. Obviously we must be able to make statements of *some* kind about exploitation, and they must be statements which go to the heart of the matter. For Marx himself, the heart of the matter undoubtedly lay in the fact (already mentioned) that the work-force in a capitalist economy, as a result of the class monopoly possessed by its employers, is compelled 'to do more work than the narrow round of its own life-wants prescribes'. It is true, I think, that if one drops this one drops Marxism; and it is also true that there is nothing in Sraffa's models of a surplus economy, as they stand, which *clearly* implies that such a state of affairs exists.[30] But I cannot see that we run any great ideological danger if we take Sraffa's models as constituting the general technical basis (as it were) of our analysis, and where necessary simply specify any additional datum that may be required.

Anyone who feels that such a procedure is objectionable should perhaps ponder on the fact that *this is very much the kind of thing which Marx himself did*. In the important but little-read Chapter XVI of Volume I of *Capital*, Marx emphasized that there is a significant sense – even if only a 'very general' one – in which surplus value rests on a natural basis:

> If the labourer wants all his time to produce the necessary means of subsistence for himself and his race, he has no time left in which to work gratis for others. Without a certain degree of productiveness in his labour, he has no such superfluous time at his disposal; without such superfluous time, no surplus-labour, and therefore no capitalists, no slave-owners, no feudal lords, in one word, no class of large proprietors.[31]

Here, in effect, Marx is outlining a simple 'model' of an economy in which the natural and technological conditions are such that the production of a surplus product, and therefore the appropriation of this product by one or another 'class of large proprietors', is *possible*. But will the potential surplus product in fact be produced? If it is produced, will it in fact be appropriated by such a class, or will it be consumed by the direct producers themselves? And if it is in fact appropriated by such a class, which class will it be and how will it manage to get away with it? To go from the *possible* to the *real*, in

[29] Cf. R. Rowthorn, 'Neo-Classicism, Neo-Ricardianism, and Marxism', *New Left Review*, **86**, 1974, p. 82.
[30] Cf. *ibid.*, pp. 84–5.
[31] *Capital*, Vol. I, p. 511.

other words, requires in every case the specification of a particular institutional datum.[32] In my own series of models, as in Marx's, a different institutional datum is specified for each. After the production of a surplus product becomes technically possible, I assume that it is in fact produced, but that at first it is consumed by the direct producers.[33] Then the crucial change occurs: a capitalist class emerges, and manages to appropriate the surplus product for itself by dispossessing the direct producers of their means of production, reducing their wages to subsistence level, and using its monopoly of the ownership of capital to force them to 'work gratis' for it during their 'superfluous time'. If this is not exploitation in the true Marxian sense, then I do not know what is.

With the specification where necessary of the appropriate institutional datum, then, and with remarkably little modification and elaboration, a sequence of Sraffian models can be made to do essentially the same job which Marx's labour theory of value was employed to do. We can start, as Marx did, with the postulation of a prior concrete magnitude which limits the levels of profit and rent. We can adopt the same kind of view about the order and direction of determination of the variables in the system as Marx did. Up to a point, the same kind of quantitative predictions about the relation between price ratios and embodied labour ratios can (if we wish) be made; and the analysis based on the models can readily be framed (again if we wish) in logical–historical terms. The same kind of scope can be left for the influence of social and institutional factors in the distribution of income; and the transformation problem (or its analogue) can be solved in passing, as it were, without any fuss whatever. In the light of all this, the fact that we do not need to tell our Sraffian equations anything at all about Marxian 'values' seems superbly irrelevant.

That is the end of what I have to say on this issue in the present essay, but it is only the beginning of what I think *ought* to be said. Given the perspective in which Marx viewed capitalism, the methodology which he thought appropriate to employ in its analysis, and the techniques which were available to him, he virtually *had* to 'start with values': he could do no other. With the aid of the new techniques which are available to us today, we can do Marx's job more effectively. But the great question is, of course, whether that job is still worth doing – in other words, whether Marx's perspective and methodology are still worth our serious attention today. It is high time that this question became the main focus of the debate.

[32] Cf. *ibid.*, p. 514: 'Favourable natural conditions alone, give us only the possibility, never the reality, of surplus-labour, nor, consequently, of surplus-value and a surplus-product.' Cf. also *Theories of Surplus Value*, Part II, p. 406: 'It is clear that though the existence of *surplus-labour* presupposes that the productivity of labour has reached a certain level, the mere *possibility* of this surplus-labour . . . does not in itself make it a *reality*. For this to occur, the labourer must first be *compelled* to work in excess of the [necessary] time, and this compulsion is exerted by capital.'

[33] Marx himself quite frequently postulates a situation of this kind: see, e.g., *Capital*, Vol. III, pp. 172–4.

VII

The 'Historical' Transformation Problem[1]

I

Why did Marx start in *Capital* with 'values', and then proceed at a later stage in his analysis to 'transform' these into the 'prices of production' at which commodities under competitive capitalism actually tended to sell? I have been suggesting for many years now that *part* of the answer to this crucial question lies in the fact that Marx's argument, although it took a logical form, was also intended to possess a significant 'historical' dimension. In putting forward this suggestion, I had never felt that I was saying anything particularly novel or original: I was as it were brought up on this line of thought, which I fondly imagined had been shared by several not unimportant commentators on Marx's work, including Engels, Böhm-Bawerk, Hilferding, and Lenin. In an article in the June 1975 issue of the *Economic Journal*,[2] however, I was taken to task for adopting this line by two economists, M. Morishima and G. Catephores, who claimed that the transformation problem in fact had no 'historical' dimension at all, and that 'for Marx . . . value was reduced to a logical category deprived of empirical historical reality'.[3] While I was not persuaded by them that my interpretation of Marx's theory had been essentially wrong or misleading, I felt that they *had* quite convincingly shown that I had not always expressed myself on this issue with a sufficient degree of clarity and consistency. The reformulation of my views in the present essay will, I hope, do something to remedy this.

II

Can Marx's *general* economic method be said to have been 'logical-historical' in character? My own affirmative answer to this question was

[1] This article is an extended (and slightly amended) version of a note which was originally published in the June 1976 issue of the *Economic Journal*, in the form of a reply to the article by Morishima and Catephores which is referred to below.
[2] M. Morishima and G. Catephores, "Is There an 'Historical Transformation Problem?'", *Economic Journal*, **85**, 1975, pp. 309–28.
[3] *Ibid.*, p. 317.

based first on *Capital* itself: the number of occasions on which Marx in that book goes out of his way to emphasize that a particular *logical* stage in his analysis corresponds to an actual *historical* stage in the development of the economy is really quite considerable; and all these instances taken together seemed to me indicative of a general method of thinking to which I felt that the term 'logical–historical' might not inappropriately be applied. My affirmative answer was also based, however, on some passages in Engels's remarkable review (1859) of Marx's *Critique of Political Economy*,[4] which still constitute the *locus classicus* on this vexed issue and which deserve extended quotation:

> Marx was and is the only one who could undertake the work of extracting from the Hegelian logic the nucleus containing Hegel's real discoveries in this field, and of establishing the dialectical method, divested of its idealist wrappings, in the simple form in which it becomes the only correct mode of conceptual evolution. The working out of the method which underlies Marx's critique of political economy is, we think, a result hardly less significant than the basic materialist conception.
>
> Even after the determination of the method, the critique of economics could still be arranged in two ways – historically or logically. Since in the course of history, as in its literary reflection, the evolution proceeds by and large from the simplest to the more complex relations, the historical development of political economy constituted a natural clue, which the critique could take as a point of departure, and then the economic categories would appear on the whole in the same order as in the logical exposition. This form seems to have the advantage of greater lucidity, for it traces the *actual* development, but in fact it would thus become, at most, more popular. History moves often in leaps and bounds and in a zigzag line, and as this would have to be followed throughout, it would mean not only that a considerable amount of material of slight importance would have to be included, but also that the train of thought would frequently have to be interrupted; it would, moreover, be impossible to write the history of economy without that of bourgeois society, and the task would thus become immense, because of the absence of all preliminary studies. The logical method of approach was therefore the only suitable one. This, however, is indeed nothing but the historical method, only stripped of the historical form and diverting chance occurrences. The point where this history begins must also be the starting point of the train of thought, and its further progress will be simply the reflection, in abstract and theoretically consistent form, of the historical course. Though the reflection is corrected, it is corrected in accordance with laws provided by the actual historical course, since each factor can be examined

---

[4] The translations from and references to this review below are to the version which appears as an appendix to the edition of Marx's *Critique of Political Economy* published by Lawrence and Wishart, London, 1971.

at the stage of development where it reaches its full maturity, its classical form.

With this method we begin with the first and simplest relation which is historically, actually available, thus in this context with the first economic relation to be found [the commodity relation – R.L.M.]. We analyse this relation. The fact that it is a *relation* already implies that it has two aspects which are *related to each other*. Each of these aspects is examined separately; this reveals the nature of their mutual behaviour, their reciprocal action. Contradictions will emerge demanding a solution. But since we are not examining an abstract mental process that takes place solely in our mind, but an actual event which really took place at some time or other, or which is still taking place, these contradictions will have arisen in practice and have probably been solved. We shall trace the mode of this solution and find that it has been effected by establishing a new relation, whose two contradictory aspects we shall then have to set forth, and so on . . .

One can see that with this method, the logical exposition need by no means be confined to the purely abstract sphere. On the contrary, it requires historical illustration and continuous contact with reality. A great variety of such evidence is therefore inserted, comprising references both to different stages in the actual historical course of social development and to economic works, in which the working out of lucid definitions of economic relations is traced from the outset . . .[5]

The letters passing between Marx and Engels during the period concerned (19 July to 26 August 1859) make it almost certain that Marx saw the relevant portion of Engels's review prior to its publication, which presumably means that he did not take exception to it. Certainly, at any rate, Engels was still expressing the same kind of view about Marx's method in the 1890s, both in his correspondence[6] and in his well-known *Supplement* to Volume III of *Capital*.

A number of commentators,[7] however, have disagreed with this assessment by Engels of the relation between logic and history in Marx's work, claiming on the one hand that it is greatly oversimplified, and on the other hand that it is inconsistent, if not with Marx's actual practice, at least with some of Marx's own methodological statements, particularly those in his Introduction to the *Grundrisse*. In the latter, for example, we find the following remarks which seem at first sight to be directly opposed to those I have just quoted from Engels:

It would therefore be unfeasible and wrong to let the economic categories follow one another in the same sequence as that in which they were

---

[5] *Ibid.*, pp. 224–6.
[6] See, e.g., his letter of 1 November 1891 to Conrad Schmidt.
[7] See, e.g., the reply by Morishima and Catephores which immediately follows my note in the June 1976 issue of the *Economic Journal*.

historically decisive. Their sequence is determined, rather, by their relation to one another in modern bourgeois society, which is precisely the opposite of that which seems to be their natural order or which corresponds to historical development. The point is not the historic position of the economic relations in the succession of different forms of society. Even less is it their sequence 'in the idea' (Proudhon) (a muddy notion of historic movement). Rather, their order within modern bourgeois society.[8]

In order to deal with this problem, which is indeed a difficult and important one, we must begin by taking a closer look at Marx's discussion of this question in the Introduction to the *Grundrisse*, with a view to setting the passage just quoted in its proper context.

The relevant section of the Introduction, entitled 'The Method of Political Economy', starts with a passage in which Marx speaks of those relatively modern systems of political economy which 'ascended from the simple relations, such as labour, division of labour, need, exchange value, to the level of the state, exchange between nations and the world market'. This ascent from the abstract to the concrete, from the simple to the complex, says Marx, is 'obviously the scientifically correct method'.[9] But, he then proceeds to ask, 'do not these simpler categories also have an independent historical or natural existence predating the more concrete ones?' 'That depends', he replies; and it is in the course of the comments which follow that he develops his views on the proper relation between logic and history in economic analysis. The first point he makes (illustrating it mainly with the legal category 'possession') is that

the simpler category can express the dominant relations of a less developed whole, or else those subordinate relations of a more developed whole which already had a historic existence before this whole developed in the direction expressed by a more concrete category. To that extent the path of abstract thought, rising from the simple to the combined, would correspond to the real historical process.[10]

His next point is that the simpler, more abstract category, although it does have a prior existence in history, may not by any means be the *dominant* category in earlier societies. Money, for example, although it plays a role everywhere from very early on, 'is nevertheless a predominant element, in antiquity, only within the confines of certain one-sidedly developed nations, trading nations'; and the category 'labour', although it 'expresses an immeasurably ancient relation valid in all forms of society', nevertheless 'achieves practical truth as an abstraction only as a category of the most

---

[8] Marx, *Grundrisse* (translated by M. Nicolaus, Penguin Books, London, 1973), pp. 107–8. Cf. *Capital*, Vol. III (Foreign Languages Publishing House, Moscow, 1959), p. 282.
[9] *Grundrisse*, pp. 100–1.
[10] *Ibid.*, p. 102.

modern society'. Thus there are certain cases, including some of considerable importance, in which

> although the simpler category may have existed historically before the more concrete, it can achieve its full (intensive and extensive) development precisely in a combined form of society . . .[11]

Let us note carefully here that Marx is *not* saying that because 'money' and 'labour' were subordinate rather than dominant categories in earlier societies, the analysis of these categories must therefore be purely logical and possess no 'historical' dimension: on the contrary, he is trying to define the *nature* of the 'historical' dimension which it will possess, and to differentiate it from that which the logical analysis of a category like 'possession' will possess. Indeed, it is precisely because so many categories which achieve their *full* validity only in bourgeois society are the end-products of a long process of historical development that, as Marx puts it,

> the categories which express its relations, the comprehension of its structure, thereby also allows insights into the structure and the relations of production of all the vanished social formations out of whose ruins and elements it built itself up. . . The bourgeois economy thus supplies the key to the ancient, etc.[12]

But what about those categories which were 'historically decisive' in some earlier form of society, but which are now subordinate? Ground rent, for example, was formerly a dominant category, because agriculture was formerly the dominant form of production. In bourgeois society, however, 'agriculture more and more becomes merely a branch of industry, and is entirely dominated by capital': thus in political economy capital (and profit) must be dealt with before landed property (and rent). In other words, the sequence *of categories such as these* in the logical analysis must be determined by 'their relation to one another in modern bourgeois society', rather than by the sequence 'in which they were historically decisive' which may be 'precisely the opposite'.[13]

Coming by this route (as Marx himself did) to the statement from the Introduction quoted on pp. 136–7, we see that when read in its context it does not contradict Engels's account in his review of the *Critique*, but merely qualifies it. On the other hand it is perfectly true that Engels's account, taken as a whole, is much less sophisticated – and less cautious – than Marx's. If Engels's account were all we had to go on, we would have no hesitation at all in attaching the label 'logical–historical' to Marx's *general* economic method. Given that we also have Marx's own account in the *Grundrisse*, however, I now think that we have rather less justification for doing so.

[11] *Ibid.*, p. 103.
[12] *Ibid.*, p. 105.
[13] *Ibid.*, pp. 106–7.

But let us be clear on one very important point. What Engels says is accurate enough as a generalization of the method employed by Marx *in the book Engels was actually reviewing*. Marx's *Critique of Political Economy* was in effect only a first instalment of *Capital*, dealing almost exclusively with commodities and money (the subjects subsequently covered in Part I of Volume I of *Capital*); and in relation to these subjects, both in the *Critique* and later in *Capital*, Marx's method can legitimately be described as 'logical–historical' in something very close to the sense which Engels had in mind when he wrote his review.[14] Similarly, when Engels returned to this methodological question in the 1890s, and adopted much the same kind of line, it was in connection with Marx's treatment of the transformation of values into prices – where, once again, Marx's method can in my view quite legitimately be described as 'logical–historical'.

What I am trying to say, to sum up, is that some commentators, including myself, in attempting to sort out the relation between logic and history in Marx's *general* economic method, have perhaps placed a little too much weight on Engels's statements, which were in effect generalizations of the method Marx employed in his analysis of commodities, money, and the transformation of values into prices. But in these fields Marx *did*, I believe, employ a method which was essentially 'logical–historical' in character. In particular, 'value' was regarded by him as one of those 'simpler' categories mentioned in the *Grundrisse* which had existed historically from very early times, but which achieved 'its full (intensive and extensive) development' only under capitalism. Marx's *logical* analysis of commodities, money, and value, I believe, and in particular his analysis of the transformation of values into prices, *was* envisaged by him as a kind of 'corrected reflection' of a real development which had taken place in history. The important question here, I believe, concerns the nature of the 'correction' he made to the reflection; and it is with this, in effect, that the remainder of the present essay will be concerned.

III

What *kind* of correspondence between logic and history would it be necessary to demonstrate in order to prove that Marx's transformation of

[14] There is no evidence to suggest that Engels, at the time he wrote the review, had seen the Introduction to the *Grundrisse* which Marx had written two years before but which he was never to publish. All that Engels probably had to go on, apart from the *Critique* itself, was Marx's letter to him of 2 April 1858 describing the plan (as he then envisaged it) of his economic work. On the basis of this letter Engels could easily be forgiven for believing that in Marx's economic work as a whole logic and history were going to be made to march hand in hand in a fairly uncomplicated way. The letter is studded with references to the relation between the two: at least three 'transitions' are described as being 'historical' as well as 'dialectical'; it is pointed out that 'the most abstract determinations, when more carefully examined, always point to a further definite concrete historical basis'; and, perhaps even more significantly, the prerequisites given for the determination of value by labour time are the same as those which Marx gives elsewhere (e.g. *Grundrisse*, p. 159) for the emergence of simple commodity production.

values into prices of production, although logical in form, also possessed a significant 'historical' dimension? It is sometimes assumed[15] that it would be necessary to demonstrate the actual historical existence (or at any rate Marx's belief in the actual historical existence) of something reasonably approximating to an independent pre-capitalist 'value-epoch' – i.e., a specific historical epoch which was *dominated* by simple commodity production[16] and in which commodities were normally exchanged at their values. *Given this assumption*, of course, the cause of these commentators is won. They have little difficulty in showing that an independent 'value-epoch' of this kind has never in fact existed; that Marx never said that it had ever in fact existed; and that if he *had* said so this would have been inconsistent with his frequent statements to the effect that it was only under capitalism that commodity production could develop to its fullest extent.

The really interesting question, however, is whether there might be some *other*, rather less obvious, kind of correspondence between logic and history which would justify us in ascribing a significant 'historical' dimension to Marx's transformation analysis. Marx himself came nearest to discussing this question directly in a long section of Chapter X of Volume III of *Capital*, immediately following his exposition of the *logic* of the transformation of values into prices in Chapter IX. In this section Marx begins by posing the 'historical' transformation problem in fairly precise terms:

> The really difficult question is this: how is this equalization of profits into a general rate of profit brought about, since it is obviously a result rather than a point of departure?
>
> To begin with, an estimate of the values of commodities, for instance in terms of money, can obviously only be the result of their exchange. If, therefore, we assume such an estimate, we must regard it as the outcome of an actual exchange of commodity-value for commodity-value. But how does this exchange of commodities at their real values come about?[17]

He goes on to illustrate what he calls the *punctum saliens* of this by postulating a state of affairs in which 'the labourers themselves are in possession of their respective means of production and exchange their commodities with one another', and in which all these commodities are exchanged 'at their real values'. Under these conditions two labourers, in a working day of given length, will each create the same amount of new value, including

[15] For example, by Morishima and Catephores in their article in the June 1975 issue of the *Economic Journal*.

[16] 'Commodities' in Marx's terminology are goods produced for sale or exchange on some kind of market by 'private individuals or groups of individuals who carry on their work independently of each other' (*Capital*, Vol. I (Foreign Languages Publishing House, Moscow, 1954), pp. 72–3). The 'simple' circulation of commodities, according to Marx's account, is characterized by the formula C–M–C (Commodities–Money–Commodities), its 'end and aim' being 'consumption, the satisfaction of wants, in one word, use-value' (*ibid.*, p. 149).

[17] *Capital*, Vol. III, pp. 171–2.

(Marx here assumes) a certain amount of what under capitalism would be called surplus value, which in this case will belong to the labourers themselves. If the amounts of means of production employed by the labourers are different, their 'rates of profit' will also be different – but under the postulated conditions this circumstance will be 'immaterial' to them, because they will think of their net receipts as a reward for their labour and not as a profit on their capital.[18] This state of affairs differs sharply from the historically (and logically) later one in which 'commodities are not exchanged simply as *commodities*, but as *products of capitals*'[19] – a situation which is normally incompatible with the exchange of commodities 'at their real values'. 'The exchange of commodities at their values, or approximately at their values', Marx proceeds,

> thus requires a much lower stage than their exchange at their prices of production, which requires a definite level of capitalist development . . . Apart from the domination of prices and price movement by the law of value, it is quite appropriate to regard the values of commodities as not only theoretically but also historically *prius* to the prices of production. This applies to conditions in which the labourer owns his means of production, and this is the condition of the land-owning farmer living off his own labour and the craftsman, in the ancient as well as in the modern world. This agrees also with the view we expressed previously, that the evolution of products into commodities arises through exchange between different communities, not between the members of the same community. It holds not only for this primitive condition, but also for subsequent conditions, based on slavery and serfdom, and for the guild organization of handicrafts, so long as the means of production involved in each branch of production can be transferred from one sphere to another only with difficulty and therefore the various spheres of production are related to one another, within certain limits, as foreign countries or communist countries.[20]

There follows immediately a statement of the conditions requiring to be fulfilled in practice if the prices at which commodities are sold are to 'approximately correspond to their values';[21] and later in the chapter Marx turns to the related problem of the conditions which in practice determine the rate at which the transformation of these values into prices of production will be accomplished.[22]

It should be carefully noted that Marx, when he argued here that the values of commodities were 'not only theoretically but also historically *prius* to the prices of production', was *not* implying the existence of an

[18] *Ibid.*, pp. 172–4.
[19] *Ibid.*, p. 172.
[20] *Ibid.*, p. 174.
[21] *Ibid.*, pp. 174–5.
[22] *Ibid.*, pp. 192–3.

independent pre-capitalist 'value-epoch' *dominated* by simple commodity production and the sale of commodities at their values. Marx was well aware of the fact that it was only under capitalism that 'all, or even the majority of products take the form of commodities';[23] and he often emphasized too that it was only under capitalism that the concept of abstract labour achieved 'full validity'[24] and that the concept of value emerged 'in its purity and generality'.[25] But he also very often emphasized that commodity production as such emerged and developed, along with 'individual moments of value-determination',[26] in pre-capitalist societies. The 'evolution of products into commodities'[27] (which was of course closely associated with the evolution of money)[28] began in a small way, according to Marx's account, on the borders of primitive communities; and 'the progressive development of a society of commodity-producers',[29] together with 'the evolution of exchange-value and . . . of social labour as universal labour',[30] continued through slavery and feudalism, normally (at any rate in the later stages) on the basis of the private ownership by the direct producers of their own means of production. When Marx said that values were 'historically *prius*' to prices of production, then, he was referring not so much to a discrete historical *period* (or 'epoch') as to a long and complex historical *process* – the process by which, as commodity production, exchange, and money evolved within the successive forms of pre-capitalist society, 'the value of commodities more and more expands into an embodiment of labour in the abstract'.[31]

For Marx, the importance of all this lay in the fact that he visualized capitalism, first and foremost, as a particular type of commodity-producing system.[32] Under capitalism, he argues, the historical process of which I have just been speaking is continued and indeed greatly intensified, so that being a commodity becomes for the first time 'the dominant and determining characteristic'[33] of the system's products. But from the point of view of economic analysis what is important is not so much this *quantitative intensification* of the process, but rather the *qualitative change* which the

[23] *Capital*, Vol. I, p. 169. Cf. Marx's *Theories of Surplus Value*, Part III (Lawrence and Wishart, London, 1972), pp. 112–13.
[24] *Grundrisse*, p. 105.
[25] *Ibid.*, pp. 251–2.
[26] *Ibid.*, p. 252. The passage in which this phrase occurs begins with the following rather significant sentence: 'As in the theory the concept of value precedes that of capital, but requires for its pure development a mode of production founded on capital, so the same thing takes place in practice' (p. 251).
[27] *Capital*, Vol. III, p. 174.
[28] Cf. *Capital*, Vol. III, p. 189: 'The value of the commodity remains important as a basis because the concept of money cannot be developed on any other foundation . . .'
[29] *Capital*, Vol. I, p. 93.
[30] *Critique*, pp. 50–1.
[31] *Capital*, Vol. I, p. 89. Cf. *ibid.*, p. 170.
[32] See, e.g., *Capital*, Vol. III, pp. 857–8, and *Theories of Surplus Value*, Part III, pp. 112–13. Cf. also above, pp. 128–9.
[33] *Capital*, Vol. III, p. 857.

system of commodity production undergoes when the 'simple commodity' becomes (as Engels put it) 'capitalistically modified'.[34] This modification, historically speaking, is effected through the medium of 'primitive accumulation', which, by divorcing the direct producers from their means of production and turning labour power itself into a commodity, effectively destroys the 'simple' or 'petty' type of commodity production characteristic of the pre-capitalist era, and thereby paves the way for the substitution of the capitalist type of commodity production.[35]

It is of the change in the mode of price determination brought about by this historical transformation of simple into capitalist commodity production, surely, that Marx's logical transformation of values into prices of production should be regarded as the 'corrected reflection'. In the logical analysis, of course, each factor is considered at what Engels in his 1859 review called 'the stage of development where it reaches its full maturity, its classical form'[36] – a turn of phrase echoed (perhaps significantly) by Marx in his description of the 'petty mode of production' in one of the key chapters of *Capital*. In its 'classical form'[37] as Marx conceived it, simple or petty production is a state of affairs (similar to that found in western Europe in the later feudal period)[38] in which a significant minority of products is produced as commodities, under fairly competitive conditions, by independent artisans and peasants who own their own means of production and who therefore think of their net receipts as a reward for their labour.[39] Marx would have claimed, I think, that in relation to simple commodity production in its 'classical form', as so defined, his assumption of the proportionality of equilibrium prices and values was a reasonably realistic one. Alternatively, if he had not been prepared to go quite as far as this, he would at the very least have emphasized (as he in fact did in one place) that in the Commodity–Money–Commodity circuit the equivalence of the values of the commodities concerned 'does not deprive the process of all meaning, as it does in M–C–M', but is rather 'a necessary condition of its normal course'.[40] And he would also have claimed that when the independent labourers lost the ownership of their means of production, and were replaced by capitalists who thought of their net receipts as a profit on their capital, it made perfectly good sense to analyse the effects of this on the

---

[34] *Ibid.*, p. 14. In *Capital*, Vol. I, pp. 169–70, Marx goes so far as to say that an inquiry into the circumstances under which 'all, or even the majority of products take the form of commodities' would be 'foreign to the analysis of commodities'.

[35] The most extensive account of this process given by Marx himself is that in the *Grundrisse*, pp. 459–515.

[36] *Critique*, p. 225.

[37] *Capital*, Vol. I, p. 761.

[38] But not in Russia (see Marx's letter of 8 March 1881 to Vera Zasulich); and not *only* in western Europe (see *Capital*, Vol. I, pp. 765–6).

[39] Cf. *Capital*, Vol. I, pp. 334, 583–4, 624, 714–15, 761–2, and 765–6; Vol. II (Foreign Languages Publishing House, Moscow, 1957), pp. 34–5; Vol. III, pp. 172–4 and 581–3; and *Theories of Surplus Value*, Part III, pp. 377–8.

[40] *Capital*, Vol. I, pp. 150–1.

mode of price determination in terms of the transformation of values into prices of production.

IV

A related point concerns the validity (or otherwise) of postulating an intermediate stage between values and prices of production – what I have myself called, in so postulating it, a 'morning-after' stage, in which it is assumed that capitalists have seized control of production and have begun 'exploiting' the workers in the Marxian sense, but that there is as yet no migration of capital from one industry to another. On Marx's assumptions, this means that commodities will still exchange at their values, but rates of profit will be unequal. It is, of course, true that one cannot claim as much 'historical' underpinning for this intermediate stage as one can for the other two, but its postulation nevertheless seems to me to be quite a useful device. With its aid the process of the emergence and appropriation of surplus value (in the Marxian sense) can readily be analysed in its 'pure' form; and the subsequent analysis of the redistribution of the sum of the surplus values among the different industries so as to equalize the rate of profit can be made to appear rather less abstract. The fact that it ignores the role of the merchant is irrelevant if what we are trying to do is to find our way through the theory as Marx himself presented it, since in his general analysis Marx normally assumes 'direct sale, without the intervention of a merchant'.[41]

I hasten to add that this device is not an invention of my own (*pace* Morishima and Catephores): there is every reason to believe that Marx himself thought (although never *very* precisely) in terms of an intermediate logical-and-quasi-historical stage of this kind. Relevant here, I suggest, is Marx's Volume I assumption (in his analysis of absolute surplus value) that the subordination of labour to capital is not at first associated with any changes in the methods of production;[42] the last sentence of the passage from Chapter X of Volume III quoted *in extenso* above (p. 141); and, in particular, the following significant paragraph which occurs two or three pages later in the same chapter:

> What competition, first in a single sphere, achieves is a single market-value and market-price derived from the various individual values of commodities. And it is competition of capitals in different spheres, which first brings out the price of production equalizing the rates of profit in the different spheres. The latter process requires a higher development of capitalist production than the previous one.[43]

---

[41] *Capital*, Vol. II, p. 111.
[42] *Capital*, Vol. I, pp. 184, 248, and 310.
[43] *Capital*, Vol. III, p. 177. Cf. *Theories of Surplus Value*, Part II (Lawrence and Wishart, London, 1969), p. 208.

Noteworthy in this connection, too, are Marx's statements in various contexts to the effect that 'the inequality of profit in different branches of industry . . . is the condition and presupposition for their equalization through competition';[44] and also his accounts of the way in which the *actual* conversion of values into prices of production 'in all capitalistically exploited spheres of production'[45] can be hastened or retarded by factors such as the mobility of capital and labour and the availability of credit.[46]

V

In conclusion, I would just say this. While I now feel that it may be misleading to speak of Marx applying a *general* 'logical–historical method' to the problem of values and prices, I am still convinced that his analysis of values and prices *did* have an important 'historical' dimension, and that it cannot be properly understood unless one appreciates this. In other words, I think there is no doubt that Marx did go about his analytical job in very much the kind of way I have described above, even if a number of the ends were left untied. Whether the job was in fact worth doing in this way, however, is quite a different question: and it is around this more interesting and fundamental issue that I hope any future debates on the historical aspects of the transformation problem will centre.

[44] *Grundrisse*, p. 761. Cf. *Capital*, Vol. III, p. 156, where Marx says that the rates of profit prevailing in the various branches of production are 'originally' very different.
[45] *Capital*, Vol. III, p. 192. The whole of the passage in which this phrase occurs is of interest in the present connection.
[46] On the role of credit in the process of the equalization of the rate of profit see *Capital*, Vol. III, pp. 192 and 426; *Theories of Surplus Value*, Part II, p. 211; and *Theories of Surplus Value*, Part III, p. 519.

PART THREE

AFTER

VIII

Value in the History of Economic Thought[1]

I

One of the main concerns of a historian of economic thought is with *traditions* or *streams* of thought. Even if we accept some kind of 'relativist' hypothesis in our interpretation of the economic thought of different historical periods, it remains true that there are always important elements of continuity in the development of thought within any particular period – and even (up to a point) from one period to another – which are bound to be of interest to historians. And since nobody can tell where a particular stream is flowing until it actually gets there, this means that each generation has to rewrite the history of economic thought in the light of the new point which it finds the stream has reached.

The present essay is concerned primarily with the Ricardian–Marxian stream of thought. My contention will be that in our own time this stream has flowed to a new point which no one could have anticipated – i.e., roughly, to Sraffa's commodity production models[2] – and that, as a result of this, a great deal of the history of value theory now has to be rewritten. In the first section of the essay I try to delineate, in fairly general terms, the kind of conceptual framework within which this re-examination of the value theories of the past might usefully be conducted. In the second section, I discuss some of the problems relating to the places of Smith and Ricardo respectively in the stream of thought concerned. In the third and final section, I deal with the question of the relation between Marx and Sraffa.

II

So far as the framework itself is concerned, the best starting point is the general view of the development of value theory put forward by Schumpeter in his monumental *History of Economic Analysis*, before which all other

[1] This essay is an amended version of a paper which was originally given at a conference of the History of Economics Society held in Chicago in May 1973, and subsequently published in *History of Political Economy*, **6**, 1974, pp. 246–60.
[2] Piero Sraffa, *Production of Commodities by Means of Commodities* (Cambridge University Press, 1960).

histories of economic thought still pale into insignificance. The two basic elements in Schumpeter's account were, first, his characterization of the Ricardian (and to a lesser extent the Marxian) analysis as a 'detour' from the main line of economists' endeavours, and, second, his emphasis on the importance and virtual uniqueness of the contribution of Walras. The argument was that the scholastic doctors had developed an analysis of value and price in terms of 'utility and scarcity' which 'lacked nothing but the marginal apparatus';[3] that this analysis 'went on developing quite normally right into the times of A. Smith';[4] that "it was the 'subjective' or 'utility' theory of price that had the wind until the influence of the *Wealth of Nations* – and especially of Ricardo's *Principles* – asserted itself";[5] and, in fact, that the salient feature of the analytical work of the whole period up to 1790 was the development of the elements of 'a full-fledged theory of demand and supply'.[6] Once the baneful influence of 'A. Smith' and more particularly of Ricardo began to assert itself, however, an unfortunate 'detour' took place.[7] Schumpeter did not go quite as far here as Jevons, who said of 'that able but wrong-headed man, David Ricardo' that he 'shunted the car of Economic science on to a wrong line',[8] but the idea was essentially the same. Ricardo's crime, according to Schumpeter, was threefold. First, Ricardo was 'completely blind to the nature, and the logical place in economic theory, of the supply-and-demand apparatus and . . . took it to represent a theory of value distinct from and opposed to his own'.[9] Second, and associated with this, Ricardo ignored or at any rate did not develop 'the rudimentary equilibrium theory' of Chapter 7 of the *Wealth of Nations*, which 'points toward Say and, through the latter's work, to Walras'.[10] And third, Ricardo's method involved an economic analysis 'in terms of social classes', as distinct from the later (and up to a point earlier) analysis 'in terms of categories of economic types'.[11] After a period of Ricardian darkness, light was eventually restored as a result of the promulgation of the Jevons–Menger utility theory, which must be seen as 'an embryonic theory of general equilibrium' and which constituted the 'ladder' by which Walras 'climbed to the level of his general-equilibrium system'.[12] All was then really over bar the shouting.

Schumpeter's view of the development of value analysis has itself 'had the wind' for many years now, and even those of us who have felt obliged to criticize certain aspects of it have probably been more influenced by it than

[3] J. A. Schumpeter, *History of Economic Analysis* (Allen and Unwin, London, 1954), p. 1054; and cf. also p. 98.
[4] *Ibid.*, p. 1054.
[5] *Ibid.*, p. 302.
[6] *Ibid.*, p. 98.
[7] *Ibid.*, pp. 474, 560, and 568.
[8] W. S. Jevons, *The Theory of Political Economy* (4th edition, Macmillan, London, 1931), p. li.
[9] Schumpeter, *op. cit.*, p. 601.
[10] *Ibid.*, p. 189; and cf. also p. 472.
[11] *Ibid.*, p. 552.
[12] *Ibid.*, p. 918.

we were aware. My own view, at the time when the *History* first appeared, was that Schumpeter had as it were post-dated the commencement of the Ricardian 'detour' by underestimating the extent to which the way had in fact been prepared in the eighteenth century for certain basic 'Ricardian' ideas; but I did not really question his opinion that the Ricardian analysis was in fact, in a certain sense, a 'detour'. So far as his three basic criticisms of Ricardo were concerned, I disagreed fundamentally with the first, but in the case of the second and third I did not see much wrong with his account of the actual *facts*: my quarrel with him here was simply that he had in effect described as 'bad' certain features of Ricardian thought which I regarded as 'good'. I felt that 'bourgeois' economics had begun to lose something of great importance when what Schumpeter called 'the prevailing tendency to get away from ... the class connotation of the categories of economic types'[13] began to show itself after Ricardo's death; and I also felt that Ricardo was to be congratulated, rather than condemned, for refusing to move in the direction of the Walrasian general equilibrium analysis, which seemed to me to represent nothing much more than a sort of setting of the seal on that 'prevailing tendency' of which Schumpeter had spoken.

I am far from wishing to disown all these criticisms today, but there are two respects in which I now think that my earlier view needs revision. In the first place, I tended at that time to see the *general method* of price determination which underlay the Walrasian theory as representing a kind of relapse into pre-scientific inquiry: the substitution, in effect, of an empty statement that everything depended upon everything else for what I then regarded as the only possible type of valid *causal* statement in value theory – namely, the postulation of some kind of (relatively) independent 'determining constant' from which one proceeded to the final conclusion by means of a simple one-directional *catena* of causes. In the second place, it seems to me that in the light of the 'Sraffa revolution' of the 1960s, the Ricardian–Marxian analysis can no longer be plausibly considered by anyone as having been a mere 'detour'. These two points are important enough to warrant our clearing the decks and trying to make a new start.

In the latter half of the eighteenth century it began to be asserted (particularly in France and Scotland) that societies tended to progress over time through a series of socio-economic stages, each marked by a different 'mode of subsistence',[14] and that this historical process eventually culminated in the emergence of what Smith called a 'commercial society', in which, as he put it, 'every man ... lives by exchanging, or becomes in some measure a merchant'.[15] The essential features of this 'commercial society' were usually assumed to be, first, that it was (or at any rate was becoming) a *capitalist* society; second, that it was marked by a highly developed *division*

[13] *Ibid.*, p. 552.
[14] See above, pp. 18 ff.
[15] Adam Smith, *Wealth of Nations* (edited by R. H. Campbell and A. S. Skinner, Oxford University Press, 1976), Vol. I, p. 37.

of labour and a high degree of *competition* on both sides of the market; and third, as a consequence of these features, that its basic economic elements were characterized by a high degree of *interdependence*. The task of the economist, as it gradually came to be envisaged, was precisely to reduce this complex and at first sight chaotic interdependence to some sort of order; and in view of the fact that the *prices* of goods and services clearly played a key role in the working of the system, this task (in its analytical aspect) tended to resolve itself into that of the *explanation* of these prices.

The latter problem, in its turn, has in the history of value theory usually resolved itself into two others which are closely interconnected but logically separable. The first is that of the 'determination' of the prices. If I may lean upon Schumpeter for a quotation once again, 'we say that we have determined a set of quantities (variables) if we can indicate relations to which they must conform and which will restrict the possible range of their values'.[16] Obviously this is a very general definition, which covers a whole host of possible variations in the actual method of 'determination' employed by the analyst. The relations to which the variables to be determined must conform may be expressed with varying degrees of precision; they may be expressed verbally or (in some sense) 'mathematically'; and their coverage may vary widely, from a small corner of the economy to the economy as a whole, and from the national economy to the world economy. It can be said, however, that two modes or frameworks of 'determination' have been of particular importance in the history of economics. First, there is that in which it is assumed that there is a single 'cause' or one-way chain of 'causes' of price. Second, there is that in which it is assumed that prices mutually determine one another in some kind of general (or 'general equilibrium') system.

But a scheme of 'determination' in this sense requires something to be added to it (or embodied in it) in order to transform it into what most of us would regard as a proper *explanation* of prices. Schumpeter illustrated this crucial point by a critical reference to Pareto's view that it was a mistake on Böhm-Bawerk's part to search for the 'cause' of interest since 'the interest rate, being one of the many elements of the general system of equilibrium, was, of course, simultaneously determined with all of them'.[17] The solution to the problem of *explaining* interest, said Schumpeter, 'calls for an explanatory *principle* just as does the position of the balls in Marshall's bowl'; and without the postulation of such an explanatory principle we cannot justifiably talk about the 'cause' or 'source' or 'nature' of interest – or for that matter of any other variable we wish to explain. Once again, this explanatory principle may take a number of different forms, and may be related in various different ways to the chosen system of determination. It may be, as it were, superimposed upon the latter from outside; or it may

[16] Schumpeter, *op. cit.*, pp. 968–9.
[17] *Ibid.*, pp. 925 and 968.

be reflected in the choice of the particular set of relations which is regarded as relevant to the problem of determination, or in the form in which these relations are expressed. It may consist in the specific postulation of some 'key' variable in the selected system of relationships, or in some other kind of indication of the order or direction of determination of the variables in this system. Clearly it will be intimately related to the nature of the particular 'vision' with which the analyst starts; clearly, too (or almost as clearly) it will be a virtually inevitable ingredient of any piece of analysis which sets out to provide an explanation of economic phenomena – even if the analyst *believes* he is saying merely that everything in his postulated scheme of relationships depends upon everything else.[18]

There are three different kinds of 'explanatory principle' in this sense which have been of particular importance in the history of economics. First, there is the kind of principle which explains prices in terms of man's activities and relations *as a producer*. Second, there are various kinds of 'demand and supply' explanation, the most significant of which (historically speaking) is that which treats the price of a commodity as being determined by 'adding up' the different expenses or costs incurred in producing it, each of these component parts of price being itself determined by (in some sense) 'demand and supply'.[19] Third, there is the kind of principle which explains prices in terms of man's activities and relations *as a consumer*. These three principles, of course, do not exist and have never existed in separate water-tight compartments. But each of them does emphasize a different aspect of the process of price determination; and it is certainly true that in the history of price theory each has been sharply distinguished from the others by its leading exponents.

The essence of the differences between opposing traditions or streams of thought in the sphere of price theory should, I believe, be sought in the first instance in differences in the explanatory principle they adopt, and not in any differences which may exist in the framework of determination. The two frameworks of determination which I have distinguished above are up to a point neutral, in the sense that either of them can be used in connection with any of the three explanatory principles. But these explanatory principles are *not* neutral in any sense: they normally embody quite different basic 'visions' of the economic process which are more or less irreconcilable with one another.

The Ricardian–Marxian tradition is distinguished from others by its acceptance of the first of the three explanatory principles. The basic idea which Ricardo, Marx, and their followers at various times have had in common is that the explanatory principle employed in value analysis should be firmly anchored to man's activities and relations *as a producer*; and it is

---

[18] On this point, see the very interesting discussion in Maurice Dobb's *Theories of Value and Distribution since Adam Smith* (Cambridge University Press, 1973), pp. 1–15.
[19] See *ibid.*, pp. 112–15.

from the standpoint of this idea that its upholders have generally sought to criticize theories of price determination based on the second and third explanatory principles. And since the second and third principles are much further removed from the first than they are from one another, it seems convenient to group them together and to speak, as Mr Dobb does, of the Ricardian–Marxian tradition on the one hand, and the traditions based on the second and/or third principles on the other hand, as 'broadly speaking, two quite distinct and rival traditions in nineteenth-century economic thought as to the order and mode of determination of phenomena of exchange and income-distribution'.[20]

Both traditions derive from one and the same source – Adam Smith. But within half a century of the *Wealth of Nations* they have separated out – the first in the work of Ricardo, and the second in that of Malthus. The first tradition continues, through the work of the so-called 'Ricardian socialists', to Marx; and thence, through the debates on the 'transformation problem', to Sraffa and the present-day Marxists and 'neo-Ricardians'. The second tradition continues, through the work of the 'orthodox' opponents of Ricardo, to Jevons and the Austrians; and thence, through Marshall's *Principles*, to the work of the modern 'neo-classicists'. Periodically, representatives of one stream of thought rise up and confront those of the other, each group taking its stand on one or other of the basic explanatory principles – although there are of course substantial differences, as between one period and another, in the way in which these explanatory principles are allowed to manifest themselves. This is of course a greatly over-simplified picture, and easy game for critics of a certain sort; but it can, I believe, provide us with the bare bones of the conceptual framework we need if we are to rewrite the history of economic thought for our own generation.

Looking at the historical development of the two traditions, we find that although they have if anything increasingly *di*verged on the question of the explanatory principle, they have increasingly *con*verged on the question of the mode of determination. It was not only those theories that explained prices in terms of 'demand and supply' and/or marginal utility which moved towards some kind of 'general equilibrium' framework of determination during the second half of the nineteenth century, but also (even if more slowly and hesitantly) those that explained them in terms of the conditions of production. In *both* cases, the postulated relations to which the variables to be determined had to conform were expressed with a greater and greater degree of precision, and more and more often in 'mathematical' terms; in both cases, their coverage was more and more widely extended; and in both cases, too, the notion of the mutual determination of prices and profits within a general system of simultaneous equations was given more and more prominence. For obvious reasons, those theoretical systems which framed the explanatory principle in terms of 'demand and supply' tended

[20] *Ibid.*, p. 112.

more rapidly in this direction than the Ricardian–Marxian systems; it is of course the great name of Walras which shines out in this connection. But it is often forgotten that Marx, operating on the basis of a radically different explanatory principle, was also advancing in the same general direction at about the same time as Walras – a curious fact which cannot be entirely explained in terms of cross-fertilization and which cries out for some kind of 'Marxian' explanation.[21]

A final point which perhaps requires emphasis in this connection is that there is no universal criterion, valid for all times and places, of the satisfactoriness or otherwise of an explanation of value – given, of course, that the basic formal requirements are adequately fulfilled. An explanation which appears satisfactory in one historical period may appear unsatisfactory in the next, for example, because the coverage of the postulated relations to which the dependent variables have to conform begins to appear insufficient. Sir James Steuart, for instance, in 1767, explained the prices of manufactured goods as the sum of

(a) the 'real value' of the commodity (i.e., roughly, 'the value of the workman's subsistence and necessary expence' and 'the value of the materials', the average level of which determined the *minimum* price), and

(b) what he called the 'profit upon alienation', which 'will ever be in proportion to demand, and therefore will fluctuate according to circumstances'. This explanation, Steuart believed, showed 'how trade has the effect of rendering fixt and determined, two things which would otherwise be quite vague and uncertain'.[22] To Smith, however, in 1776, such an explanation appeared to be far from rendering prices 'fixt and determined': one could arrive at a much more satisfactory and 'determinate' explanation by extending the coverage of the postulated relations to include the mobility of capital between industries, which enabled one to define the limits of the profit constituent in price much more precisely. Somewhat similarly, to our modern eyes a solution of the Marxian 'transformation problem' in terms of a three-department schema looks much less satisfactory and 'determinate' than a solution in terms of an *n*-department schema. On the other hand, it may be (and often in fact is) the nature of the basic explanatory principle (as distinct from the extent of the coverage of the postulated determining relations) in the work of one period or person which appears unsatisfactory to another. Jevons, for example, criticized Cournot on the grounds that the latter 'does not *recede* to any theory of utility, but commences with the *phenomenal* laws of supply and demand';[23] Malthus criticized Ricardo on the grounds that the latter did not appreciate that 'the great law of demand and supply is called into action to determine what Adam Smith calls

---

[21] Cf. *ibid.*, p. 20: "A general equilibrium 'model' of an economy is at least unlikely to be forthcoming until the growth of market relations and of economic mobility has reached the level of development that they had begun to do in mid-nineteenth century England."

[22] Steuart, *An Inquiry into the Principles of Political Oeconomy* (London, 1767), Book II, Chap. 4.

[23] Jevons, *op. cit.*, p. xxxi (my italics).

natural prices as well as what he calls market prices';[24] and Marx constantly criticized contemporary 'bourgeois' economists on the grounds that they did not 'penetrate through' to the real social forces (i.e., the conditions of production) which in his view underlay market phenomena. Thus the question of the satisfactoriness or otherwise of an explanation of value is in part a question of the extent to which the postulated determining relations appear appropriate to the particular stage in the development of the economy which has been reached, and in part – usually in larger part – a question of the nature of the particular 'vision' which the value theorist has decided to adopt.

III

I want now to discuss a few selected problems which begin to arise as soon as one starts looking at the development of the Ricardian–Marxian tradition in the light of the interpretative principles I have just been describing. In this section, I shall be concerned in particular with problems relating to the places of Smith and Ricardo in the stream of thought concerned.

Smith's position in relation to the Ricardian–Marxian tradition is of course a rather ambiguous one. In many respects – possibly in most – there is no doubt that he must be regarded as a precursor of that tradition. For Ricardo and Marx, Smith provided a new and vitally important framework of class stratification; an equally new and important emphasis on the role of production relationships between socio-economic groups in the process of the 'determination' of economic phenomena; a new concept of surplus (in value terms) which Smith developed as a substitute for the Physiocrats' concept; and a theory of the 'cause' or 'real measure' of value which, although he himself described it as no longer applicable in a fully developed capitalist society, was destined to be of the utmost importance in its capacity both as a specific theory and as the crystallization or embodiment of a specific explanatory methodology.[25]

There are other aspects of Smith's work, however, which are less easy to fit in. I have in mind here especially his generalized picture of the interdependence of the elements in the economic system, and in particular of the interdependence of the prices of finished goods and the class incomes into which their 'cost of production' was conceived to resolve. The terms in which Smith conducted his discussion of this interdependence were such as to give a certain impetus to the development of explanatory principles oriented towards 'demand and supply' (and later towards demand alone) and can thus be said to have given aid and comfort to the non-Ricardian stream. On the other hand, in so far as his discussion pointed in the general direction of the 'Walrasian' concept of the mutual and simultaneous

[24] Malthus, *Principles of Political Economy* (2nd edn., London, 1836), p. 71.
[25] Cf. above, pp. 16–17.

determination of variables in an equational system, it can presumably be said to have been in the ultimate interests of both streams.

It was this latter aspect of Smith's work that Schumpeter singled out for special praise. 'In Chapter 6 of the First Book of the *Wealth of Nations*', he wrote, 'A. Smith decomposed the price of products into three components: wages, rent, and profit. In Chapter 7, these prices are built up again from these same components.' And in a footnote here Schumpeter added: 'The arrangement referred to embodies A. Smith's manner of recognizing the fact of general interdependence between the elements of the economic system and constitutes one of his greatest merits in the field of pure analysis.'[26] It was this part of Smith's work, as we have already seen, which in Schumpeter's view pointed 'toward Say and, through the latter's work, to Walras'. Before we finally make up our minds about the *extent* to which it pointed toward Walras, however, there are two points which we should remember about Smith's analysis.

The first point emerges when we compare the basic economic models of Smith and Turgot. Both economists assumed that there were five different ways of utilizing a stock of money so as to procure a revenue: two 'passive' ways (lending it out at interest or using it to buy a piece of land) and three 'active' ways (employing it to set up as a capitalist entrepreneur in agriculture, merchanting, or manufacture). In Turgot's model, the mobility of capital between *all* its five alternative uses was emphasized, and the working of the economic system was explained in terms of the manner in which the rewards accruing to capital owners, in spite of the fact that they were normally unequal in all these different uses, were nevertheless kept in 'a kind of equilibrium' by means of transfers from one use to another in response to market changes. In Smith's model, by way of contrast, although mobility within the sphere of 'active' uses was emphasized, and mobility within the sphere of 'passive' uses fully recognized, transfers of capital *between* these two spheres played little part. Profit rates in the 'active' sphere were brought to an equality by means of transfers of capital, and in the 'passive' sphere a similar mechanism kept rent and interest in an appropriate relation to one another. When it came to the question of the relationship between rent and interest on the one hand and profit on the other, however, Smith based his explanation not so much on the mobility of capital between its 'passive' and 'active' uses, as on the facts

(a) that interest was 'derived from' or 'paid out of' profit, and

(b) that rent was essentially what was left over from the net product of land after the 'normal' profit due to the capitalist farmer had been deducted.[27] Even in this, the most 'Walrasian' part of his analysis, then, Smith

---

[26] Schumpeter, *op. cit.*, p. 557.

[27] Cf. R. L. Meek, *Studies in the Labour Theory of Value* (2nd edition, Lawrence and Wishart, London, 1973), pp. iv–vii, where this point is developed (in a slightly different context) and the appropriate references are given.

apparently felt it proper to make a deliberate break in the postulated chain of economic interdependence.

The second point relates more directly to Chapter 7 of the *Wealth of Nations*, which Schumpeter specially commended. Surely this chapter does not really point *very* definitely toward Walras, or even toward Say? The main theme of the chapter is simply that, if we take the 'ordinary or average rate' of wages, profit, and rent as *given* in any particular society (or 'neighbourhood'), the forces of competition will tend to bring the day-to-day market price of a commodity into conformity with its 'natural price' – i.e., with a price just sufficient to provide wages, profit, and rent at this (given) 'ordinary or average rate'. The question of what actually *regulates* the 'ordinary or average rate' is dealt with in the following chapters, where the main argument is that the rate is 'naturally regulated . . . partly by the general circumstances of the society, their riches or poverty, their advancing, stationary, or declining condition; and partly by the particular nature of each employment'.[28] An appreciable amount of scope is left for the influence of physical, social, and institutional factors; the orientation of the analysis throughout is dynamic rather than static; and the *main* emphasis is not on the reciprocal interdependence of factor prices and commodity prices, but rather on the way in which the latter depend upon the former. 'It is because high or low wages and profit must be paid', Smith says, 'in order to bring a particular commodity to market, that its price is high or low.'[29]

Moving on now to Ricardo, let me yet again use Schumpeter as a stalking-horse in order to introduce the points which I want to make. Schumpeter, as we have seen, accused Ricardo of being 'completely blind to the nature, and the logical place in economic theory, of the supply-and-demand apparatus', and of taking the latter 'to represent a theory of value distinct from and opposed to his own'.[30] But these charges cannot really be justified. Ricardo was perfectly well aware of the fact that prices were fixed within a demand-and-supply framework; what worried him was that some of his contemporaries (e.g. Lauderdale, Say, and Malthus), in their discussions of the value problem, appeared to be saying little more than this. In other words, theories of value based on 'demand and supply' *were at that time in fact being put forward* as theories 'distinct from and opposed to' Ricardo's own.[31]

'You say demand and supply regulates value', Ricardo wrote to Malthus in October 1820, '– this, I think, is saying nothing'.[32] It was 'saying nothing',

[28] *Wealth of Nations*, Vol. I, p. 72.
[29] *Ibid.*, p. 162. Rent, of course, as the context of this statement shows, was regarded by Smith as price-determined rather than price-determining.
[30] Schumpeter, *op. cit.*, p. 601.
[31] As already noted above, a certain impetus was given to the development of such theories by the terms in which Smith had conducted his discussion of the interdependence of economic quantities.
[32] *Works of David Ricardo*, edited by P. Sraffa, Vol. VIII (Cambridge University Press, 1952), p. 279.

in Ricardo's view, for two interrelated reasons. First, any self-respecting theory of value, in his opinion, had to make some kind of explanatory statement about the *level* at which the forces of 'demand and supply' fixed the prices of commodities in the 'normal' case. But, second, this explanatory statement could not consist (as it often did with Malthus) merely of a proposition to the effect that 'demand and supply' fixed prices at a level determined by the average rates of wages, profit, and rent *which were then in their turn also determined by 'demand and supply'*. It was not so much the fact that such an explanation appeared to contain an element of circularity which worried Ricardo,[33] as the fact that in his opinion an explanatory principle based merely on 'demand and supply' was too weak to support the corollaries which a theory of value ought properly to enable one to draw, and that it left too little scope for the influence of social and institutional (as distinct from purely 'economic') factors in the process of the determination of prices in general and of class incomes in particular. There is little doubt that Ricardo saw his own analysis of distribution as constituting an *alternative* theory to those which were oriented towards the notion that, as Malthus put it, 'the component parts of [the long-run equilibrium price of commodities] are themselves determined by the same causes which determine the whole'[34] – i.e., by 'demand and supply'.

The question of why Ricardo's own, stronger, explanatory principle should have been based upon embodied labour is up to a point a separate one. The two easiest answers – which may each contain a certain element of truth – are that Ricardo chose embodied labour either *faute de mieux*, or because Smith had rejected it. Another answer which is sometimes given, and which in my opinion contains no element of truth whatever, is that he chose it for some kind of 'moral' or 'political' reason associated with the Lockean tradition. When he himself attempted to explain the philosophy lying behind his choice, Ricardo emphasized the fact that 'mankind are only really interested in making labour productive', and that 'facility of production is the great and interesting point'.[35] And probably it was indeed the capacity of embodied labour to reflect the difficulty or facility of *production* of a commodity which led him, right to the end, to claim that 'in fixing on the quantity of labour realised in commodities as the rule which governs their relative value we are in the right course'.[36] At any rate, it is certainly true that from the historical point of view it was the general explanatory principle lying behind the labour theory – the idea that economic analysis should start from man's activities and relations *in production* – rather than the theory as such, which was destined to be of lasting significance.

[33] This fact *did* worry James Mill: see the latter's *Elements of Political Economy* (3rd edn., London, 1826), p. 98.
[34] Malthus, *Principles*, p. 78. Cf. Ricardo's interesting comments on this in *Works*, Vol. II, pp. 52–3.
[35] *Works*, Vol. IX, pp. 83 and 100.
[36] *Ibid.*, Vol. VIII, p. 344.

IV

In this final section, I want to say something about the place of Sraffa in the stream of thought we are discussing, and in particular about the relationship between Sraffa and Marx. Does Sraffa's work represent, in effect, a rehabilitation and further development of the ideas of Marx, or is it just another manifestation of Cambridge commodity fetishism? In what I say on this highly controversial issue I shall try to cut through the religion and the mathematics and go back to fundamentals. What I propose to do is simply to reduce the Marxian and Sraffian models to their most elementary component parts, put them side by side, and let the comparison speak for itself.

First, however, let me try to define a little more precisely what I believe to be the basic common characteristics of the theories of value and distribution put forward by Ricardo, Marx, and Sraffa – those common characteristics which warrant our speaking of their work as constituting a single 'stream' or 'tradition' of thought. Essentially, as I have already suggested, they are united by the fact that they all explain prices and profits in terms of what we may call the 'conditions of production' – meaning by this both the technological conditions and the sociological conditions. Essentially, too, they are united by the fact that they have, as it were, a common enemy, in the shape of the 'adding-up' approach to the problem of price determination – the idea that the prices of commodities are formed by adding up wages, profit, and rent, each reckoned at their normal rates, and that these three quantities are determined independently of, and in a sense prior to, the prices of the commodities.

But we can be more specific than this. In their basic models, all three economists in effect envisage a set of technological and sociological conditions in which a net product or surplus is produced (over and above the subsistence of the workers, which is usually conceived to be determined by physiological and social conditions). The magnitude of this net product or surplus is assumed to be given independently of prices, and to limit and determine the aggregate level of the profits (and other non-wage incomes) which are paid out of it. The main thing which the models are designed to show is that under the postulated conditions of production the process of the distribution of the surplus will result in the simultaneous formation of a determinate average rate of profit and a determinate set of prices for all commodities.

It may be said that this pattern is rather difficult to detect in Ricardo; and up to a point I would accept this. I do feel, however, that there are sufficient indications of this general manner of thinking in Ricardo's work to justify us in regarding him as a founder-member of our Trinity. Of particular importance here, of course, is his proposition that profits depend upon the 'proportion of the annual labour of the country [which] is devoted to the support of the labourers'[37] – a proposition whose ubiquity led Mr Dobb to

[37] *Works*, Vol. I, p. 49.

suggest that we may see in Ricardo's basic theory of prices and profit, at least if it is interpreted in terms of the Dmitriev equation and if commodities are substituted for 'values', something very like 'the nucleus of the Sraffa system'.[38] But whatever may be the situation with regard to Ricardo, the pattern I have delineated is *not* difficult to detect in Marx and Sraffa – and this is the theme which I wish now to develop.

So far as Marx is concerned, enough has been said above[39] about his 'transformation' of Volume I 'values' into Volume III 'prices of production' to enable us to dispense here with the preliminary explanations of his procedure which might otherwise have been necessary. *In effect*, as we have seen, Marx wrote

$$(c_1 + v_1)(1 + r) = a_1 p_1$$
$$(c_2 + v_2)(1 + r) = a_2 p_2$$
$$(c_3 + v_3)(1 + r) = a_3 p_3$$
$$r[\Sigma(c + v)] = \Sigma s$$

and solved for p_1, p_2, p_3, and r, thereby implicitly recognizing that when one proceeded from values to prices it was no longer true to say that prices and profits were determined, as it were, in each industry separately: the price of a particular commodity, and the general level of profit, could now be affected by changes in men's activities and relations as producers *anywhere* in the system. What Marx did *not* recognize, however, was the importance of the fact that his method of transformation transformed only outputs, and not inputs, from values to prices. It was this defect in his analysis which eventually became the subject of the great 'transformation problem' debate. The solutions put forward by Bortkiewicz and Winternitz relied on the assumption that the three Departments were (respectively) the capital goods industry, the wage goods industry, and the luxury goods industry. All one then needed to do was to apply the coefficient p_1 not only to the output a_1 but also to the inputs c_1, c_2, and c_3, and the coefficient p_2 not only to the output a_2 but also to the inputs v_1, v_2, and v_3, thus obtaining the following basic system:

$$(c_1 p_1 + v_1 p_2)(1 + r) = a_1 p_1$$
$$(c_2 p_1 + v_2 p_2)(1 + r) = a_2 p_2$$
$$(c_3 p_1 + v_3 p_2)(1 + r) = a_3 p_3.$$

The three prices and the rate of profit were then mutually and simultaneously determined, provided that one included in the system a fourth equation expressing either the equality of total profits and total surplus values, or the equality of total prices and total values, or the assumption that one of the commodities was the *numéraire* in which the prices of the others were reckoned. Finally, after much water had flowed under various ideological bridges, Francis Seton showed, on the basis of an ingenious input–output

[38] M. H. Dobb, *op. cit.*, pp. 116–17, 177–8, and 258–9.
[39] Pp. 105–10.

schema (in value terms), that the analysis could readily be generalized for an n-industry economy in which it was no longer assumed that the ultimate use of each product was invariable and predetermined by its industry of origin. It was still true, it appeared, that in such an economy the process of the distribution of the surplus would result in the simultaneous formation of a determinate average rate of profit and a determinate set of prices for all commodities.

Sraffa, in the first two chapters of his *Production of Commodities by Means of Commodities*, puts forward three basic models – the first of a subsistence economy, the second of an economy producing a surplus over subsistence which is assumed to go entirely to a capitalist class in the form of profit, and the third of an economy producing a surplus over subsistence which is assumed to be shared between the capitalist class and the workers. It is the second, of course, which corresponds to the Marxian model we have just outlined, and this is the only one of the three which we shall need to deal with here.

Let us begin with a simple three-sector model, in which the annual inputs and outputs are expressed in physical terms:

240 qr. wheat + 12 t. iron + 18 pigs → 600 qr. wheat
90 qr. wheat + 6 t. iron + 12 pigs → 31 t. iron
120 qr. wheat + 3 t. iron + 30 pigs → 80 pigs.

The inputs on the left-hand side of these 'equations' are assumed to include not only the physical means of production required, but also the wage goods consumed by the workers. The input coefficients are assumed to be fixed, as are also the outputs which appear on the right-hand side. It will be evident that this economy is producing a surplus each year consisting of 150 qr. wheat, 10 t. iron, and 20 pigs. It is assumed that this 'social surplus', or rather the value of it, is distributed to the capitalists in the form of profit, and that the *rate* of profit will have to be equal in each industry. The problem is to build on this 'physical' basis a model which will determine, mutually and simultaneously,

(a) a set of unit prices for wheat, iron, and pigs which will permit the production process to be carried on in this way and at this level in the following year; *and*

(b) an average rate of profit which, at these prices, will distribute the whole of the given physical surplus among the capitalists.

Let us call the average rate of profit r, and the price of a quarter of wheat p_w, of a ton of iron p_i, and of a pig p_p. The counterpart in price terms of the above set of physical 'equations' will then be the following:

$$(240p_w + 12p_i + 18p_p)(1+r) = 600p_w$$
$$(\ 90p_w + \ 6p_i + 12p_p)(1+r) = \ 31p_i$$
$$(120p_w + \ 3p_i + 30p_p)(1+r) = \ 80p_p.$$

Sraffa, in his earlier models, makes the systems determinate by selecting one of the commodities as the *numéraire*. If we set, for example,

$$p_i = 1$$

the above system becomes determinate, and the values obtained for the rate of profit and the prices will obviously satisfy the two basic conditions we have just laid down.

It will be clear that there is a very close analogy between this Sraffian model and the Bortkiewicz–Winternitz model delineated above. And the analogy becomes even closer if we compare the Sraffian model with the simple three-sector Seton-type model considered in an earlier essay in the present volume.[40] In both cases, the postulated system produces a 'social surplus', the magnitude of which is assumed to be given independently of prices; the process of distribution of this surplus is shown to result in the simultaneous formation of a determinate average rate of profit and a determinate set of commodity prices; and the aggregate profits (reckoned at this average rate) received by the capitalists are just sufficient to enable them to purchase the 'social surplus' (valued at these prices). The only difference is in the unit in which the quantities in the equations are expressed, and this seems to me to be more a difference in emphasis than a difference in substance. The use of embodied labour as the unit in the 'Marxian' model emphasizes the fact that what the capitalists are enabled to purchase with their aggregate profits is the fruit of the 'superfluous time'[41] of the labour force; the use of physical units in the Sraffian model emphasizes the fact that what they are enabled to purchase is the surplus product of the system. And these are, surely, two sides of the same coin.

There are three other points, of a slightly more esoteric nature, which may be made in this connection:

(a) Sraffa's analysis of the role of 'basics' and 'non-basics' is closely analogous to the earlier consideration of a fact that emerged in the course of the Marxian 'transformation problem' debate – the fact that the rate of profit was determined independently of the conditions of production of commodities like the luxury goods in the Bortkiewicz–Winternitz model, which do not enter as inputs anywhere in the system.

(b) Sraffa's analysis of the 'standard commodity', and the main use to which he puts it, is closely analogous to Marx's analysis of the commodity produced with capital of an organic composition equal to the social average, and the use to which *he* puts it.[42]

---

[40] Above, pp. 118–19. The Bortkiewicz–Winternitz model can of course be regarded as a special case of this Seton-type model – the case in which k_{13}, k_{23}, and k_{33} are all equal to zero.

[41] See above, p. 132.

[42] It can readily be shown that there is a simple relationship between the average rate of profit in the economy as a whole on the one hand, and the rate of surplus value *in the production of the standard commodity* on the other hand. (Cf. R. L. Meek, *Economics and Ideology and other Essays*, pp. 175–8; and J. Eatwell, 'Controversies in the Theory of Surplus Value: Old and New', *Science and Society*, **38**, 1974, p. 301). It can plausibly be argued that this is essentially the same kind of relationship as that which Marx postulated between the average rate of profit

(c) The stadial form of Sraffa's analysis lends itself, probably designedly, to a logical–historical interpretation. It is possible to build a longer series of Sraffa-type commodity production models which accurately mirror and usefully extend Marx's own stadial analysis, leaving the same kind of scope for the influence of social and institutional factors in the distribution of income, and solving the 'transformation problem', as it were, in passing.[43]

The sub-title of Sraffa's book is 'Prelude to a Critique of Economic Theory', and in his preface he says: 'It is . . . a peculiar feature of the set of propositions now published that, although they do not enter into any discussion of the marginal theory of value and distribution, they have nevertheless been designed to serve as the basis for a critique of that theory.'[44] This invitation to battle has been accepted, but so far hostilities have taken place on a fairly narrow front: the debate has concentrated on the relevance of Sraffa's demonstration of the possibility of the double-switching of techniques to the 'capital controversy', in the context of a critique of the marginal productivity theory of distribution. What this *may* lead to, sooner rather than later, is a widening of the area of confrontation to cover value theory in general. If it does, attention may well be turned more specifically to the feature of Sraffa's analysis which I have emphasized above – namely its novel use, within a production-oriented framework of determination, of something very like the traditional Ricardian–Marxian explanatory principle.

---

in the economy as a whole and the rate of surplus value *in the production of the commodity produced by capital of average organic composition*. Before too much emphasis is given to this point, however, I think it should be borne in mind that the model with which Marx himself explained the transformation of values into prices in Vol. III of *Capital* was one in which the organic composition of *none* of the commodities concerned was equal to the social average (cf. above, p. 106). It was only later in his exposition, after he had done all the donkey-work, that he drew attention to the relationship just mentioned. And his main purpose in doing so, I think, was to prepare the way for his discussion, in Chap. XI of Vol. III, of 'Effects of General Wage Fluctuations on Prices of Production' – i.e., of the problem of the apparent contradiction between 'values' and prices *in the form in which it appeared to Ricardo*. The analogy in question, therefore, seems to me to be rather more relevant to the question of the connection between Sraffa *and Ricardo* than to that of the connection between Sraffa and Marx.

[43] Cf. above, p. 131.
[44] Sraffa, *op. cit.*, p. vi.

IX

Marginalism and Marxism[1]

Marginalism and Marxism may seem at first sight a very stale subject for debate, of interest only to antiquarians and the celebrators of centenaries. What possible good can it do, it may be asked, to discuss the relation between two theoretical systems which were first put forward a whole century ago, neither of which anybody today accepts without considerable qualification? We do not bother to discuss the bimetallism-versus-mono-metallism issue today: why then 'Marginalism and Marxism'? There are two justificatory points, I think, which can usefully be made before we start our task.

First, Marxism is much more than a mere collection of economic doctrines which can be *compared* with those of marginalism: it also contains within itself a set of broad *interpretative* criteria, of a highly idiosyncratic character, which were designed to evaluate and explain the origin of other theories. This does not mean, however, that there is only one unique 'Marxist' interpretation of, say, marginalism, which is faithfully accepted by all Marxists and regarded by them as valid for all time. The Marxist canons of criticism are sufficiently broad to allow several different interpretations, all of which can properly be said to be 'Marxist' in character. Also, it is obvious that the spirit in which these interpretative principles are applied may vary considerably. At some times and places they may be applied in a 'vulgar', dogmatic way; at others in a sophisticated, more flexible way. In our own time, 'Marxism' is no longer necessarily tied up, as it was in the years between the wars, with the defence of the day-to-day political and economic policies of a large modern state. The decline of Stalinism in the USSR has made it possible for the modern generation of Marxists to be much more free and adventurous in their use of Marx's canons of criticism. Thus the reapplication of these canons to the problem

---

[1] This essay owes its origin to a paper given at a conference held at Bellagio in August 1971. It was subsequently published, in amended form, in *History of Political Economy*, 4, 1972, pp. 499–511. No further amendments of substance have been made in the present version.

of the origin and nature of marginalism need not necessarily yield the same old conclusions: there may well be something new to be discovered.

Second, it is not only Marxism which has developed and changed. Marginalism, too, has altered over the years. The essential point here is so simple that it is easy to overlook it. When a new doctrine like marginalism first appears, a Marxist critic of it is necessarily limited in his available points of reference. He is bound to interpret it in relation only to the older doctrines which it has succeeded in replacing, and the immediate needs which it appears to serve. As it develops and changes over time, however, and possibly comes to serve new needs unforeseen by its founders, the Marxist critic acquires new points of reference. He can now look back at the doctrines of the founders with the benefit of hindsight, and what he now sees may well be rather different from what he saw before.

Let us begin by discussing a feature of marginalism[2] which all Marxists, whether with or without this hindsight, have always claimed is *a*, if not *the*, leading characteristic of the doctrine. This is the way in which it in effect set the seal upon that crucial historical process of *abstraction from the socio-economic relations between men as producers* which began in theoretical economics in the years following Ricardo's death.

This point has now been made so often by Marxist – and other – historians of economic thought that it is unnecessary to do more here than summarize it very briefly. The classical economists, broadly speaking, believed that if the phenomena of the market were to be fully understood, the analyst must begin by 'penetrating below the surface' of these phenomena to the underlying relations between men in their capacity as producers, which in the last resort could be said to determine their market relations. The classical labour theory of value was in essence an analytical embodiment of this methodological principle; and the classical theories of distribution, which laid much stress on the class relationships between the recipients of factor incomes, were also closely bound up with it. In the years after Ricardo's death, however, a fairly rapid retreat from this attitude began, at any rate in more orthodox circles. In value theory the new trend was marked in particular by the emergence of a subjective theory of value based in one way or another upon 'utility', and in distribution theory by what Schumpeter called the 'prevailing tendency to get away from . . . the class connotation of the categories of economic types'.[3]

The so-called 'marginal revolution' set the seal upon this development in a distinctive and decisive way. The new starting-point became, not the socio-economic relations between men as producers, but the psychological relation between men and finished goods. Jevons proclaimed that his

[2] From the Marxist point of view, the word 'marginalism' is really something of a misnomer, since it relates more to the *method* of the doctrines concerned than to their *content*. 'Subjectivism' would perhaps be a better word. Cf. Oscar Lange, *Political Economy*, Vol. I (translated by A. H. Walker, Pergamon Press, New York, 1963), p. 235 n.

[3] J. A. Schumpeter, *History of Economic Analysis* (Allen and Unwin, London, 1954), p. 552.

theory 'presumes to investigate the condition of a mind, and bases upon this investigation the whole of Economics'.[4] Menger emphasized again and again 'the importance of understanding the causal relation between goods and the satisfaction of human needs'.[5] And both these authors in one way or another embodied this new methodological principle in the proposition that, as Walras put it, '*rareté* is the cause of value in exchange'.[6] 'The theory of exchange based on the proportionality of prices to *intensities of the last wants satisfied*', wrote Walras, '. . . constitutes the very foundation of the whole edifice of economics.'[7] It was in this striking way, then, that the primary focus of attention in the theory of value was shifted from the relations between men as producers to the relations between men and goods. And in the new theory of distribution which gradually developed, quite largely on the basis of the inspired hints of the three founders themselves, the tendency was in the same general direction – towards the notion that the socio-economic relations between the classes which supplied land, labour, and capital had nothing *essentially* to do with the respective rewards which the market process afforded them.

Marxists were bound to see this abstraction from the relations of production as representing a 'scientific' retreat, just as the marginalists were bound to see it as a 'scientific' advance. The trouble was that in the debate which ensued between the two schools it was very difficult to separate real, substantive issues from purely semantic ones. Marxist critiques of marginalism are studded with comparisons between the 'superficial' mode of approach which confines itself to the sphere of market exchange and the 'scientific' mode which 'penetrates through' to the real social forces lying beneath the surface. Marginalist literature, similarly, is full of references to the 'superficial' character of analyses which do not 'recede to' – i.e., penetrate through to – utility,[8] and to the 'scientific' necessity of separating out the 'purely economic' relations from those others (mainly 'political')

---

[4] W. S. Jevons, *The Theory of Political Economy* (4th edition, Macmillan, London, 1931), p. 15.
[5] Carl Menger, *Principles of Economics* (translated by J. Dingwall and B. F. Hoselitz, Free Press, Glencoe, Illinois, 1950), p. 58.
[6] Léon Walras, *Elements of Pure Economics* (translated by W. Jaffé, Allen and Unwin, London, 1954), p. 145. I think it is going a little too far to describe this proposition, as Professor Jaffé does, as 'simply a . . . pious restatement of his father's doctrine' and 'no more than an *obiter dictum*' (*ibid.*, pp. 512–13). It is true, of course, as Professor Jaffé in effect states, that in the context of Walras's general equilibrium theory as such the psychological relation between men and finished goods is only one of the elements of the market process as a whole; and that it is in a sense meaningless to ask, when confronted with a formal statement of the interconnections between *rareté*, cost of production, and value, which is *the* cause and which are the effects. But if we are going to lay any stress at all on Walras's doctrine of 'maximum satisfaction' – which Walras himself would surely have wanted us to do – it seems improper to regard his notion that '*rareté* is the cause of value' as a mere excrescence uppn the main body of his doctrine.
value' as a mere excrescence upon the main body of his doctrine.
[7] *Ibid.*, p. 44. This statement appeared in the preface to the 4th edn. of the *Elements* (1900).
[8] Cf. Jevons, *op. cit.*, p. xxxi: 'His [Cournot's] investigation has little relation to the contents of this work, because Cournot does not *recede* to any theory of utility, but commences with the *phenomenal* laws of supply and demand' (my italics).

with which they happen to be associated in the actual world.[9] Much of this, on both sides, is pure semantics. It has taken us all a long time to realize that we do not get very far by merely pinning derogatory labels on our opponents' work, and that the real proof of puddings of this sort must always be in the eating.

Associated with this abstraction by the marginalists from the relations of production, Marxists have always maintained, were certain elements of 'apologetics' and 'ideological illusion'. These are very sinister-sounding words; in juxtaposition, they tend to conjure up a picture of a conscious conspiracy to further the interests of the bourgeoisie by glossing over certain crucially important aspects of capitalist reality. Possibly there have been some Marxists who have believed that this did actually happen, but they have in fact been very few. Three points may be made in this connection.

In the first place, the marginal revolution was hardly a conspiracy, and certainly not a conscious one. Schumpeter was correct enough, at any rate up to a point, in saying that the new theories *emerged* as 'a purely analytical affair without reference to practical questions'.[10] It is true that they emerged, at any rate in large part, by way of reaction to the prevailing labour and cost theories of value, and that the founders were very well aware of the dangerous uses which were currently being made of these theories in certain quarters.[11] But this was hardly a *major* preoccupation among the founders, however much it may later have become so among some of the followers.

In the second place, there is the question of whether and in what sense the doctrines did in fact 'further the interests of the bourgeoisie'. They were certainly used explicitly by at least one of the founders to defend free competition; and Walras was probably correct in claiming that his was the first real *proof* of the beneficence of free competition which had ever been attempted.[12] Among the successors and popularizers, of course, this kind of use – or misuse – became much more frequent. Some at least of the successors were obviously more anxious than the founders had been to use the new theories to attack Marxism. Wieser's *Natural Value*, for example, was in intention and effect a sustained polemic against the Marxian and Rodbertian systems; and the marginal productivity theory of distribution, when it eventually emerged in its more or less complete form, was widely and consciously used – in particular by J. B. Clark – to attack the Marxian exploitation theory. In the face of such facts as these, it is not really relevant to argue, as Schumpeter does, that there was nothing in the new theories to serve apologetics any better than the older theories. *In good logic*, it is true, no political or ethical conclusions could in fact be

[9] Cf. Schumpeter, *op. cit.*, p. 551.
[10] *Ibid.*, p. 888.
[11] Cf., e.g., Menger's comments in chap. 3, sec. E, of his *Principles of Economics*, pp. 165–74. See also Jevons's 'primer' of *Political Economy* (London, 1878), pp. 5–6 and 10–11.
[12] Walras, *op. cit.*, p. 256.

drawn from them – but that is hardly the point. The fact remains that it took a long time for this to be realized, and that apologetic use *was* extensively made of them during this period, and is still – even if less frequently – being made of them today. It is also true, of course, that equalitarian conclusions were occasionally drawn from marginal utility theory, notably (albeit rather disastrously) by Pigou, and that George Bernard Shaw tried to build what Engels called a 'vulgar socialism'[13] on the basis of the work of Jevons and Menger. But surely such uses were aberrant, and quite apart from the main stream. Mrs Robinson no doubt goes rather too far in claiming that 'the whole point of *utility* was to justify *laisser faire*',[14] but it would be even more misguided to claim that it was not in fact very often put to this use.

In the third place, there is the question of whether the new theories did in fact encourage economists to gloss over important aspects of capitalist reality. In a certain sense, there is no doubt that they did. Leaving aside their general abstraction from socio-economic production relations, which the marginalists expressly or implicitly claimed to be irrelevant to the central economic problem, the fact remains that during the period dominated by the marginalists there was a tendency to remove from the agenda, or at any rate to relegate to a low position on it, certain important problems – notably those of development and the under-employment of resources, and (to a lesser extent) monopoly – which were of great practical importance by any standards, and which constituted the very subject-matter of Marxian economics. Associated with this, in most cases, was the conspicuous absence of any concrete specification about technological change, and the habitual assumption that entrepreneurs were essentially an equilibrating rather than a disequilibrating force[15] – a feature which constituted one of the major differences between marginalism and Marxism.

Something more must be said about this third point before we leave it. It can be quite plausibly argued that the omission or soft-pedaling of such problems was in no way apologetic or reprehensible – that the new men, having decided that a fresh start was necessary with a radically new approach, simply *began* with the particular problem to which this new approach could most directly and readily be applied, i.e., the static problem of scarcity, so admirably defined by Jevons in the 'Concluding Remarks' to his *Theory of Political Economy*.[16] This, it may be said, was never intended to be anything more than a beginning; one had to learn to walk in the new direction before one could run in it. Jevons himself, after all, believed that 'dynamical branches of the Science of Economy may remain to be developed',[17] and had no hesitation in using his theory of capital

[13] Engels's comment occurs in his preface to Vol. III of Marx's *Capital*.
[14] Joan Robinson, *Economic Philosophy* (Watts, London, 1962), p. 52.
[15] Cf. Leo Rogin, *The Meaning and Validity of Economic Theory* (Harper, New York, 1965), pp. 431 and 443–4.
[16] Jevons, *op. cit.*, p. 267. The relevant part of his statement is quoted on p. 173 below.
[17] *Ibid.*, p. vii.

to throw light on the doctrine of the falling tendency of the rate of profit;[18] Walras attempted, however unsatisfactorily, to 'dynamize' his theory; and Menger was quite prepared to agree that the establishment of 'laws of development' in economics was 'per se by no means unjustified', even if 'still quite secondary'.[19] In the light of these facts, I am now not sure that the one or two rather tentative attempts I have myself made to interpret the rise of marginalism in terms of the emergence of the problem of scarcity in the real world were really very persuasive. One *can* talk here, of course, about Mill's belief that the stationary state was just around the corner; about Jevons's curious propensity to view the supply of coal and even of paper as very limited;[20] about the Great Depression and the accompanying tendency among economists to regard capitalism as having ended its growth process;[21] and so on. But the hints about this which I have at various times flung out in footnotes have never been taken up – and perhaps rightly not. The idea that economics must always necessarily be confined to the economics of scarcity was not really an inherent part of the new philosophy. What requires explanation is not only the fact that the founders concentrated on scarcity, but also – and more importantly – why so many members of the new school, having, as it were, cut their teeth on the scarcity problem, were unable to transcend it, thereby often giving the impression that they were unconcerned with those great problems of capitalist reality which worried the man in the street.

Let us now change our perspective, and look back at the rise of marginalism with the benefit of that hindsight which I spoke of earlier. If we do this, what leaps to the eye is a certain feature of contemporary reality which marginalism did not gloss over, but which on the contrary it for the first time enshrined in economic theory. This was, quite simply, the more or less universal prevalence, in all spheres of economic activity and among all economic agents, of what Weber called 'the spirit of capitalism', reflected in marginalist doctrine by the extension of the principle of economic rationality to cover the behaviour of households as well as that of firms.

This is a point emphasized by Oscar Lange in Volume I of his remarkable textbook, *Political Economy*, which was first published in 1959 in Poland. The principle of economic rationality, says Lange, asserts simply that if we want to attain the maximum degree of realization of an end we must *either* use our given means with maximum efficiency *or* attain our given end with a minimum outlay of means. This principle, which seems so obvious to us today – and which was indeed first adumbrated two centuries ago, by Quesnay – is in fact something which is historically conditioned

[18] *Ibid.*, pp. 253–4.
[19] Carl Menger, *Problems of Economics and Sociology* (translated by F. J. Nock, University of Illinois Press, Urbana, Illinois, 1963), p. 119.
[20] And also – as Professor Coats did at the Bellagio conference – about the contrast which must have struck Jevons very forcibly between the great empty spaces of Australia and the narrow boundaries of Britain
[21] Cf. Wesley C. Mitchell, *Lecture Notes* (Kelley, New York, 1949), Vol. 2, p. 59.

and which emerges very slowly (both in reality and in the reflection of this reality in theory) until capitalism arrives on the historical scene and speeds the process up. Prior to this, economic activity tends to be largely traditional and customary in character, rather than 'rational' in the relevant sense – however much this may have been undermined by the introduction of what Marx called 'commodity production' and money exchange. With the eventual arrival of capitalism, however, 'rational' behaviour comes to prevail in the sphere of gainful activity – particularly of course in the individual capitalist enterprise, the scene *par excellence* of 'rational' calculation. But *household* activity, generally speaking, still tends (at any rate for a certain period) to retain much of its former traditional and customary character. Only when 'the spirit of capitalism' has become all-pervasive does it begin to appear plausible to assume that household activity, too, is 'rational' in the relevant sense.[22]

From this point of view, then, the significance of marginalism lies precisely in its assumption that household activity, as well as the activity of capitalist firms, is conducted in accordance with rational, maximizing principles – meaning by this, as Lange puts it, that there is a uniform aim which is the object of maximization and which integrates all the particular aims which correspond to different needs.[23] In most of the earlier marginalist models, the thing that was assumed to be maximized by households was of course 'utility', conceived on a more or less hedonistic basis. 'To satisfy our wants to the utmost with the least effort', wrote Jevons, '– to procure the greatest amount of what is desirable at the expense of the least that is undesirable – in other words, *to maximise pleasure*, is the problem of Economics';[24] and he clearly regarded it as an 'inevitable tendency of human nature' that individual consumers should behave in accordance with this principle.[25] Later, however, this 'utility' which consumers were assumed to maximize came to be interpreted in a broader way which Lange calls 'praxiological', meaning by this that 'utility' was conceived as 'a degree of realization of the aim of economic activity, independent of the nature of the aim'.[26] We are all familiar with the major landmarks in this historical transition from 'utility' to 'preference'. The important point about it, from the viewpoint of the present discussion, is that when the change takes place, marginalism is in effect transformed into a kind of logic of rational economic choice. And the generality of this logic is of course increased further when, as with Robbins and von Mises, 'economics' comes to be defined as the study of *any* kind of human behaviour governed by the principle of economic rationality, thereby being

[22] Cf. Lange, *op. cit.*, pp. 148–72 and 250–2. See in particular p. 251: 'The essence of the subjectivist trend . . . consists in the fact that it treats household activity as behaviour according to the economic principle.'

[23] *Ibid.*, p. 253.

[24] Jevons, *op. cit.*, p. 37.

[25] Cf. *ibid.*, pp. 59 and 95.

[26] Lange, *op. cit.*, p. 235.

reduced in effect to a mere branch of the general study of the logic of rational activity as such – i.e. of praxiology.

This last stage in the development of the marginalist trend is of course condemned by Lange, as implying the final self-liquidation of political economy. It is not of course that Lange objects to praxiology as such: on the contrary, his chapter 'The Principle of Economic Rationality' in *Political Economy* is full of its praises, and two of its branches in particular – operations research and programming (in the broad sense) – are recognized by him to be of exceptional and growing importance in relation to the economics of control, especially under socialism. What he really objects to is that the marginalist trend should in the final outcome have led political economy into becoming a mere *branch* of praxiology. Political economy, he believes, should properly be an independent science, to which praxiology (especially its programming constituent) should be no more than an auxiliary – an important auxiliary, no doubt, but an auxiliary none the less. Look what a fearful fate awaits you, Lange is saying, if you are unwise enough to abstract from the relations of production instead of making them your starting-point. Praxiology will then become not your servant, but your master.

But this is hardly the whole of the story, and from the point of view of our present discussion Lange's account stops short of the real denouement. It would be quite wrong to see the marginalist trend as leading *only* to the Robbins–von Mises dead end. Marginalism, with its emphasis on the general principle of economic rationality and on the special importance of *consumer* rationality, directly inspired (or at any rate paved the way for) certain other very different and much more significant developments. I am thinking here, of course, particularly of welfare economics. Most of the partial welfare economics of Marshall was directly based on the concept of marginal utility; and the general welfare economics which we teach today owes a great deal to the inspiration of marginalism – as well as, of course, to the brilliant analysis of general equilibrium made by one of its founders. As early as Pareto and Barone it became apparent that the principles of economic rationality which had been one of the main concerns of the earlier marginalist writers could be used not only as a basis for understanding what actually happened in a free enterprise system, and not only as a basis for checking the rationality of such a system, but also as a basis for deciding what ought to be *made* to happen under a controlled system. And the development of programming was hardly an independent development either: it emerged precisely in order to deal with the problem of the guidance of rational action in cases to which for one reason or another the marginal calculus was not applicable.

The fact that the marginalist doctrine, so often used in earlier days to justify free competition, has developed in such a way that it now serves as a basis for the economics of control, should not surprise us unduly. Welfare propositions in fact lay at the very heart of marginalism, right from the beginning. The starting-point of every economy, says Menger, is 'the goods directly available to economic subjects'. The ultimate goal of all human economy is 'to assure the satisfaction of our direct needs'. What we can do to maintain our life and well-being is to travel the road from this starting-point to this goal 'in as *suitable* a way as possible, i.e., in our case, in as *economic* a way as possible'. Under such circumstances, 'only *one* road can be the *most suitable* . . . In other words, if economic humans under given conditions want to assure the satisfaction of their needs as completely as possible, only *one* road prescribed exactly by the economic situation leads from the strictly determined starting point to the just as strictly determined goal of economy.'[27] And Jevons, somewhat similarly, describes 'the problem of Economics' in the following words: 'Given, a certain population, with various needs and powers of production, in possession of certain lands and other sources of material: required, the mode of employing their labour which will maximise the utility of the produce.'[28] The clear implication of such statements as these – which do not by any means stand alone – is that a solution of 'the problem of Economics' must necessarily involve a formal description of the 'most suitable road' from the means to the end – i.e., the formulation of optimum conditions for maximizing welfare. And propositions of this type were of course frequently put forward by the founders. Given the aims and pre-conceptions of the latter, however, it was inevitable that these propositions should have been mixed up with others of a different type, relating to what would in fact happen in markets of a certain kind given certain assumptions about individual motivation. The result is that it is often difficult to decide whether a particular marginalist proposition relates to what *ought* to happen, to what actually *does* happen, or to what *would* happen if (for example) the individuals concerned tried to maximize their net satisfactions. The welfare rules were there, however, and in time, when the need arose, it was not too difficult to abstract them from their free-enterprise in-tegument, develop them, and put them to uses which would have surprised and shocked their original propounders.[29]

The marginalist trend, then, which began in such bitter opposition to Marxism, has in the end resulted in the production of a congeries of theories, concepts, and techniques which have become an indispensable auxiliary to Marxism – and an auxiliary, moreover, whose importance increases, rather than diminishes, as measures of central control over the economy are widened in scope. The great question today, indeed, is whether, at any rate in a socialist economy, this end-product of marginalism ought properly to be regarded not as a mere auxiliary to Marxism but rather as its successor.

[27] Menger, *Problems of Economics and Sociology*, pp. 216–18.
[28] Jevons, *op. cit.*, p. 267.
[29] Not Menger, perhaps: see his very interesting and prescient remarks on the economics of socialism in *Problems of Economics and Sociology*, p. 212.

The point here is that Marxian political economy, like the classical systems out of which it grew, was concerned in the main to make generalizations about the economic regularities and tendencies which were characteristic of a market economy. These regularities and tendencies, it was assumed, emerged as a kind of unintended net resultant of the interaction of the independent buying and selling activities of millions of individual economic agents. Thus the generalizations at which this political economy arrived could be presented as *laws*, which were conceived as operating objectively, autonomously, and independently of human will and consciousness, like the laws of the physical sciences.[30]

Under socialism, however, the scope of operation of economic 'laws' of this traditional type – and therefore the applicability of any of the traditional systems of political economy – must necessarily be greatly reduced. There will still of course be numerous *technical* 'laws' to be taken account of in the business of production; certain 'laws' of consumer behaviour will no doubt still be relevant; and certain classical and Marxian generalizations about the processes of social change may still up to a point be applicable. But is not that just about as far as it goes? When it comes down to really basic things like the allocation of resources, the pattern of prices, and the strategy of overall development, can one under socialism really speak of the existence of 'laws', operating independently of human will and consciousness, *of the type which classical and Marxian political economy were specifically designed to deal with*? Those who have claimed that such 'laws' do in fact still operate under socialism (e.g. Stalin) seem to me to have really said nothing much more than that there are certain basic economic realities which the planners have to take proper account of if they want to avoid getting into a mess. And Marxian political economy cannot give us *very* much help in taking account of them; it is precisely here that we have to bring in welfare economics, programming, operations research, cybernetics, etc. – i.e., the whole panoply of praxiological principles which, as we have seen, is the end-product not of the Marxian but of the marginalist trend.

What is the moral of all this? That marginalist economics is a more useful guide to action in a socialist economy than Marxian economics? That all roads lead, not to Rome, but to the economics of control? Both of these, up to a point, I suppose – but also one rather more specific and less stereotyped one. The important point about marginalism is that it was based on the notion of a general principle of economic rationality which embraced both the profit-maximizing activities of firms and the utility-maximizing (or preference-maximizing) activities of consumers, but in which the former were made in an important sense secondary and subordinate to the latter. For an economics of control appropriate to a rational and democratic age to emerge, the existence of a principle of this type

[30] Cf. below, pp. 177–9.

was a *sine qua non*. And such a principle was not available anywhere else. In particular, it was not available in Marxian economics. Marx and Engels had, it is true, sketched out the general nature of the allocation problem under socialism a dozen times – the problem of the comparison of the 'useful effects' of goods with one another and with the quantity of labour required for their production, as they used to call it – but for various worthy reasons they had never attempted to specify the conditions of a rational solution of this problem. Thus the principles of rationality and associated techniques employed by the marginalists were the only ones available when the need for an economics of control arose in practice. It mattered not that these principles had originally been used to explain – and often to defend – what actually happened under competitive capitalism. With or without – more usually without – the appropriate 'Marxian' modifications, they were snapped up and used as a guide to what ought to happen in a controlled economy. So the final moral, perhaps, is that the devil not only *can* quote Scripture for his purpose, but *will* do so when the need is urgent and there is nothing else ready to hand.

X

The Rise and Fall of the Concept of the Economic Machine[1]

An inaugural lecture, as I understand it, is the proper place for a new professor first to don the mantle of the historian and look at the past of his subject; then to change into the mantle of the prophet and speculate about its future; and, finally, to do the thing which academics seem to find especially difficult to do – at any rate in their own fields as distinct from those of their colleagues – to make a personal stand. All this I propose to do tonight under the umbrella of the somewhat gnomic title I have been misguided enough to select for this lecture, 'The Rise and Fall of the Concept of the Economic Machine'.

But first, if you will allow me, I would like to draw your attention to the remarkable similarity between this long procession of professors appearing before you at Leicester to give their inaugural lectures, and another procession of professors in Scotland some time ago. That this Scottish procession *did* consist of professors is surely proved by the fact that a contemporary observer – the King of Scotland, no less – conjured them by that which they professed. First in the procession, you will remember, came an armed head. Second, in the place which I occupied in the original programme of these lectures, there came – some of my closer colleagues may think fittingly – a bloody child. And so the procession went on, until the observer gave a *cri de coeur* which may yet be echoed in this theatre:

> What! will the line stretch out to the crack of doom?
> Another yet? – A seventh? – I'll see no more: –
> And yet the eighth appears . . .
> Horrible sight! . . .
> Infected be the air whereon they ride;
> And damn'd all those that trust them!

Curiously enough, it is with another, much later group of Scottish profes-

[1] An inaugural lecture delivered at the University of Leicester on 12 November 1964, subsequently published (in 1965) by Leicester University Press.

sors that the story of modern economics – and, indeed, of modern social science as a whole – really starts. It is with Professors Adam Smith and John Millar of Glasgow University, and Professors Adam Ferguson and William Robertson of Edinburgh University, that the *science* of society really begins in an organized way. For it was they who first began consciously and consistently to visualize society as a kind of gigantic machine, a vast and intricate mechanism whose innumerable cogs and belts and levers were related to one another in certain defined ways. This social machine, like all machines, worked in an orderly and predictable manner, and produced results of an orderly and predictable character – results which could be said to be 'subject to law' in much the same way as falling bodies, say, or fish in an aquarium, were 'subject to law'. Thus was born the truly revolutionary notion that the things which actually happened in society reflected the working of certain law-governed, mechanistic processes, 'autonomous' and 'objective' in the sense that they operated independently of the wills of individual men.

To many contemporaries, this whole idea seemed extremely shocking, and indeed even blasphemous. Society and its history were surely made by human beings, not by falling bodies or fish; and had not Heaven bestowed free will upon human beings? The revolutionaries replied that history was indeed made *out of* the wills and actions of millions of free human beings: these wills and actions in fact constituted the basic elements of the machine. But these elements were linked with one another in the machine in such a way that the overall results which the machine produced were often quite different from the consciously desired ends of the individuals concerned. Individual men tried to better themselves by improving their tools and techniques of production: one of the unexpected net resultants of their actions which the machine produced was a more or less regular sequence of different systems of law and government. Individual men tried to get as much profit as possible from the capital at their disposal: out of their actions the machine created a rational allocation of resources and the phenomenon of overall economic growth. The butcher, the brewer, and the baker, together with their clients, sought nothing but their own self-interest, and sought it independently of one another: the machine saw to it that these private vices were transmuted into public benefits, so that everyone got his dinner. The first task of the social scientist, then, according to the revolutionaries, was to make an objective study of the complex mechanism which produced these surprising results, and to formulate the laws and principles governing its operation. The fact that men in their social life were 'subject to law' did not mean either that free will was an illusion or that the Heavens were empty: Providence still worked through men, but it did so in a rather more roundabout way than had previously been thought. Providence had so arranged it that the operations of the individual elements in the system were coupled to one another in such a way that the system as a whole worked for the good of mankind.

Why this great intellectual revolution should have taken place in Scotland, and at this particular time, is clearly a subject which will occupy the writers of Ph.D. theses for centuries. Speaking as a naturalized Scot, I am of course inclined to attribute it to the innate superiority of the Scottish people, who in the latter half of the eighteenth century were still relatively uncontaminated by the English influence. Academic honesty compels me, however, to admit that the Scottish Historical School had certain predecessors in France and even in England. The notion that social and economic processes were law-governed in a mechanistic way was developed fairly fully by the French Physiocrats; and a few English writers, most notably John Locke and Dudley North, had attempted some sort of 'explanation of economic affairs based on the operation of self-stabilizing mechanisms'[2] even before the eighteenth century had begun. It was in the work of Smith, Millar, Ferguson, and their associates, however, that the idea first took proper root and began to be deliberately nurtured. Adam Smith, tracing out the social origins of morality, the regularities observable in the history of law and government, and the law-governed processes operating in economic life; John Millar, penetrating to the inner causes of differences in social rank, and re-writing the whole history of the British constitution in the light of the new approach – people like these were the real revolutionaries, the true fathers of the great twin sciences of economics and sociology.

One of the earliest discoveries made by those who investigated the operations of the social machine was that it seemed to treat as primary certain basic features of the *economic* life of society. The results which the machine produced at any given time in the spheres of, say, law, government, politics, and morals seemed to be dependent upon the particular way in which men got their living at the time. 'Subsistence is the primary object of all societies', wrote Quesnay in the margin of one of Mirabeau's manuscripts. 'This object must never be lost sight of in the constitution of governments: everything else is only modification.' 'In a certain view of things', said Smith to his Moral Philosophy students at Glasgow, 'all the arts, the sciences, law and government, wisdom, and even virtue itself tend all to this one thing, the providing of meat, drink, raiment, and lodging for men, which are commonly reckoned the meanest of employments.' What was urgently wanted, it was evident, was a special, separate study of what Marshall was later to call 'mankind in the ordinary business of life'. So Smith and Quesnay, from being philosophers and sociologists, blossomed out as economists, and began to make a special investigation into the operation of law-governed processes in the economic sphere. Economics separated itself out from the general study of society; and the concept of an *economic* machine separated itself out from the general concept of a social machine. The primary elements of this economic machine consisted of the activities of human beings in their capacity as producers and exchangers of

[2] W. Letwin, *The Origin of Scientific Economics* (Methuen, London, 1963), p. 181.

Smith saw the economy as influencing all other spheres

goods and services; and the machine worked – in an orderly, law-governed way, of course – to produce results which were often quite different from the intentions of the individuals engaged in these economic processes. Market prices rose and fell quite irrespective of the desires of individual buyers and sellers; profits were reduced to a minimum in spite of the attempts of individual producers to increase them to a maximum; social prosperity was a sort of mechanical by-product of private parsimony. When economists today talk about the 'price mechanism', about the 'motive force' of the economy, about the 'multiplier' and the 'accelerator', or about the economy as a 'control system', they are clearly using – without even thinking about it, so familiar has it become – the traditional concept of the economic machine.

Let us pause for a moment in our story to salute the achievement of the pioneers. In a world which still believed, by and large, that the economy would fall into anarchy if it were not held together and regulated by deliberate acts of government policy, it was no easy thing to assert that it could in fact regulate itself, without any government intervention at all, in an orderly, law-governed way. It is true, of course, that in saying this the pioneers were in a sense merely generalizing from certain basic changes which were actually taking place in the economy at the time. The rapid development of market exchange and the price system, and the economic unification they brought with them in the more advanced countries, were creating a type of economic system which was in fact beginning to work more or less automatically, like a gigantic machine. But all this was still really only in the process of becoming: and to discern what is becoming, as distinct from what is, requires not merely accuracy of observation but also the addition of genius. It is of importance too, I think, that the founders of the social sciences were not only great but also good men. One thinks of John Millar supporting the Americans in their War of Independence, taking an active part in the struggle to abolish slavery, and defending the high ideals of the French Revolution even in its later stages – all in defiance of the fierce contemporary witch-hunt. And one thinks of Adam Smith writing those brave words about his late friend David Hume which he knew very well would bring the wrath of the ecclesiastical Establishment down upon him.

The economy may work in an automatic, law-governed way, like a machine, but what is law-governed is not necessarily good. Whether the machine ought to be left alone or not is something which can properly be decided only after its manner of operation, and the results it produces, have been thoroughly analysed. The classical economists duly carried out this analysis, and came to the conclusion that the machine could in fact be safely left alone. Indeed, they said, if the government tried to interfere with the activities of the individual elements of the machine, or with the way they were linked together, it would almost certainly make things worse rather than better. There were important exceptions to this, of course – a socialist can quote the *Wealth of Nations* for his purposes – but *laissez-faire* was still the general rule which governments ought to adopt. And historically speaking this was undoubtedly the proper rule for them to adopt at that time, given that the main economic problem on the agenda was the development of under-developed countries.

For half a century after the publication of the *Wealth of Nations*, no serious doubts were expressed about the utility of the concept of the economic machine, or about the essential beneficence of the results it produced. Malthus and Ricardo may have differed radically in their accounts of the way in which the machine worked, and Malthus was certainly prepared to countenance rather more interference with its operation than Ricardo; but it was not really in very much more than this that they disagreed. Economics was going through its peaceful period. For some odd reason, I have always felt that the atmosphere of this period was perfectly summed up in a rather delightful anecdote from Harriet Martineau's *Autobiography*, in which she describes a visit she paid to Malthus:

> A more simple-minded, virtuous man, full of domestic affections, than Mr. Malthus could not be found in all England. . . . Of all people in the world, Malthus was the one whom I heard quite easily without my trumpet; – Malthus, whose speech was hopelessly imperfect, from defect in the palate. I dreaded meeting him when invited by a friend of his who made my acquaintance on purpose. . . . When I considered my own deafness, and his inability to pronounce half the consonants, in the alphabet, and his hare-lip which must prevent my offering him my tube, I feared we should make a terrible business of it. I was delightfully wrong. His first sentence – slow and gentle with the vowels sonorous, whatever might become of the consonants – set me at ease completely. I soon found that the vowels are in fact all that I ever hear. His worst letter was *l*, and when I had no difficulty with his question, – 'Would not you like to have a look at the lakes of Killarney?' I had nothing more to fear.[3]

But this rather touching serenity was merely the calm before the storm. After Ricardo's death, when the Combination Acts were repealed and the so-called Ricardian Socialists began to speak for a working class becoming conscious of its new strength, economics became a battlefield – and it has remained so ever since. First Sismondi, then the Ricardian Socialists, then Marx, then Marshall and Pigou, and finally Keynes, disputed in various degrees the alleged tendency of the economic machine to produce beneficent results. The machine, they said, was instituted not by God but by man, and like all man-made things it shared in the imperfections of man himself.

---

[3] Quoted from Keynes, *Essays in Biography* (Macmillan, London, 1933), p. 132.

Some of the results of its operation were good, but others were bad. It produced a grossly inequitable distribution of income, said Sismondi and the Ricardian Socialists. It produced monopoly, instability, and stagnation, said Marx. It produced an irrational allocation of society's resources, said Marshall and Pigou. It produced chronic underemployment of these resources, said Keynes. Some of these results were new: they were the products of important changes taking place in the internal constitution of the machine. Others were old: their condemnation by the critics was the product of changes taking place in men's moral attitudes, rather than in the machine. But all the results, it was agreed, were produced by a machine-like organism; none of the critics threw any doubt on the utility of the concept of the economic machine. Quite the contrary, in fact: the production of bad results which no individual could conceivably want, like prolonged slumps, was adduced as irrefutable evidence for the existence of a machine of the classical type. Keynes's system was perhaps the most machine-like of them all: indeed, actual physical machines, in which coloured water runs in a highly diverting way through numbers of curious glass tubes, are today used in some of the more affluent departments of economics to illustrate Keynes's theory. And Marx, of course, made a brilliant effort to re-unite the economic machine with the social machine from which it had originally sprung.

Keynes and Pigou make rather strange bedfellows, and Pigou and Marx even stranger ones. Is it really very useful to link them together as I am doing now – the revolutionaries with the reformists, the lions with the lambs – when all that actually unites them is a common belief that the results which the economic machine produces are not necessarily beneficent? I am doing this tonight because I think – if I may now change invisibly into my prophet's robes – that this is what future historians of economic thought are going to do. My point here is that the economics of the future is going to be based very much less than it is now on the concept of the economic machine: in fact over large areas of the field it is going to presuppose the absence of any automatic mechanism at all for the performance of certain basic economic tasks. This will bring about a revolution in the nature and content of economics more profound and far-reaching than any other which it has experienced in the whole of its history. In the light of this revolution, the main characteristic of all economics from Smith to Keynes will be seen as the centrality of the concept of the machine. The economists of this period will be divided up according to whether they believed or did not believe in the beneficence of the results produced by the machine; and the significance even of this division will gradually diminish as time goes on.

The revolution of which I am now speaking is not something of the vague and misty future: its beginnings are perfectly evident now to anyone who knows where to look. The concept of the economic machine is already in a state of decline. And it is in a state of decline in economic theory for the simple reason that it is in a state of decline in economic reality. In the real world today the areas in which the economic machine does not operate are steadily becoming wider and more important. In some countries – most notably those of the Communist world – the machine has in large part been deliberately destroyed. But in the West, too, the relative size of the area within which we can expect the machine to perform basic economic tasks is now fairly steadily diminishing. This is partly because of the increasing adoption of interventionist policy measures designed to promote economic stability and growth, although these measures are as often as not intended rather to make the machine work better than to supersede it. Of much more importance is the recent emergence of large and complex public enterprises, such as those in this country which produce our electricity, our coal, our railway services, our roads, our hospitals, and much of our education. Significant, too, is the growth in size of individual privately owned firms, which has greatly increased the importance and complexity of the task of controlling the interrelations between the numerous branches, plants, and workshops of which the firm consists. This was always of course an area in which by the nature of things the machine's writ could not run: all I am saying is that the *extent* of this area has greatly increased in our own time. The combined effect of all these developments, taking the East and the West together, is that men are now becoming obliged to solve deliberately and consciously a large number of quite crucial problems of economic choice which in former days were either relatively insignificant or which the machine automatically solved for them.

This new social need is reflecting itself in several different ways. In the first place, it is reflecting itself in a quite unprecedented increase in the demand for the services of economists, in both the private and the public sector of the economy. The newspapers today are full of advertisements for economists who are experts in management studies, operational research, statistics, programming, urban transportation, town planning, electricity economics, marketing, and so on. It is pleasant to see one's subject suddenly becoming useful as well as respectable, and its practitioners becoming well paid; the only trouble, of course, is that until supply catches up with demand it is going to continue to be desperately hard to obtain enough people to do the mundane job of teaching it. In the second place, the new social need is reflecting itself in certain very important changes in the field of economic theory. Here two recent developments are of special significance. The first is the evolution of certain new mathematical techniques, often subsumed under the generic title of 'operations analysis', which are designed to assist in the deliberate solution by private and public managements of a number of difficult problems of economic choice. The second is the development of the comparatively new branch of economics known as 'welfare economics', a substantial part of which now consists in attempts to formulate a set of rules or criteria by which the various economic situations open to society at any given time may be ordered and compared from the point of view of their relative desirability. The important thing about these new developments is that they are mainly designed to help us make the right economic choices in situations in which the economic machine cannot be expected to make them automatically for us. As a result of these developments – and, of course, as a result of the extended use of computers to obtain optimal solutions to economic problems – economics both in the East and in the West is being fairly rapidly transformed into a science – or perhaps an art – of economic management, or social engineering. Just as in the eighteenth century, a radical change in social and economic organization is giving birth to a radical change in the nature and function of economics.

But is this change which is taking place in economics really so radical? Is it not true that economists have always been in a sense social engineers, concerned quite simply to make the world a better place? Well, it is certainly true that the cold, hard-hearted economist lampooned by Swift, Peacock, and Ruskin, has always been a mere figment of the literary imagination. But there seems to me to be a great difference between trying to make the world a better place by altering (or not altering) the cogs and belts and levers of a machine, and trying to make the world a better place by scrapping the machine and doing in a planned and purposive way the jobs which it used to do. In each case, it is true, you need a set of criteria – in the first case to evaluate what the machine does, and in the second case to guide what *you* do – and it is probable that some of the criteria evolved by the machine-minders and the machine-menders will turn out to be capable of use by the machine-breakers as well. In the socialist world commonwealth of the future, there may well be more statues of Pigou than of Keynes or even of Marx. Socialism, after all, almost by definition, has no Keynesian slumps; Marxism, as Oscar Lange once said, cannot teach us much about running a central bank; but socialism does have a Pigouvian problem of allocating scarce resources among alternative employments in a rational manner. Even admitting all this, however, there surely does remain one really essential difference between the new situation and the old – that the analysis of spontaneous, mechanical, law-governed processes is bound to play a much smaller rôle in economics as the machine itself comes to play a much smaller rôle in the real world. Since the very core of traditional economics, as it has come down to us from the eighteenth century, consists in an analysis of these spontaneous processes and a statement of the laws which govern them, it follows that economics as a discipline is bound to change quite radically in both content and form. This is already happening before our very eyes: let anyone who doubts this ask himself whether there is really very much in common between the traditional textbook analysis of the operation of the price mechanism, and the modern techniques which have been developed for use in the fields of capital budgeting, operations research, and cost–benefit analysis. In these very wide and important fields, in both the East and the West, economists are beginning to join with mathematicians, engineers, and accountants in large numbers to solve the new and exciting tasks which society is setting them with the aid of new and exciting tools and techniques.

Is the traditional economist's occupation gone, then? Did this University make a grave error when it appointed me, a non-mathematician interested mainly in the working of the economic machine, to the Chair of Economics? I am glad to say that I have managed to think up enough reasons for me to be able to answer 'no' to this question with something like a clear conscience. In the first place, while it is true that economic laws of the spontaneous type upon which economics has traditionally concentrated are going to become of much less importance, certain other objective necessities which are sometimes dignified by the name 'economic laws' will continue to exist and to be the concern of economists. I am thinking of things like the so-called 'law of diminishing returns' in Western economics, and the so-called 'law of the balanced, proportionate development of the national economy' in modern Soviet economics. But I have to admit that there is not really very much here for the economist to get his teeth into. It does not help me very much, as an amateur gardener, to be told that after a point the size of my roses will increase less than in proportion to the amount of manure I put on them, even if this statement is decked out in the form of a general 'law of diminishing returns'. Nor, I am sure, does it help Soviet planners very much to be told that they cannot have their cake and eat it too, or that they must cut their coat according to their cloth, even if these statements are decked out in the form of a general 'law of the balanced, proportionate development of the national economy'. It may raise the morale of Soviet economists to maintain that their economy is subject to bigger and better laws than ours, but many of their so-called 'economic laws of socialism' seem to me to consist either of elementary platitudes about certain aggregates which have to be kept in balance, or of mere definitions. However, we in the West are hardly in a position to throw stones here: and it may well be that we are now entering an era when it will be useful to give the name 'law' to *any* objective necessity, whether spontaneous or non-spontaneous, which acts as a constraint upon the activities of the new class of social engineers. Some of these constraints may come to appear much more subtle and interesting than they do now, and we should perhaps not worry overmuch if they are not 'laws' within the strict meaning of the term which we have come to accept. One should always remember the sad story of the professor of philosophy, a logical positivist, who, travelling home in the bus one day, found himself crushed against the side of the bus by a gigantic navvy. 'Would you mind giving me some room?', the professor asked. And the reply came: 'What do you mean, room!'

In the second place, there are many countries in the world where the machine's influence is still powerful, and is likely to remain so for quite a long time yet. This is true of Britain, I think, even if we assume that the present government's programme will be fully carried out. Parts of this programme, such as steel nationalization, will undoubtedly make important inroads into the sphere of operation of the machine: but certain other parts of the programme, if they succeed in their aim, will merely have the effect of making what is left of the machine work more efficiently and equitably than before. In so far as this is so, the study of spontaneous laws of the traditional type, in which old-fashioned economists like myself are wont to indulge, will remain of considerable importance. And even in the case of the nationalized sector, a training in traditional economics will by no means be useless. Consider the economic competition which is developing at the moment between the nationalized gas and electricity industries, for example: if this is permitted to continue, is it likely to have *very* different effects from the competition which takes place between large privately owned monopolies? And it may well be that as the nationalized sector is extended certain new spontaneous laws, of a mixed economic and sociological type, will begin to operate. Here we have a fine happy hunting ground for economists like myself and for sociologists with a similar interest in spontaneous law-governed processes.

In the third place, even in countries like the USSR, where the influence of the machine is much less powerful than it is in the West, the scope for the analysis of spontaneous processes remains rather wider than most people think. It is true that the operation of the machine in the USSR is very considerably restricted by the fact that the allocation of resources to the different industries is carried out not by a price mechanism but by the government. But something like a 'price mechanism' still to some extent governs the exchanges of goods between town and country, as anyone who has seen supply and demand working in a Russian collective farm market will readily appreciate; and there is still something like a 'market', in the traditional sense, for consumers' goods and for labour. In addition, if there do in fact exist long-term laws of social development, of the type with which Marx concerned himself, these are presumably still operative in some form or another in the USSR. Here, then, is fertile ground for the generation of quite a good crop of spontaneous socio-economic laws. The late Joseph Stalin, you may remember, occupied himself with this subject during the last year or so of his life, producing a very perceptive little book about it called *Economic Problems of Socialism*. It is a great pity that at this precise time Stalin was also occupying himself in cooking up the Doctors' Plot: this has unfortunately led to his ideas about economic laws under socialism receiving much less attention than they deserve. Personally, I feel a sentimental attachment to Stalin's book, since it marked the transition from what you might call the charismatic phase of my life; and I am eagerly looking forward to its coming rehabilitation – the book, I mean, not the charismatic phase.

In addition, of course, there is the current movement in the USSR towards the creation of a new kind of economic machine, designed to do at least part of the job that the old one did, but on the basis of public rather than private ownership of the means of production. The new Liberman proposals do not of course envisage the abolition of central planning or anything like it: but they do seem to envisage a significant increase in the power of individual factories to decide upon the particular assortment of goods they produce, and to settle appropriate prices for them with the shops that are going to sell them, as well as an increase in the use of profit as a success indicator. If these proposals mean anything at all, they must mean that something like a price mechanism, even if a muted and modified one, is to be introduced in the USSR to help ensure that the pattern of production reflects consumers' tastes. In so far as this is in fact done, an economic machine will ride again in the USSR, and men in some parts of their economic life may again become 'subject to law' in something very like the old classical sense. It would be wrong to exaggerate the importance of this: when the computers come to be applied to central planning in a big way it may well be found that a Liberman-type machine is not as necessary as it appears to be now. But to the extent that the proposals are in fact put into effect, there will be at least *some* spontaneous law-governed processes for economists to investigate.

For all these very good reasons, then, I think that my colleagues were not in fact wrong in appointing me: there are going to be enough economic laws of the old familiar kind about the place to keep me busy for quite a long time yet. But to say this is merely to put the revolution which is occurring in economics into its proper perspective: it is by no means to deny its importance. In a significant sense, the prophecies of Bukharin and Preobrazhensky, who in Russia in the 1920s foretold the impending doom of economics in its traditional form, *are* in fact coming to be fulfilled. The fantastic upsurge in mathematical economics, operations research, and econometrics during the last decade is something much too far-reaching and universal to be dismissed as a mere fashion: it can be interpreted only in terms of the response of a new generation of economists to a new world-wide social need which traditional systems of economic analysis are unable to cope with. My own recognition of this incapacity of the traditional systems dates, oddly enough, from a visit to Poland with a delegation of British economists in 1956. This was a vintage year for economic discussion in Poland: the lid had suddenly been taken off, and the economists were discussing quite crucial issues with tremendous frankness and enthusiasm. While we were in Cracow, Mrs Joan Robinson, who was one of the members of our delegation, gave a lecture to the local economists, the majority of whom were Party members. I was interested in the subject of the lecture, and obtained a special dispensation from Mrs Robinson to enable me to attend. That night, at dinner, I was sitting next to Mrs Robinson and opposite to Oscar Lange. 'How many orthodox Marxist economists would you say were at my lecture this afternoon?',

Mrs Robinson asked Lange. Lange thought for a moment, and then smiled, and said: 'Well, there was Mr Meek . . .'

Given that the revolution is upon us, then, and that economists are already walking (with novelists) along the corridors of power, what attitude should we adopt towards it? It would be wrong, I think, to ignore what is going on, or to try to remain neutral. What is happening, after all, is surely of some importance: man is at last beginning to master the machine which has hitherto controlled his economic destiny. He is doing this in two ways – first, by preventing the machine from operating at all in certain important fields where he thinks that decisions ought to be consciously and purposively made; and second, by taking action to ensure that the results which the machine produces in the remaining fields coincide with his aims. The first, as we have seen, is the truly revolutionary way; but the second, if man's intervention is vigorous enough, may sometimes become almost indistinguishable from it. Personally I find all this extremely exciting. Man, as Engels prophesied, is beginning to emerge from a situation in which he was dominated by the laws of his own social activity into a situation where these laws are dominated by him, so that he can at last begin, with full consciousness, to make his own history. This era has opened, whether we like it or not, and the clock cannot be put back. All that is at issue is whether man, with the power to make his own history now at his command, will make it well or ill. And this will depend quite largely upon the trustworthiness of the tools and techniques of scientific decision-making with which economists and other social scientists supply him.

'The age of chivalry is gone', wrote Burke. 'That of sophisters, economists, and calculators, has succeeded; and the glory of Europe is extinguished for ever.' May I conclude with a word of reassurance to those who, upon hearing what I have been saying tonight, are a little concerned about the glory of Europe? It is true that in the age which lies ahead of us many economists – and other social scientists too – will become calculators, in the sense that the tasks which they will be set will more and more require them to be proficient in mathematics and statistics. But I do not think that the glory of Europe is likely thereby to be substantially diminished. For one thing, as I have tried to show, there will still be plenty of scope in the new age for mathematical innocents like myself who want to continue working along traditional lines; the neurotics and ideologists, praise be, will still be able to quarrel interestingly about the criteria which the calculators ought to use; and if the calculators are obliged to study social and political institutions and processes along with their mathematics there need be little fear of their being misled by sophisters. Finally, we should remember what it is that the economists and calculators are trying to do. They are trying, in essence, to *economize* – to make the best possible use of the scarce resources at man's disposal. It has always puzzled me that this kind of aim should be regarded almost as an ultimate value when it is pursued in art, literature, and music, and yet as somehow sordid and ignoble when it is pursued in the ordinary business of life. Even if the object of the economist were simply to economize for its own sake, and nothing more, this would surely not be an ignoble pursuit in a world where many millions of people are still starving. Man, after all, does not live by freedom alone. But the economist does not, of course, preach affluence for its own sake. He preaches it for the sake of the good life which is impossible without the leisure which affluence brings with it. Economists, as Keynes once said, are 'the trustees not of civilization, but of the possibility of civilization'.

INDEX